Social Work Practices

Contemporary Perspectives on Change

Karen Healy

SAGE Publications
London • Thousand Oaks • New Delhi

First published 2000

SAGE Publications Ltd
6 Bonhill Street
London EC2A 4PU

SAGE Publications Inc
2455 Teller Road
Thousand Oaks, California 91320

SAGE Publications India Pvt Ltd
32, M-Block Market
Greater Kailash – I
New Delhi 110 048

British Library Cataloguing in Publication Data

A catalogue record for this book is
available from the British Library

ISBN 0 7619 6271 9
ISBN 0 7619 6272 7 (pbk)

Library of Congress catalog card number available

Typeset by Keystroke, Jacaranda Lodge, Wolverhampton.
Printed in Great Britain by Biddles Ltd, Guildford, Surrey

For Rachael

Contents

Acknowledgements

I am grateful for the generous support and encouragement I have received from many people over the course of this work. My special thanks go to Ingrid Burkett, Graham Floater, Sue Goodwin, Mal McCouat, Joan Mulholland and my colleagues at the University of Sydney. I thank Professor Jan Fook, Professor Peter Leonard and Dr Colin Peile for their rare gifts of intellectual generosity and leadership. I am deeply grateful for their openness to differences, whole-hearted support of this project and for their ongoing affirmation of the importance of critical social work practices. Thanks to Karyn Walsh for friendship, mentoring and intellectual challenges, and to the young women who participated in the anti-violence project for giving so much in their insights about social work practices. I wish to acknowledge Queensland Health, who provided the original funding for the young women's anti-violence project and thus provided me with a fabulous opportunity to study activist practices in detail.

Thanks to Karen Phillips, editor at Sage, for her encouragement of this work and for carrying on our e-mail conversation across the world! Finally, my heartfelt thanks to Julie Conway, Rachael Healy and Dennis Longstaff for their love and friendship, which meant that, even when I was going out on a limb, I never felt really alone.

This is my original work. I do draw, in small part, on two previously published papers. I thank the editors of the journals mentioned for permission to reproduce aspects of these papers:

K. Healy, (1998) 'Participation and child protection: the importance of context', *The British Journal of Social Work*, 28 (6): 897–914.
K. Healy and J. Mulholland (1998) 'Discourse analysis and activist social work: investigating practice processes', *Journal of Sociology and Social Welfare*, 25 (3): 3–27.

1   Social Work: Contemporary Challenges

Throughout the history of modern social work activists have sought to articulate the radical potential of social work. Through their critical interrogations these thinkers have contributed to the evolution and, in some instances, the subversion of social work. Very often, however, social workers experience difficulty in translating an activist commitment to practice, and the gulf between theory and practice has grown wider despite a claim to 'praxis' in much of the contemporary social work literature. Rather than something that helps social workers understand and develop practice, theory is often experienced as, at worst, authoritarian or esoteric and, at best, an addition to practice rather than something useful to it. The venture I am embarked on in this book is to demonstrate the opportunities recent theoretical developments provide for different ways of thinking about and doing progressive social work. I will use the opportunities these contemporary theories provide for destabilizing the oppositions that have become part of the modern social work landscape, and in so doing my intention is to assist social workers think through the challenges of practising critically in the contemporary contexts of transition.

The focus of this book is an important one at this point in the history of critical social work. As we enter a new millennium, it is timely for critical social workers to reflect on the legacy bestowed via the theoretical and practice impulses that have nurtured the emergence of activist practice approaches in the latter half of the twentieth century. It is also an opportunity to take stock of the momentous contests that now beset social workers committed to progressive social change.

The contemporary climate: post-Fordist abyss or grounds for hope?

The dramatic socio-economic transformations that have occurred internationally over the past two decades provide a very different landscape for social work than when critical practice theories first came to prominence in the 1960s. Massive social and economic upheaval attendant with globalization and the large-scale withdrawal of the welfare state mean that all certainty about basic social service provision is gone and the possibilities for a progressive reorganization of welfare services seem bleak. Indeed activists who have long critiqued state welfare now look on nervously at the dismantling and restructuring of a minimalist welfare state. The language of managerialism, which first entered welfare discourse in the 1970s, has achieved ascendancy (L. Davies, 1990). As terminology such as lean production, re-engineering, purchaser/provider splits, inputs and outputs is now common parlance in the organization of social services, it is perhaps not an exaggeration to claim that the 'McWelfare' state has arrived! The role of social workers is stripped of complexity as their functions are reduced to a bare minimum and to the management of service users' 'cases'. As Parton (1994b) writing from within the British context observes: 'social workers reconstituted as care-managers, are required to act as co-ordinators of care packages for individuals' (p. 99).

Despite resistance to postmodern perspectives amongst many critical social workers, it is increasingly difficult to ignore the challenges levelled through them. Postmodern insights draw activists inexorably towards a recognition of the oppressive effects of the utopian ideals that have guided us. Bauman (1992) asserts that 'We, the residents of the postmodern habitat, live in a territory that admits no clear options and strategies that can even be imagined to be uncontroversially correct' (p. 185). Postmodernists reject visions of massive social transition as a chimera and demand, instead, greater caution and constraint in the formation of critical practice objectives and processes.

It is easy to be pessimistic as the certainties that once guided activism provide little succour in the face of the challenges before us. Yet, I contend there are some, highly limited, grounds for optimism. As the truth claims and grand plans of critical social work give way under the force of political and theoretical challenges, new directions are emerging. Some of these are admittedly bleak as we stare into the abyss of a post-Fordist welfare state where the social work role is reduced to piecemeal, patch-up work with no hope of a better tomorrow. At the same time, however, the contests posed at the turn of this century can draw activists to a new pragmatism focused on local, contextual and modest proposals for change activity. Despite the activist critique of the esoteric nature and language of poststructuralism, critical elements of this school can invite the re-examination of the practical problems confronting social workers and services users in relation to local issues of power, identity and processes of change, and it is to the exploration of these possibilities that this book is committed.

In this book I will use a two part strategy. In the first part, I will overview the often unspoken but also uncontested assumptions on which critical social work depends and the consequences of these strategies for representing and performing social work practice. The second part of the strategy involves the examination of the possibilities and limitations of critical poststructural theories for thinking differently about power, identity and change in practice. My investigation will incorporate social work practice examples. It is envisaged that the use of these practice examples will increase the relevance of the current theoretical debates to the reworking and diversification of critical practice approaches.

Critical social work

While a critical tradition has been present since the birth of professional social work, it was not until the 1960s that a distinct body of critical practice theories emerged. Since that time, critical authors have persistently challenged the occupational self-image of social work as a caring profession by emphasizing the complicity of social workers in the reproduction of the oppressive conditions within the practice context and beyond it (Rojek et al., 1988; see also Sarri and Sarri, 1992). According to many activists, traditional social work assumes individual culpability for the difficult personal and social circumstances faced by clients of the welfare state. By contrast, critical social workers claim to redirect practice towards the elimination of the original structural causes of problems faced by service users.

Despite the diversity of critical social work, virtually all of these practice models draw on the critical intellectual traditions and radical social movements that gained prominence during the late 1960s and the 1970s. A variety of critical influences have contributed to powerful critiques of social work and, in some instances, to the development of alternative modes of social work (Fook, 1993; Rojek et al., 1988). There is a broad range of models that can be identified as critical, these include: anti-racist and multicultural social work, anti-oppressive and anti-discriminatory social work, feminist social work, various strands of community work, Marxist social work, radical social work, structural social work, and participatory and action forms of research. Notwithstanding the significant differences and, in some instances, antagonisms between these models, critical social work approaches share an orientation towards radical social transformation.

In this book, I will use the term 'critical social work' or 'activist social work' to refer to practice models that incorporate an emancipatory social change orientation. Critical social work approaches emphasize:

- a commitment to standing alongside oppressed and impoverished populations (Leonard, 1994, p.17);
- the importance of dialogic relations between workers and service users;
- the role of social, economic and political systems in shaping individual experiences and social relationships, including interactions within the practice context (Leonard, 1995, pp. 10–15);
- a commitment to the 'study of change, the move toward change' and the provocation of change (Fine, 1992, p. 220). Critical practice is orientated towards the transformation of processes and structures that perpetuate domination and exploitation (Leonard, 1994, p. 17).

Marginalizing dissent in critical social work

My purpose in this book is to contribute to the reworking and diversification of critical social work understandings and practices. In order to achieve this aim, it is necessary to dismantle some of the orthodoxies that have developed about what critical social work 'is'. This is a difficult task, not only because of the complexities of progressive social work in contemporary society, but also because of the often unspoken and yet unquestionable status of many of the central truth claims of critical social work. It is astounding that while activist social workers are scathing of orthodox social work and profoundly self-critical about their own relations to the consumers of social services, there remains an 'amazing confidence' in the emancipatory potential of critical practice models (Rojek et al., 1988, p. 55).

Some of the difficulty in mounting a critique from *within* activist social work arises from the representations of activist practice as inherently different from and, indeed, opposed to orthodox social work. Frequently, these oppositional representations quell dissent about critical social work by contributing to the view that those 'who are critical of radical positions must, by that fact, be for traditional forms of theory and practice' (Rojek et al., 1988, p. 2). Even the difficulties experienced by social workers in bringing an emancipatory orientation to bear in their work fail to lead to critical re-evaluation of the central claims of activist practice approaches. It is as though these practices are innocent of marginalization and silencing of any kind. Instead, the dissonance between critical visions and the practices of social work is attributed to a range of reasons other than the limitations of the discourses themselves. The lack of translation of radical ideas to critical practice is attributed to a variety of reasons, including: the social control function of social workers; the limited commitment to radical change amongst social workers; the lack of political sophistication of social workers (see Ife, 1997, p. 169); and, even, the limited change aspirations of the consumers of social services (see Dixon, 1989; Mowbray, 1992).

In rethinking critical social work, I begin with the proposition that critical social work, as it is currently constituted, marginalizes dimensions of activist social work. While the critical models on which activists draw allow insights that are important to social workers, they often leave little space in which to voice the contradictions, uncertainties, contextual variability within activist practice contexts and the specific demands associated with social work practice, particularly in conventional settings. The silencing of the local features of practice is not an oversight but, rather, it is intrinsic to the ways in which critical social work has represented social work practice and practice processes.

First, despite a claim to praxis, activists are often highly prescriptive about what counts as critical practice. For example, critical practices are described as 'anti-authoritarian' and 'oppositional' (see Ife, 1997, pp. 74–5, p. 184). Very often these definitions carry with them implicit assumptions about where social workers will practice. This insensitivity to diverse practice contexts contributes to representations of activism that privilege certain kinds of practice sites, such as small community based settings, over other contexts, particularly the multidisciplinary (and multi-ideological) bureaucratic and privatized settings where most contemporary social work practices are performed. Moreover, these definitions contribute to modes of activism in which the typical demands and expectations of social work practice are ignored, if not seen as impediments to change practice. All too often, critical theories seem to avoid the urgent questions of how to bring an activist orientation to bear in settings where the overt use of worker power and authority is not only unavoidable but, in fact, central to the work that social workers do. Even the use of power mandated *through* critical practice theories, such as the exercise of power required to initiate consciousness raising, collective processes, the sharing of skills and the dispersion of power itself, is underplayed, if acknowledged at all, in critical social work authors' reflections on practice (Healy and Mulholland, 1998).

Second, the representations of workers and service users as opposites can obscure the other ways workers and service users relate to each other in practice. The caricature of the privileged social worker and the disadvantaged client leads to gross overgeneralizations about power, identity and change processes in social work practices. In activist discussions of practice, social workers are represented as replicas of other forms of professional practice, such as medicine, law and education, with little regard for the diversity of social work practices, the profession's ambivalent relation to positivist human sciences and its gender composition, features that differentiate it from many other contemporary human service disciplines.

Third, the fixed definitions of social change devalues the change activity in which social workers are typically engaged. Critical traditions foreground social super-structures in analysis and action. The dualistic construction of the structural and local spheres leads logically to the conclusion that the local practices of social work are limited if not counterproductive for radical social change (see Dixon, 1989; Mowbray, 1992). Quite simply, radical analyses can overlook the emancipatory potential in everyday social work practices by establishing standards that devalue much of the change activity in which social workers are involved. At the same time, the emancipatory potential of other practice contexts is exaggerated because of a failure to acknowledge the extent to which the historical context of social services impacts on the kinds of practice processes that are possible (Larbalestier, 1998).

Critical poststructural theories can make an important intervention in terms of highlighting and destabilizing the orthodoxies that have become unquestioned features of modern critical practice discourses. In its emphasis on the local and the contextual, critical poststructural theory can begin the reworking of critical practice theories by destabilizing the opposition between social totality, where the causes and solutions to social problems are assumed to be, and the localities where social work actually occurs. This destabilizing work can help social workers to extend and diversify what counts as social change and hence what qualifies as critical social work practices.

A poststructural turn in critical social work

In analysing the relevance of contemporary 'post' theory to social work I refer to critical poststructural theories, particularly the work of Foucault and the radical poststructural feminists, rather than other aspects of postmodernism. The reason for this orientation is that the work of these poststructural authors provides useful tools for destabilizing and reworking the social work theories, whilst retaining an orientation towards progressive political practices. Although the terms 'postmodernism' and 'poststructuralism' are often used interchangeably, there are differences between them. Here I will overview these similarities and the differences as a way of alerting the reader to the orientation taken in this book.

One of the difficulties in differentiating between postmodernism and poststructuralism is that many of the authors associated with these bodies of thought contest their inclusion in them. The diversity of ideas amongst thinkers so named leads Foucault (1988b) to remark: 'I do not understand what kind of problem is common to people we call postmodern and poststructural' (p. 34). Nonetheless, there are some common themes that delineate postmodern ideas from those associated with poststructuralism.

Both schools contest the grand narratives of modernity, particularly the attempts to explain and transform the social whole. However, the basis of the critique differs between the schools. On the one hand, postmodernists are disillusioned with modernity. Lyotard (1984) contrasts the Enlightenment claims to human better-ment with the violence and oppressions that have occurred in the name of progress. Moreover, postmodern authors contend that the contemporary conditions of constant change and upheaval exceed the capacity of the grand theories of modernity to understand or direct action (Bauman, 1992). Postmodern theories are founded on the claim that the contemporary conditions of transformation are so fundamental that the new conditions must be named and new cultural forms developed in order to understand and engage with these uncertain times (Kenway, 1992, p. 121).

By contrast, poststructural theory challenges the failure of contemporary social and political discourses to come to terms with the constitutive power of language. Poststructuralists are particularly critical of the humanist aspects of Enlightenment thought, which are based on assumptions about the coherence of individual identity and which place humans centre stage in determining the course of history. Butler (1995) distinguishes between postmodernism and poststructuralism in the following way:

> There is a difference between positions of poststructuralism which claim that a subject never existed, and the postmodern positions which claim that the subject once had integrity but no longer does. (p. 48)

In short, the problem with modern understandings is that they give too much priority to individual action as the engine of change and too little attention to the power of discourses in shaping the social realities we experience. The poststructural emphasis on the constitutive properties of language calls into question the key assumptions, such as notions of identity and change, on which modernist social work theories, whether conservative or radical, have rested.

Despite their profound scepticism of humanism, poststructural theories have adopted a less dismissive position than postmodernists in relation to the Enlighten-ment ideals of autonomous action and the possibilities of progressive forms of social change. Foucault (1991f) argues that: 'One doesn't have to be "for" or "against" the Enlightenment . . . one has to refuse everything that might present itself in the form of a simplistic or authoritarian alternative' (p. 43). The focus here is on interrogating and diversifying approaches to progressive change rather than abandoning these ideals altogether. In contrast to the grand and utopian visions that have underpinned activist social work theories, poststructuralism denotes approaches to social change that are anti-dogmatic, pragmatic, flexible and con-textually sensitive and that require activists to adopt a critically self-reflexive attitude towards the effects of their emancipatory ideals. If there can be said to be an aim of poststructural emancipatory politics it is towards the creation of conditions for ongoing dialogue and contestation. As Yeatman (1994) states: 'the ideal state is not the overcoming of domination once and for all but ongoing imaginative and creative forms of positive resistance to various types of domination' (p. 9)

There is enormous diversity within poststructural thought and certainly not all of it can help extend progressive political practices. Even amongst those authors whose work develops critical poststructural perspectives, there is a lack of consensus about many key assumptions and directions for action. The task of drawing implications for critical forms of social work is complicated by this lack of commonality, the complexity of the various bodies of work and the disparate interpretations of the work of poststructural thinkers. For these reasons, it is generally more useful to talk about individual thinkers rather than the field of poststructuralism. In this work, I have elected to focus on the work of Foucault and radical poststructural feminist thinkers, Hélene Cixous, Elizabeth Grosz and Moira Gatens because of their interest in activist politics and the processes of power, identity and change.

The poststructural orientation of this work

One claim on which this book rests is that critical social workers, like the orthodox social workers they critique, are closed to the dynamism and diversity of social work practices. The attempts of orthodox and radical social workers alike to locate an essence of social work evades the possibility that there is no such 'thing' as social work independent of the contexts in which it is constituted. In this analysis I will use poststructural insights to challenge the search in both orthodox and critical forms of social work for a core to practice. I propose that the destabilizing influence of poststructuralism can challenge the orthodoxies that are as much a part of 'radical' social work and its 'conventional' other. Through this contest, poststructuralism can contribute to more democratic and open-ended interchange between the theoretical and practical dimensions of social work.

The use of poststructural theory to rethink critical practices is controversial. Amongst many critical social workers there is a concern that poststructural ideas can obscure the material realities of disadvantage and, moreover, that these theories can leave activists bereft of political strategy (see Rees, 1991; Hewitt, 1993; Kenny, 1994; Taylor-Gooby, 1994). Smith and White (1997) contest the relevance of poststructuralism for critical social work practice thus:

> In minimizing the continued role of the state, and in collapsing all ideology and subjectivity into discourse, the often grim, lived realities of oppressed groups may be reduced to 'difference' and, in the process, pressing social imperatives may become obscured. (p. 294)

Many activists are concerned about the nihilistic and conservative implications of poststructural philosophies. These thinkers question the utility of poststructuralism on the grounds that it offers few truths or directions for practice and threatens to undermine the emancipatory ideals that have provided the foundations for critical social work. It fails to provide a framework for progressive practice because it is unable to 'specify possible mechanisms of change and . . . to state why change is better than no change' (Parton, 1994b, p. 110).

The use of poststructural theory I am proposing does not involve a straightforward adoption of these perspectives. Rather, I am using the opportunities poststructuralism provides for destabilizing the truth claims about what social work is, particularly what counts as emancipatory practices, so that a diverse range of progressive practices may emerge. My focus here is primarily on extending social work and, in accordance with this orientation, it is also necessary to interrogate the limitations of poststructural theory for social work practice. The reader should bear in mind that just as many of the critical theories on which social workers draw have not been developed with social work practice in mind, neither do most poststructural thinkers have any knowledge of social work practice. For example, Foucault (1991a, p. 304) cites social workers alongside a range of other modern professions such as law and medicine whose gender composition, knowledge base and professional power are quite distinct from social work. While I acknowledge the importance of Foucault's critique of professional helping as a tool for the surveillance and discipline of oppressed populations, it has been necessary to 'use Foucault against himself' (Sawicki, 1991, p. 108) on the grounds that he too has adopted a universalist critique of the helping professions which fails to grasp the dynamism and diversity of social work practices.

Using social work practice to build critical practice theory

In this book, I will demonstrate how the practices of social work can inform and extend critical practice theories. Despite an espoused emphasis on praxis amongst activist social workers, it is increasingly rare that the specifics of day to day practice directly inform the development of practice theories. Indeed, the search for the truth about social work practice seems to occur anywhere but in the practices of social work. An over-reliance on modern theories, from the psychoanalytic through to the sociological, has led to authoritarian theorizing approaches in which the practices of social work are marginalized as sites of knowledge building. As Rojek et al. (1988) claim,

> In recent years, social workers have been invited to locate their activities in the context of (a) capitalist society, (b) patriarchal society, and (c) the community. Such grand claims have been made on behalf of each concept, often by writers who are not full-time social workers and sometimes by writers who have never set foot in an agency office. (p. 161)

A dissonance endures between theories of emancipation and the practices of social work, including critical practice. There are many losses for social workers arising from this lack of practice based and practice relevant theorizing, not the least of which is the virtual absence of formal knowledge about progressive practice in conventional practice contexts and the operations of power even within activist practice sites. By contrast, the analysis that is developed in this book is developed, in part, within specific contexts of practice. My intention is to *use practice to interrogate theory and vice versa.*

Importantly, this analysis is not confined to particular practice situations. By theorizing with reference to practice examples, I aim to provide illustrations of the dynamism of power, identity and change that not only are unaccounted for, but which *cannot* be accounted for, in current theorizations about critical social work. By highlighting some of the limitations of emancipatory theories for social work practice I intend to open the critical canon to the complexities and contingencies of activist social work practices. I envisage, also, that by my grounding the analysis with reference to practice problems and illustrations, readers may be encouraged to consider the possibilities and limitations for critical work in their own contexts of practice. This orientation, of course, is not to deny the importance of critical visions for better practice, but to insist that if these ideals are to be meaningful for practice they must engage with the *practices* of social work. In other words, my intention is not to eliminate the influence of critical social theory, even grand theory. Rather, I question the status these theories have gained as objective and unquestionable truths and, in so doing, create more fertile conditions for dialogue between theories of activism and the practices of critical social work. Thus, I intend to contribute to the transformation of what is often a monologue or at least two separate conversations into a more dynamic interchange.

What you can expect: an overview of the book

There are three elements of the book. These are:

- an overview of critical social science and poststructural theories and their implications for emancipatory practices;
- the empirical investigation of power, identity and change in conventional and critical practice contexts;
- discussion of the implications of 'post' theories for reinventing critical social work and a discussion of future directions for critical social work theory and research.

In Chapters 2 and 3 I focus on social science theories and their influence on emancipatory political practice. In Chapter 2 I overview the critical social science tradition; this incorporates many of the theoretical perspectives that underpin radical social change movements and practices, such as Marxist and feminist theories. Here I outline how the key assumptions of this tradition have shaped analysis and action in a range of critical social work models. In the third chapter I provide an introduction to critical poststructural theories. While the diversity of postmodern and poststructural thinking is acknowledged, here I emphasize the implications of two areas of poststructural thought, the work of Foucault and radical poststructural feminist thinkers, particularly Hélène Cixous, that I will analyse further throughout the work. In this chapter, I explore the implications of these thinkers' works for emancipatory politics.

In Chapters 4 to 6, I investigate the relevance of poststructural theories for activist social work practices. In Chapter 4 I canvass the positive and negative appraisals of poststructuralism within the activist social work literature. I then outline how poststructuralism may assist activist social workers to rethink the assumptions underpinning current modes of emancipatory practice and to develop approaches to activism that are more open ended and responsive to the contingencies of social work.

Chapters 5 and 6 ground the debate about critical and poststructural perspectives through practice illustrations from both conventional and activist practice settings. In discussing critical practice I draw extensively from a site of practice in which a core group of young parenting women were involved in analysis and action about young women's experiences of violence. Referring to this practice context and also to statutory social work practice, in Chapter 5 I critically interrogate critical social work notions of power. While acknowledging the insights that critical discourse makes possible, here I demonstrate the perspectives that are suppressed, including: the application of critical perspectives to statutory social work practices; the productive operations of power *within* critical contexts; and the limits of the categories of power and powerlessness to describe the experience and exercise of power in social work practice.

Chapter 6 involves an investigation of the possibilities and the limitations of the radical change strategies endorsed by critical social work. In this chapter, I explore some of the contradictory and complex effects of critical strategies, particularly the emancipatory and silencing effects of consciousness raising, collective identification and oppositional activity. I discuss how poststructural perspectives can address some of these silencing effects by promoting practice approaches that are cognizant of specific practice contexts and the local aspirations of those people whom critical social workers aim to work alongside.

The final two chapters draw together themes from the theoretical and practical investigation of post theories and social work practices to identify the use of this 'school' for critical forms of social work. In Chapter 7 I outline how the profoundly destabilizing effects of post theories can assist in the reconstruction of social work practice approaches that are open to the uncertainties and contextual variability of contemporary human service practices. I do not intend to endorse an 'anything goes' approach to activism. Rather, I aim to promote the diversification of what counts as activism and who counts as capable of contributing to critical practice theories, and so to renew activist appreciation of everyday and diverse practices of social work as sites of critical understanding and action.

Conclusion

At the dawn of the twenty-first century, critical social workers face momentous challenges to the grand visions and ambitions that once sustained activist practices. Under the sway of internal and external critique, activist social workers face the sobering reality that the dreams of a better future on which contemporary social movements and critical welfare practice draw all too easily become the nightmares for those they claim to liberate. As progressive social workers, we cannot ignore the need for major structural changes. Yet, if we are to avoid the totalizing and authoritarian practices to which the grand plans of modernity have led, we must learn to celebrate apparently minor and local victories in favour of those who are marginalized. At the very least, the insights of 'post' theories urge a revaluing of local changes as different from, and certainly not 'less' than, the aspirations of total transformation which have long guided activism. Amongst critical social workers, there is dissension and, for some, hopelessness about which way to turn. My intention in this book is to open critical social work to the diverse directions in which critical poststructural theories can take it and, in so doing, assist activists to think through the possibilities for progressive practices into the new millennium.

2 The Legacy of Our Past and the Nature of Our Present

Although critical social work, in its various contemporary forms, is a relatively recent arrival in the history of social work, radical elements have long existed within the field. The caricature of the psychoanalytically orientated social worker (dressed in the mandatory twin-set and pearls) belies the activism of those who, throughout the history of contemporary social work, have worked creatively and with determination for progressive change. Some of these earlier activists are well known to the profession. For example, Jane Addams's (1961) work on philanthropy and social settlement in America, which was published a century ago, provides one illustration of critically orientated social service work. While occasionally the voices of our predecessors (see Parker, 1961; Reynolds, 1963) and historical analyses of social welfare practices (see Kravetz,1976; Franklin, 1986; Van Krieken, 1992) challenge generalizations about the deep-seated conservatism of our forebears, by and large their critical practice remains undocumented and unacknowledged.

It was not until the late 1960s and early 1970s, under the heady sway of progressive social movements and critical social theories, that a distinct and internally diverse critical social work canon emerged (Rojek et al., 1988, p. 45). During this epoch, a burgeoning alternate public sphere provided the intellectual and the political foundations that were of immense importance to social workers as they embarked on the critical redirection of practice theory. The intellectual antecedents of contemporary critical social work are multifarious and incorporate a broad band of critical social theories including: feminist theories, Marxism, community development, radical educational theory (especially the work of Freire), anti-psychiatry, radical sociology, critical theories about race and ethnicity, and liberation theology.

Critical social workers defined themselves against the individualistic ethos of orthodox social work theories, particularly the psychoanalytic theories that gained pre-eminence in mainstream social work from the 1920s to the 1970s (Rojek et al., 1988, pp. 20–1). Critical social welfare theorists challenge views that hold welfare clients partially, if not entirely, culpable for the difficult personal and social circumstances many of them face (see Cloward and Fox Piven, 1975; Weatherley, 1987; Mullaly, 1993). Critical practice theorists foreground the social origins of oppression in their analyses and practice responses. Activists contrast their own approaches to orthodox social work as they emphasize the values of equity and justice for oppressed populations. Critical practice theory spans a diverse range including: anti-racist and anti-oppressive social work, radical community work, feminist social work, Marxist social work, participatory action research, radical social work, and structural social work.

Given the divergent origins of critical social work, deep differences and, indeed, antagonisms within this canon are to be anticipated. For instance, feminist workers have offered extensive critiques of the gender blindness inherent to radical social work models (Hanmer, 1977; Marchant, 1986), while anti-racist social workers have emphasized the racism that continues even in critical social work discourses (Dominelli, 1989). Similarly, there is fierce contention about practice methods amongst activists. There is debate about the privileging of collective practice approaches over the interpersonal practice methods that are most commonly encountered in social work practice. In response to this debate a significant body of literature has emerged attesting to the relevance of activist ideas to casework and clinical practices (see Bricker-Jenkins et al., 1991; Fook, 1993).

Despite their obvious variations, what these critical approaches to the practice share is their foundation in the critical social science paradigm. This is not to suggest that the practice approaches can be entirely explained by this paradigm. For example, Peile (1991, p. 145) points out that although feminist approaches are often based in the critical social science paradigm, they also move beyond it (see Van den Bergh and Cooper, 1986; Sands and Nuccio, 1992). The point, however, is that within each of these models of practice there is a general endorsement of critical social science understandings about the nature of the social world and human existence.

In this book I am primarily concerned with critical practice theory and, here, I begin with an illumination of the often unspoken but also unquestioned theoretical foundations of activist social work. The examination turns initially to our theoretical past, that is towards the antecedents of the contemporary critical social science theory on which activist social work draws. In this first section I will discuss the foundational work of Hegel and Marx and I will consider the twentieth century developments of critical theories. Although this material is dense, it provides important insights about the origins of the taken-for-granted truths on which activists, including anti-racist, feminist and radical social workers, depend. I will then move to an investigation of our present. I outline key elements of the critical social science paradigm which inform much contemporary critical social work theory. In making links to these historical origins, I outline the fundamental tenets of critical practice theory. For although it is certainly true that critical practice theories are remarkably varied in the practice processes they promote, they can be shown to share pivotal assumptions about power, identity and processes of change. It is important to make these claims plain not only in order to understand what critical social work 'is', but also to investigate how it can be transformed.

Critical theory: the origins of critical social science

Critical theories are concerned with possibilities for liberatory social transformation. In realizing this vision, critical theorists emphasize the relationship between theory and practice. For them, a key point of critical theory is not just to understand the world but to change it (Marx, 1972e, p. 109; Mies, 1983, p. 123; Fay, 1987, p. 4). This approach situates the theorist and practitioner *within* struggles for political change. As Fraser (1989) comments,

A critical social theory frames its research program and its conceptual framework with an eye to the aims and activities of those oppositional social movements with which it has an identification. (p. 113)

Approaches such as Marxism, some forms of feminism and liberation theology, are examples of critical social science theories (Fay, 1987). An important aspect of the critical theories is their emphasis on the abilities of humans, through their self-conscious and collective action, to achieve the emancipatory vision of a society free from domination.

Critical social theories have their foundations in the Enlightenment ideal of a society based on human equality and freedom. Enlightenment philosophy, which blossomed in the eighteenth century, emphasized the importance of reason and human action in shaping society (Fay, 1987). Enlightenment thought stressed the activist character of human beings; that is, it is recognized that although humans are shaped by society they are also capable of transforming it.

The contribution of Hegel to critical theory

The work of Hegel, an Enlightenment philosopher, is of major importance in the formation of the critical paradigm. Hegel's notion of the dialectic diverged from traditional philosophical claims regarding the separation of thinking from reality, and thus allowed for the development of a materialist philosophy (Engels, quoted in Tucker, 1972, p. xviii; Marcuse, 1955). Firstly, Hegel's dialectic challenges the notion of objective truth or reality. Hegel (1910, 1977) insisted on a dialectic relation between thought and reality. For Hegel, the subject transforms the object it observes (Wartenberg, 1993, p. 109). In this dialectical view, there is no such thing as a separate reality, unaffected by the observer. For Hegel, truth and self-consciousness are interlinked. As Marcuse (1955) summarizes Hegel's position:

The world is an estranged and untrue world so long as man does not destroy its dead objectivity and recognise himself and his own life 'behind' the fixed form of the things and laws. When he finally wins his self-consciousness he is on his way not only to truth of himself but also of his world. (p. 113)

For Hegel, self-conscious reason enables humans to recognize their dialectic relation to the world. In this view, the individual's thought is not separate from reality but is actively involved in creating it.

A second aspect of the dialectic is that everything is in a process of becoming. For Hegel, each entity contains its opposite, so each thing is essentially self-contradictory. In the process of becoming, there is a dialectic conflict between the apparent reality and its self-contradiction. In the dialectic tension between the two poles, new syntheses emerge to resolve the contradiction and they then become part of further dialectic contest. For Hegel, the entire history of civilization can be understood in terms of this dialectical process between thesis, contradiction and synthesis (Forster, 1993, p. 132). There can be no static reality. For Hegel, reality 'defies formalisation and stabilisation, because it is the very negation of every stable form' (Marcuse, 1955, p. 144). Critical social theory, then, is concerned with grasping the potential of a thing rather than what a thing apparently 'is'.

A third aspect of the dialectic conception is that of totality. For Hegel, all events and experience occur in relation to the social totality. According to Peile (1991),

> Within the dialectic view, things are only concrete if they are embedded in their context, in relation to other objects. These relationships are not parts of a whole which can be considered separately. Rather, they are moments of a totality where the moments can only be understood when the relationship of each relationship to the rest are known. (p. 68)

While Hegel emphasizes context in understanding experience, he is also explicit about the form that context takes. That is, Hegel gives primacy to the notion of a totality of consciousness of which all things are a part, and his view is that experience can only be understood in relation to this. For Hegel, each thing bears a direct relation to the totality and so can only be understood in relation to it.

Hegel's notion of the dialectic, and the conceptions of the social totality that are associated with it, provided key philosophical forms that have been incorporated into critical social theory. However, critical social theorists profoundly disagree with the idealistic emphasis of Hegel's philosophy (Peile, 1991, p. 70). In the view of these theorists, Hegel's work does not adequately reflect the material dimensions of reality (see Marcuse, 1955). Thus, although critical theorists incorporate Hegel's philosophical foundation, they have considerably reworked these concepts to emphasize the material because it is this which profoundly structures all facets of social reality, including individual thought.

Marx and the materialist dialectic

The work of Marx is central to a range of modern critical social theories. Indeed, Marx is commonly credited with founding the critical theory tradition (Kellner, 1989). Although acknowledging his philosophical debt to Hegel, Marx emphasized the material dimension of the dialectic (Marcuse, 1955). This inversion of the dialectic has profound implications which continue to be influential in contemporary critical social science theories and social movements.

Firstly, Marx considered that in capitalist society, the mode of production causes alienation between thought and reality (Marx, 1972c, p. 133). This disconnection affects everyone; however, Marx viewed it as having the most profound consequences for the proletariat whose production of the material world is obscured. For Marx, the condition of the working class is one of complete alienation. Fay (1987) describes Marx's view as being that:

> Alienated creatures are ones who do not recognize the world they have created as their own world, but rather take it as something 'just there', something given, something alien and powerful with which they must deal. (p. 53)

For Marx, the complicity of the proletariat in their oppression is due, in part, to their lack of consciousness about their productive capacity. Importantly, their achievement of self-consciousness is necessarily a class rather than an individual activity (Marx, 1972c, p. 157). Marx argued that revolutionary transformation requires the proletariat to recognize their shared contribution to the social order, and their shared interest in overcoming it. The abolition of the mode of labour, which in Marx's view is the true interest of the proletariat, is fundamental to ending the alienation of both classes (Marcuse, 1955, p. 291). In this sense, for Marx, the proletariat are the 'true' class, for their shared concerns represent the interests of society as a whole.

Secondly, like Hegel, Marx adopted a view of the social totality as comprised of opposites. However, unlike Hegel, Marx identified these opposites as having a social and historical identity, that is the proletariat and the bourgeoisie (see, for example, Marx, 1972a, p. 104). Repeatedly, Marx emphasized oppressive power relations and the essentially contradictory character of the interaction between these two classes. For Marx, the history of society could be understood in terms of this struggle. Marx and Engels (1972) state in their introduction to the Communist Manifesto that:

> The history of all hitherto existing society is the history of class struggles. Freeman and slave, patrician and plebeian, lord and serf, guild-master and journeyman, in a word, oppressor and oppressed, stood in constant opposition to one another. (pp. 335–6)

There is some contention amongst theorists about the extent to which Marx actually intended to prioritize the struggle between distinct classes. For example, Resnick and Wolff (1987, p. 50) contend that Marx was concerned with class processes as only one of a range of social and cultural processes through which society is produced. Nonetheless, it is clear that in his own writing, Marx referred extensively to the opposition between the working class and bourgeoisie. Thus, a plausible interpretation of Marx's world view, and one adopted by many later critical social theorists, is that of society as based on a fundamental struggle between opposing classes.

Thirdly, whereas Hegel emphasized that self-consciousness is the ultimate end point of the dialectic, Marx considered that human liberation requires the transformation of material reality. In particular, Marx's vision of the classless society requires the fundamental transformation of the mode of production. For Marx, and later for Engels, communism provided the social framework through which the correct relation between humans and the material world could be achieved (Marx, 1972c, pp.157–64). In this relation, humans recognize themselves as the creators of the material world rather than the hapless subjects of it (Marx, 1972d, p. 320). Moreover, Marx emphasized that rather than being a negation of the human individual, communism provided the only possible foundation for individual expression. For Marx (1972c), the inequitable relations of capitalist and pre-capitalist relations excluded the masses from 'cultivating their individual gifts' through their mode of labour (p. 161). For Marx, this communist revolution must involve the proletariat acting for themselves as a class. In the capitalist mode of production, the proletariat are separated from recognizing their true position; however, their lived experience of oppression provides a fundamental understanding and motivation for revolutionary activity (Marx, 1972a, p. 105). Action is directed then to developing the capacity of the proletariat to act upon their shared class interests.

Twentieth century developments of critical theory

Marx's influence on twentieth century critical social theory has been profound. The contemporary development of Marx's work, in Western political theory, has taken two key paths (Resnick and Wolff, 1987, p. 40). The first is the classical Marxian view which continues to emphasize the economic deterministic aspects of Marx's theory. However, some theorists reject this classical view as 'too narrowly reductionist' to be useful for understanding and transforming capitalist society (Resnick and Wolff, 1987, p. 40). In this second school of thought the work of the Frankfurt school, including Horkeimer, Adorno, Marcuse and Habermas, can be located. Indeed, the Frankfurt school are commonly associated with the development of twentieth century critical theory. The critical theoretical work of the Frankfurt school has focused on tracing the linkages between the economic, political, social, cultural and psychic realms (Kellner, 1993, p. 47). Nonetheless, in concert with the work of Marx, these theorists continue to refer to the social structure, particularly capitalism, as a prime source of oppression.

Habermas is a key influential figure of the contemporary Frankfurt school theorists. Despite the disillusionment of many in the Frankfurt school, Habermas defends the project of Enlightenment as an unfinished rather than an unrealizable ideal (Lechte, 1994, p. 187). In contrast with the economic focus of Marx's writings, Habermas's work is fundamentally concerned with communicative action. Much of Habermas's work deals with processes of the dialogue. In his attempts to understand the possibilities for genuine debate and consensus, Habermas has investigated the limitations to rational communication (see Habermas, 1978). Habermas (1978) contends that truth is possible, but that it is distorted through various social and psychological processes. Rather than reject the notion of truth, then, Habermas has sought to articulate the conditions in which truth can emerge. Some of the conditions he has identified include those of intersubjective understanding, shared knowledge and mutual accord amongst conversational participants (Bernstein, 1983, p. 186). Habermas's critical theories prioritize communication because, in his view, the achievement of a true democracy requires genuine public participation in political dialogue (Kellner, 1989, p. 206; see also Habermas, 1983). Thus, for Habermas, one contribution critical theory can make to social transformation is to promote authentic public debate and consensus on issues of human need (Kellner, 1989, p.162).

Some of the developments in the critical theory of the Frankfurt school are relevant to contemporary activist social work. In particular, while the Frankfurt school theories continue to emphasize oppressive relations of capitalist society, they also discuss contemporary social processes of domination. For example, the Frankfurt school exponents argue that, in the twentieth century, relations of domination are assimilated into modern cultural forms (Kellner, 1989, p.189). Nonetheless, the influence of the Frankfurt school on critical social work theory has been minor. One reason for this is the obtuse style of the Frankfurt school theorising, particularly in the work of Habermas. The theoretical density of the work and the lack of links made in Habermas's theorizing to the practice of social change, limits its usefulness to the theoretical and practical realities of critical social work. A further reason is that in the later writings of the Frankfurt school, an increasing disillusionment with the possibilities of social change was evident. For example, Horkeimer, and Adorno came to believe that reason had been corrupted via its incorporation into the very structure of capitalist society (Kellner, 1993, p.48). Similarly, in his later writings Marcuse argued that the basic class antagonisms had been channelled such that they no longer served as the basis for revolutionary action (Leonard, 1984, p.204). The general disillusionment of the Frankfurt school with the possibilities of change has meant that the work of these theorists appears to provide little guidance for the transformative aspirations of critical social workers.

Critical social science

The critical social theories that have most influenced activist social work may be banded together under the term 'critical social science'. This variant of critical social theory emphasizes the foundational belief of Enlightenment thought that through reason and action people can fundamentally reorder their private and collective life circumstances (Fay, 1987, p. 3). Fay (1987) defines this framework:

> Critical social science is an attempt to understand in a rationally responsible manner the oppressive features of a society such that this understanding stimulates its audience to transform their society and thereby liberate themselves. (p. 4)

In concert with Marx's epistemological stance, critical social science is primarily concerned with linking thought and action. For critical social scientists, rational reflection provides a vital base for radical action. Action is directed towards mobilizing the oppressed to engage in processes of fundamental personal and social transformation.

Whilst Marxist theory continues to be an important influence, critical social science refers to a range of theories not explicitly related to Marx or to the later critical theories of the Frankfurt school (Fay, 1987, p. 5). One way critical social science theories diverge from the work of these thinkers is that they do not necessarily prioritize capitalism as *the* overarching system of oppression. For example, some critical social science theories focus instead on patriarchy or imperialism as fundamental sources of domination. Indeed, various forms of feminism (particularly radical feminism, socialist feminism, Marxist feminism and eco-feminism), anti-racist theories, liberation theology, and Freire's pedagogy of the oppressed can be referred to as critical social science theories (see Fay, 1987).

Conceptual contributions of critical social science to activist social work

Despite the diversity of the content of critical social science approaches, these models share a number of features (see also Fay, 1987). In this discussion, I will outline four of the characteristics of critical social science that have particular relevance for activist social work.

Critical social theories seek to explain the social order

In their explanations of the social world, critical social science theories give primacy to the understanding of society as a totality. The various critical social science theories apprehend the social structure in different ways. For example, Marxists refer to the social totality as capitalism, radical feminists identify patriarchy as a primary social system (Wearing, 1986), and some anti-racist activists nominate the systems of imperialism (and the concomitant Eurocentric ideals) as fundamentally determining the social order (see, for example, Schiele, 1994). For critical social scientists, then, the overarching social structure is considered to fundamentally order social relations at institutional and personal levels. For this reason, critical social theorists adopt a descending order of analysis in that local experiences are believed to be the effects of an overarching social structure.

The social totality to which critical social scientists refer i entity. The particular form the totality takes is not perman but rather represents particular dialectical social processes, w Through their analysis of the nature of the totality, critical s provide insights for social transformation.

A conflict perspective is central to the understanding of power relations

From a critical social science perspective, power relations within the social totality are identified as fundamentally conflictual (Mullaly, 1993, p. 141; see also Lukes, 1974). Critical social theorists stress the power dimension of dialectical struggle between opposing social groups. This view insists that the conflicting interests of the opposed classes are fundamentally irreconcilable and that the power of the elite is maintained at the expense of the powerless (Lukes, 1974, pp. 12–13). For example, Mullaly (1993), a structural social worker, describes patriarchal-capitalist society as 'a system of winners and losers, with power and privilege going to the winners and alienation and oppression going to the losers' (p. 145). Thus, according to the conflict perspective, the power of individuals or groups reinforces and reflects structural inequities. Amongst the various critical social science approaches there is an enormous range of positions about the sites of power and the relations between them. However, critical social scientists are united in seeing power as fundamentally linked to domination (Sawicki, 1991, p. 20).

Critical social theorists dispute the manner in which the power of the elite is exercised. For some, particularly Althusser, Balibar and Poulantzas (discussed in Lukes, 1977, pp. 15–17), the position and power of the oppressor and oppressed are structurally determined. Thus, both groups can be said to be the 'effects' of the social system rather than the creators of it (Balibar quoted in Lukes, 1977, p. 16). Thus, although the elite clearly gain from the structural arrangements, they, like the powerless, are determined by it. A more common view espoused by critical social scientists is that there is a dialectical relationship between power and overarching social structures (see Fay, 1987; Lukes, 1977). In this dialectic relation there is:

> a web of possibilities for agents, whose nature is both active and structured, to make choices and pursue strategies within given limits, which in consequence expand and contract over time. (Lukes, 1977, p. 29)

This position, that humans both produce and are produced by the society, is based on an activist conception of human beings. For although humans are shaped by the social structure, they are also recognized as capable of altering it.

As social actors have some power to maintain or change the system, critical analysis is intended to identify those whose interests are met via the maintenance of the current social order. For although the activist conception of humans ascribed to by critical theorists means that both the oppressor and oppressed contribute to social arrangements, the powerful are seen to have an ongoing interest in its maintenance. In this sense, greater responsibility for the unjust social order is attributed to the powerful. Lukes (1974) argues that, 'The point . . . of locating power is to fix responsibility for consequences held to flow from the action or inaction of certain specifiable agents' (p. 56). Thus, although the powerful are recognized as structurally determined to some extent, they also have a vested interest in ensuring that the structural arrangements continue to work for their gain. Hence, social change practice involves fundamental confrontation of the elites.

An emphasis on rational self-consciousness as a precursor to change

A third aspect of the critical social science model is the promotion of rational, self-conscious thought in the process of personal and social liberation. In accordance with Marx's materialist dialectic it is recognized that the material reality will fundamentally structure, though not entirely determine, the individual's self-understanding (Corrigan and Leonard, 1978, p. 177). The complicity of the oppressed in their own oppression is, to a large extent, secured via the dominant ideologies of the particular society. Wearing (1986) defines ideology as 'a set of ideas and beliefs or world views which serves the interests of powerful groups in societies and perpetuates in various ways . . . the subordination of the powerless' (p. 34). For critical social theorists the subordination of the powerless occurs primarily through the false ideological propositions to which they adhere (Fay, 1987, p. 70). Nonetheless, despite the acquiescence of the oppressed, the fundamental conflict in society does not disappear. It is this latent conflict that the critical social theorists aim to expose and utilize as the motivation for social change. Thus, social transformation requires a consciousness raising process whereby the oppressed can critically examine the dominant ideologies of the society.

Consciousness raising strategies are aimed at assisting the individuals to identify the ways in which the social structure shapes their experience of disadvantage (see, for example, Freire, 1972). This reflective activity is orientated towards challenging the naturalized and self-limiting self-definitions and world views that have been internalized by the oppressed. In this critical reflection process, the disadvantaged are enabled to reject the dominant ideological positions as they come to recognize their genuine and ultimately shared interests. For critical social theorists, this awareness means that the oppressed are liberated to make more authentic choices about their lives, and more importantly, contribute to the creation of a social order that meets their genuine needs (Fay, 1987, pp. 74–5). Consciousness raising is thus considered as a fundamental precursor to radical social action.

The participation of the oppressed in the process of change

Critical social theories aim to empower their audience to transform the social order (Fay, 1987, p. 23). This means that the critical social science theory must have an action orientation and that this process of change must be intelligible to the oppressed (S. Leonard, discussed in Mullaly, 1993, p. 142). Critical theories emphasize the ability of people, particularly the oppressed, to transform their collective life circumstances. For critical social scientists:

> Enlightenment consists in the development of the powers of critical thinking and the will to use these powers to fashion the nature and direction of life . . . It wishes its audience to overcome their powerlessness, to re-fashion its collective arrangements to meet its true interests and ideals. (Fay, 1987, p. 67)

For example, Marx (1972c) emphasizes that through self-conscious and collective action, the working classes can transform capitalist society. In short, then, critical social science stresses the capacity of humans to transform society to an ideal state. This ideal, for critical social theorists, is a society free of all forms of domination and oppression. It is this emancipatory intent, along with the belief in the capacity of human reason and action to achieve it, which characterizes critical social science (Fay, 1987, ch. 3).

The development of a critical approach to social work

Activist approaches are, in part, built on a critique of orthodox social work. Activists expose the inherently political nature of social work and, particularly, the role of social work in processes of social control (see Bailey and Brake, 1975; Leonard, 1975).

Although this critique of the dominatory dimensions of social work practice appears to have arisen amongst Marxist social workers (Rojek et al., 1988, p. 51), it is certainly not confined to them. Activists of all ilks denounce conventional social work as a vehicle for the systemic domination of the oppressed (see Galper, 1980; Dominelli and McLeod, 1989; Mullaly, 1993) . In the following sections I will consider some key elements of the critique of orthodox social work that have emerged in the critical literature. These elements are:

- the critique of the individualistic focus of orthodox social work;
- emphasizing the inequities that underlie the worker–client relationship;
- the critique of professionalism.

Critiquing the individualistic focus of orthodox social work

Critical practice theorists critique the individualistic focus of orthodox social work (Fraser, 1989, p. 179; Mullaly and Keating, 1991, p. 51). Cloward and Fox Piven (1975) emphasize that:

> We have to break with the professional doctrine that ascribes virtually all of the problems that clients experience to defects in personality development and family relationships. It must be understood that this doctrine is as much a political doctrine as an explanation of human behavior. It is an ideology that directs clients to blame themselves for their travails rather than the economic and social institutions that produce many of them. (p. xxiii)

In the initial development of critical practice canon, in the 1960s and 1970s, radical social workers frequently emphasized the direct connections between an individualizing practice focus and social work's role as 'society's gate-keeper of the status quo' (see Middleman and Goldberg, 1974, p. 7; Throssell, 1975). As the welfare state recedes there is less debate about the role of the state in quelling dissent. Nonetheless, activists continue to seek a shift in the focus of practice to the 'first causes of oppression' in the overarching social structures such as capitalism, patriarchy and imperialism (DeMaria, 1993, p. 52).

Acknowledging the fundamental inequities between workers and clients

Activist social workers stress the inequitable character of the interactions between workers and 'clients' (see Laursen, 1975, pp. 58–9). Lowenstein (quoted in M. McNay, 1992) asserts that:

> The relationship between men and women, between races, between different social classes, and between helping professions and their clients are all variations of unequal power relations in society. (p. 55)

The fundamental and inevitable inequities between workers and clients, then, are considered to replicate and reinforce broader processes of oppression (Moreau, 1979, p. 81). Typically, in activist social work theories, workers and clients are represented as opposites. One way in which the oppositional representation of workers and clients is expressed is through the frequent portrayal of social workers as entirely naive to lived experiences of their clients (see Cloward and Fox Piven, 1975, pp. xxvii–xxviii; DeMaria, 1993, p. 60). E. Wilson (1977) contends that, 'it is hard for some social workers to imaginatively grasp the extent of hardship faced by their clients' (p. 8).

In accordance with the deductive approach taken to the analysis of power relations, it is understood that the middle class and professional status of the social worker confer on them greater power and authority than are supposed by those with whom they work. Indeed, it is frequently argued that even when the social worker shares certain experiences of oppression with the client (such as the experience of gender oppression) they are, nonetheless, more powerful than the oppressed populations with whom they work. Feminist social workers Dominelli and McLeod (1989) assert that,

> the traditional relationship between the helper and the helped is based on a hierarchical assumption that women clients need help because they are in some way inferior and women workers can offer help because of their superior qualities – be they knowledge, understanding, well-integrated personalities or a combination of all three (Wilson, 1977). As most social workers are middle class and most clients working class, this working assumption tends to reinforce ideas of class superiority. (p. 62)

From a critical social science viewpoint then, the professional power and authority of the worker is regarded as immutable and disabling. Further, even though activists occasionally acknowledge the constrained access to professional power experienced by workers, this is not seen to contribute to more equitable and mutual relations between workers and clients. In fact, Mullaly (1993, p. 162) contends that the limited general power of the worker may lead them to exploit the power differential between themselves and service users.

The ideology of professionalism and domination

While activist social work emphasizes the dissonant structural locations of workers and service users, an important aspect of the activist critique of social work focuses specifically on the ideology of professionalism. Fook (1993) argues that ideology upholds 'the belief that professionals are experts who know more than their clients about their problem situation and the means to deal with it' (p. 60). Activists contend that the ideology of professionalism is pervasive both in public institutions and within the community more generally and that this ideology supports a hierarchical relation between workers and clients (Cloward and Fox Piven, 1975; see also Fabricant, 1988; Routledge, 1993).

A key plank of the activist critique of professionalism is that this ideology leads to the privileging of technical and exclusive knowledge over the other forms of knowledge, particularly that of lived experience (see Dominelli and McLeod, 1989, p. 32; Mullaly, 1993, p. 174). In their critique of professionalism, activists frequently conflate the power exercised by social workers with other forms of professional power, such as that exercised by doctors, lawyers or counsellors (see, for example, Throssell, 1975; Andrews, 1992). For instance, Middleman and Goldberg (1974) critique the 'social worker's control over clients in social service systems' as corresponding to 'doctors' control over health systems, [and] teachers' control over parents in educational systems' (p. 4).

The transformative agenda of activist social work

Activist social work is orientated towards radical transformation in both the processes and goals of social work practice. While activists seek to develop more equitable relations between themselves and their clients, their concerns about equity are certainly not confined to this. Indeed, activists are motivated by a vision of a just society. As Pritchard and Taylor (1978) see it,

> If it [social work] is to achieve anything other than transitory success it must be motivated both by a desire to achieve socialist, environmental change *and* by an understanding of the forces that have brought our society to its present position. (p. 111)

However, the degree of change required and the role the social worker can be expected play in the transformation process vary considerably. Amongst activist social workers there is debate between the reformist and revolutionary approaches to practice. Some activist social workers aim towards the radical reform of society. This position is sometimes aligned with a democratic socialist stance (Pritchard and Taylor, 1978, p. 112). The radical casework approach of Fook (1993), and Middleman and Goldberg's method of structural social work (1974), are two examples of this position. Whilst social workers from within the reformist tradition recognize the need for fundamental structural change, they also insist that significant change in favour of oppressed populations can, and indeed must, be achieved within the current social order (Pritchard and Taylor, 1978, p. 112). For example, Middleman and Goldberg (1974) focus on the structural context of individual pain and advocate change to the structures of social service delivery; however, they do not demand the overthrow of patriarchal-capitalist society (Mullaly, 1993, p. 122).

In contrast to the reformist tradition, another group of activist social workers argue that activist practice should be primarily orientated towards revolutionary social transformation (Dominelli, 1995, p. 143; see also DeMaria, 1993; Dixon, 1993; Mullaly, 1993). These activists reject the reformist tradition on the grounds that justice for oppressed populations cannot be achieved without the complete transformation of the social order (Pritchard and Taylor, 1978, p. 113). These social workers contend that the reformist activity of social workers is not only limited for social change practice but, further, that this approach may actually contribute to the perpetuation of relations of oppression.

Despite the tensions between the reformist and revolutionary orientations, both share key ideas about the orientation to analysis and action that should be adopted by critical social workers. These central features include:

- the prioritization of the social structure in the analysis of problems;
- a shift from a focus on individual pathology to a concentration on oppression;
- the development of egalitarian practice processes;

- adoption of practice strategies that recognize and challenge the structures of oppression;
- the role of the social worker in activist practice.

The prioritization of the social structure

At the core of critical practice theory lies the analysis of the social structure. There is considerable diversity beyond this, however, as critical practice theorists draw on different analyses of the social structure. The early approaches to radical practice, in the late 1960s and 1970s, were significantly inspired by Marxist theory and, as such, class was the central conceptual category in the analysis and response to oppression (see, for example, Leonard, 1975; Throssell, 1975; Corrigan and Leonard, 1978). Over the past two decades, however, activist social work has been challenged by feminist and anti-racist activists to acknowledge sources of oppression beyond that of class.

Feminist social workers presented a powerful critique to the Marxist analysis that guided much of the early activist practice models. Although the concerns of many feminists extend beyond issues of gender, the work of feminists has had a significant influence on a plethora of activist models, including in particular structural and Marxist approaches to practice (see Fook, 1993). Although there is considerable variation in their theoretical positions, feminist activists, particularly those working from socialist feminist, Marxist feminist or radical feminist frames, nominate patriarchy as an overarching system of oppression (see Nes and Iadicola, 1989). By including an analysis of patriarchy, feminist social workers have been able to demonstrate the systemic character of women's oppression and the inclusions of gender issues in the analysis of oppression. Notwithstanding the continuing gender blindness amongst some activist social workers, it is apparent that feminist approaches have made significant inroads into the analysis of oppression across a broad spectrum of activist practice models (see Mullaly, 1993). Yet, even so, feminist social work theorists have been reluctant to take on the contemporary transformations of feminist theories in the humanities and social sciences, much of which is critical of a unified notion of patriarchy (for an exception, see Sands and Nuccio, 1992).

Anti-racist social workers have mounted a considerable challenge to activist social work, also. Anti-racists theorists have claimed that social work, including activist practice, has a history of institutionalized racism (Dominelli, 1989; Petruchinia, 1990). Moreover, some anti-racist theorists assert that many forms of critical social work continue to obscure the racial oppression faced by a significant number of welfare clients (Hutchinson-Reis, 1989, p. 168). Anti-racist social workers point to the impact of colonization and the continuing Eurocentrism on the oppression suffered by non-Anglo-Saxon populations. It is argued that disadvantaged racial and ethnic groups share collective histories of oppression and a disadvantaged structural location. Shah (1989) and Hutchinson-Reis (1989) argue that black people hold a common history and experience of society and that this distinction should be acknowledged in activist analysis and response to oppression.

Anti-racist theorists, then, centralize the dialectic conflict between privileged and non-privileged racial identities. In so doing, they demonstrate the racial blindness that endures even within activist approaches to social work.

For some time, feminist and anti-racist activists have offered compelling critiques of the class-based analyses that were favoured in radical and Marxist social work models. However, there is a wide variety of oppressions that does not fit neatly within the tripartition of class, gender and race oppression, and further it would seem that certain forms of oppression can be obscured by these categorizations. For example, lesbian women, including lesbian social workers, have argued that feminist social work has not adequately acknowledged their specific experiences of oppression (see Aronson, 1995). In the contemporary context, then, activist social work has been challenged to develop analyses that can acknowledge and incorporate the concerns of variously oppressed groups, such as gay and lesbian populations, disabled people and the aged (Langan and Lee, 1989, p. 3).

These challenges to activist social work have developed in the critical social science paradigm. For while critical practice theorists debate the nature of the social totality, they accept, as a basic organizing idea, that the totality actually exists. In general, the activist response to the protestations of the variously excluded oppressed identities has been to incorporate them into an expanded understanding of the social totality. This process of inclusion has taken two main forms. Some activists continue to prioritize one system of oppression as more profound than others. For example, Dixon (1993), a feminist community worker, argues that gender relations must be kept to the fore, whilst some radical social workers (such as Routledge, 1993) appear to prioritize the class system. The far more common response, however, is to view the social totality as comprising multiple systems of oppression (see Mullaly, 1993, p. 127). Hence, many activists are extremely vigilant in their incorporation of multiple sources of oppression, such as those of ageism, heterosexism and disablism in their analyses of social experience.

In the analysis of multiple systems of oppression, the relationship between these systems is commonly recognized as mutually reinforcing and overlapping. Moreau (1990) states that 'While retaining their own specific features and not minimising their differences in severity, all forms of oppression are based on an identical ethos of domination and subordination' (p. 64). The view that the problem lies in the dominant social structure allows activists to regard the various emancipatory aims of oppressed groups as ultimately reconcilable. Indeed, implicit in the activist vision of a society 'free from domination of any kind' (Dominelli, 1995, p. 143) is the assumption that the diverse calls for liberation can be met within a transformed society.

From individual pathology to social oppression

The notion of oppression is a key analytic tool of critical social workers. This concept enables social workers to move away from the notion of personal inadequacy as the cause of disadvantage, and instead to focus on the structural dimensions of individual or group experiences. Mullaly (1993) states that oppression occurs when a person experiences frustration, restriction or damage 'because of his or her membership in a particular group or category of people, for example, blacks, women, poor people, gays and lesbians' (p. 157). In this section, I will outline how critical practice theorists have applied the concept of oppression to the analysis of the experiences of social work clients.

Firstly, in activist social work theory, the analysis of individual oppression occurs by reference to the position of the individual or group within the social structure (Gibson-Graham, 1995, p. 179). Social identities, then, are classified by reference to broad social categorizations, such as class, gender, ethnicity and disability. These categorizations are essentialist in that the shared interests and power of certain individuals or groups of individuals, such as 'woman', or 'disabled' or 'ethnic' people, 'are said to be the necessary objective effects of a pre-given social structure' (Carrington, 1993, p. xiv). Thus, various populations are understood to share a common identity and experience (see Day, 1992, p. 16).

Secondly, relations of oppression are represented as fixed and unilateral (Dixon, 1993, p. 27; Mullaly, 1993, p. 157). For example, Moreau (1979) argues that:

> Structural social work is concerned with the ways in which the rich and powerful in society define and constrain the poor and the less powerful – the ways in which whites define native peoples and blacks, men define women, heterosexuals define homosexuals, adults define children, the young define the aged, and so-called normal people define the deviant. (p. 78)

According to this schema, certain identities are *necessarily* dominant over others. Various forms of activist social work emphasize particular relations of domination; for example, some Marxist workers emphasize the antagonistic relation between the middle class and the working class. Nonetheless, it is understood that experiences of oppression and relations of domination are fixed within an overarching social structure and, thus, can be deduced from the analysis of these arrangements.

Thirdly, the various axioms of oppression to which an individual may be subject due to their gender, class, race, sexuality and so forth are understood to overlay one another. Although many critical practice theorists contend that one form of oppression cannot be regarded as more burdensome than any other form of oppression (see, for example, Dominelli and McLeod, 1989, pp. 7–8; Moreau, 1990, p. 63) many activists consider the degree of oppression experienced by the individual to be concomitant with the *number* of oppressions experienced. For example, Dominelli and McLeod (1989) discuss the 'quadruple oppression' of race, gender, class and sexual orientation that affects black lesbian working class women (p. 65; see also Maguire, 1987, p. 115; Shah, 1989, pp. 178–9; Dixon, 1993, p. 27). Hence, while activists do not necessarily prioritize particular oppressed statuses over others, it is assumed that oppressed statuses 'add up' in the same direction and, hence, one can be doubly or triply oppressed (Yeatman, 1993).

The development of egalitarian practice processes

Critical practice theory promotes a fundamental 'shift in power from established political, economic and cultural elites and towards oppressed and powerless people'

(Galper, 1980, p. 61). In response to feminist critiques of hierarchical power dynamics that continued even in critical practice processes, they challenged activists to develop greater consistency between the goals and processes of practice. Increasingly, then, critical practice theory is orientated towards the goal of fostering equity between workers and participants within the context of practice (Dixon, 1989, p. 88; Mullaly, 1993, pp. 154–6; Thorpe, 1992, p. 26).

The activist concern with the transformation of power relations in the practice context is twofold. Firstly, the stress on increased equity can be seen as part of prefigurative strategy of activist social work. Prefigurative strategies aim for the realization in the current context of those forms of social relations, particularly equitable relations, that would characterize a transformed social order (Dominelli and McLeod, 1989, p. 9; Thorpe, 1992, p. 26; Dominelli, 1995, p. 135). Secondly, the transformation to equitable relations is central to honouring the activist conception of humans that lies at the heart of the critical social science paradigm. This ontological assumption translates in practice into a recognition of the capacity of all humans to participate equally in the processes that affect them (Galper, 1980, p. 118). This process, whereby the worker acknowledges the client's knowledge and capacities, is regarded by many activists as being empowering of itself (see Fook, 1993, p. 102).

According to the critical social science analysis, the social worker is innately more powerful than the client. The achievement of egalitarian practice relations requires a transfer of power from the worker to the participant (Fabricant, 1988) and there is some onus upon the worker to effect the transfer of power. For example, in reflecting on her collaborative research with Guatemalan women, Lykes (1988) asserts:

> My recognition of my (powerful) position enhanced my sensitivity to the power differential between researcher and participant and led to my efforts to develop strategies for empowering participants to redress this imbalance. (p. 179)

In the remainder of this section I will focus on three strategies commonly advocated by activist social workers for the achievement of more egalitarian practice relations. These are:

- the diminution of differences between workers and clients;
- the revaluing of the participant's knowledge;
- ensuring the accountability of the worker to the client.

The diminution of differences between workers and clients

Critical practice theory advocates the diminution of the distinctions between workers and service users, and two key strategies are often emphasized. The first is that workers may seek to reject those markers of status and authority that differentiate them from the client. Social workers may do this: by refusing to use professional jargon (Cloward and Fox Piven, 1975; Andrews, 1992, p. 34); by adopting the dress and language practices of the oppressed populations with whom they work (E. Wilson, 1977, p. 8); and by ensuring that they work with those issues and populations with whom they have an 'identification' (Chesler, 1991, p. 764). Some workers also suggest that the use of appropriate self-disclosure can help to facilitate the reduction of power differences (Fook, 1993, p. 104).

A second way in which activists may contribute to the reduction of differences between themselves and clients is through the adoption of a radical egalitarian stance. This stance is widely embraced in contemporary activist social work theory (for exceptions, see Alinksy, 1969; Dixon, 1989). The radical egalitarian stance makes a practical commitment to the values of power-sharing and client leadership often promoted in activist theory (see Ward and Mullender, 1991, p. 28; Dominelli, 1995, p. 142). As the unequal distribution of skills is thought to be 'inevitably correlated to the unequal distribution of power' (Phillips, 1991, p. 123), radical equity involves workers and service users in learning from each other as they share knowledge, skills and tasks at all stages of the practice process (Moreau, 1990, pp. 56–7; Mullaly, 1993, pp. 173–5). Although activists do acknowledge that the differences in power and skill are likely to remain, an ideal of the complete removal of all distinctions endures. For example, Dominelli (1995) claims that:

> [an egalitarian attitude] makes it easier for women to work cooperatively and collec-tively with each other. However, it does not guarantee the absence of power differentials amongst them, only that their presence will be acknowledged and worked upon. (p. 136)

Thus, from this view, it would seem that power differences are regarded as inevitably negative to the goal of equitable practice relations. Indeed, although Dominelli recognizes the presence of these differences, her view is that these must be 'worked on', by which she appears to mean that these differences must be diminished as far as possible.

Revaluing of the participant's knowledge

In critical practice the lived experience of the client, particularly their lived experience of oppression, is recognized as a rich source for knowledge building and activism. Indeed, it would appear that this knowledge is often regarded as a more valid source of information than the technical or 'scientific' knowledge of the professional (see Stoecker and Bonacich, 1992). Explicitly valuing the lived know-ledge of the oppressed in activist practice represents 'an acknowledgement and concrete expression of the people's superior knowledge of their own context and the desire of the researcher (or worker) to learn from them' (Mathrani, 1993, p. 351).

The emphasis in the activist literature on the revaluation of the client's lived experience reflects that one's position within the social structure fundamentally determines one's view of it. This view, referred to as standpoint epistemology, arises from the Hegelian insight into the dialectic relation between thought and 'reality' (Harding, 1987, p. 26). The revaluing of the lived experience of the oppressed is based on the premise that this lived knowledge enables a more holistic view of the world than that available to those located in a privileged position within the social structure (Swigonski, 1993, p. 172). Thus, the importance of valuing the knowledge of the oppressed lies in their capacity to offer different and more complete perspectives than those that could be gained from a position of relative advantage. Hartsock (1990) further claims that the voices from the margins will develop more inclusive epistemological approaches and world views. This is because the marginalized are unlikely to mistake their perspectives as universal (Hartsock, 1990, p. 172). In short, the standpoint position inverts the privilege traditionally accorded to professional knowledge. According to this view, the lived experience of oppression is seen to provide a fundamental source for the understanding of society and social change processes.

Ensuring the accountability of the worker to the client

A third way in which activists seek to contribute to more equitable practice relations is through ensuring that the worker is primarily accountable to the client (see Moreau, 1990; Healy and Walsh, 1997). According to activists, this contrasts with the loyalty of conventional social workers to the bureaucracies for whom they work and the ideology of professionalism that they seek to uphold. One way in which this accountability can be achieved is through maximizing information to the client and by developing mechanisms whereby the client can challenge the worker. As Middleman and Goldberg (1974) state:

> the worker should not have goals or methods that he [sic] keeps secret from the client. The mandate to establish a contract with each client or set of clients requires the worker to state his intentions explicitly. This not only insures the client's right to decide whether or not the worker's intended behavior is acceptable, but it also insures the worker's awareness of what he is about. (p. 34)

Moreover, Moreau (1990) argues that workers should seek to facilitate the accountability of welfare agencies to the people they serve. This could include such things as instigating adequate feedback and grievance mechanisms (Moreau and Leonard, discussed in Mullaly, 1993, pp. 174–5). The primary allegiance of the worker is to the service user rather than to their organization or to the state.

Strategies for change in critical social work

Activists promote practice strategies which recognize and respond to the structural causes of injustice. In this section, I will outline two strategies commonly promoted in the activist literature. The first strategy, that of consciousness raising, is common to both the reformist and transformational approaches to activist practice. The second strategy is concerned with the promotion of collective and oppositional identifications and, in some instances, the promotion of collective action. The chapter will conclude with a discussion of the role of the activist worker in social change practice.

Consciousness raising

A key strategy for change widely advocated by activist social workers is that of consciousness raising. The term 'consciousness raising' refers to a process of critical reflection whereby the oppressed move from a position of self-blame to an understanding of the structural origins of their suffering (Finn, 1994, p. 26; Gutierriez, 1995, p. 229).

The critical reflection process is connected to the lived experience of the oppressed. In this process, individuals come to understand that their lived experience of suffering is related to their membership of a particular oppressed group, such as 'women' or 'blacks'. Consciousness raising can involve a 'renaming' of experience so that the political dimensions of one's individual experience of disadvantage or suffering are made explicit (Van den Bergh and Cooper, 1986, pp. 7–8; Dominelli and McLeod, 1989, p. 32). In addition, activists insist that in the consciousness raising process, critical reflection and action are linked as the changed consciousness comes to bear on the transformed action of the oppressed (Leonard, 1975, p. 54; Carr and Kemmis, 1986, p. 144). Consciousness raising strategies reflect a number of critical social science principles.

Firstly, according to a dialectic view the world of the material and the ideological are joined. Activists claim that changed consciousness is a fundamental precursor to fundamental structural change (see Freire and Moch, 1990, p. 9). Feminist social workers Bricker-Jenkins et al. (1991) argue that:

> much of feminist practice begins with an examination of those values and beliefs that impede individual/collective self-actualisation and then seeks to create material conditions that embody a different configuration – one that makes it possible for all persons to grow to their full potential. (pp. 275–6)

By changing the world view of the oppressed, consciousness raising strategies both motivate and provide direction for social change activity. In particular, changed activity is not confined to notions of personal empowerment but rather incorporates notions of social transformation. For instance, Bricker-Jenkins et al. emphasize the importance of changed material conditions.

Secondly, consciousness raising strategies reflect the critical social science view that humans are essentially rational and, thus, changes in thought will be reflected in transformed action. Consciousness raising strategies, then, are based on a view that through a process of critical self-reflection people can develop a critique of their self-understandings and social practices, such that they can change the way they live (Fay, 1987, p. 39). Indeed, a fundamental premise of the consciousness raising strategy is that the process will not be confined simply to rational reflection but will extend ultimately to fundamental change both in the personal relationships of which one is a part and in the broader social contexts.

Thirdly, activists acknowledge the importance of their own self-reflection as a basis for action. Activists insist the consciousness raising process must involve a dialogic process between workers and clients (Galper, 1980, p. 14; Mullaly, 1993, pp. 165–6). Despite the emphasis on a dialogic stance, however, it is apparent that many practitioners have a very clear understanding of what they consider to be the true nature of people's experience. For instance, activists frequently refer to their role as 'pointing out' or 'unmasking' 'realities' (see, for example, Leonard, 1975, p. 60; Moreau, 1990, p. 56; Kelly, 1995, p. 98). Some researchers and practitioners have sought to combat the potential tyranny of the critical stance via the incorporation of a self-reflexive stance on the part of the researcher/practitioner (Mies, 1983; Harding, 1987; Swigonski, 1993). Self-reflexivity refers to a dialectical process whereby the practitioner/researcher reflects upon his/her position in relation to the knowledge development process and continually integrates this awareness into further knowledge building and action (Myerhoff and Ruby, quoted in Schrijvers, 1991, p. 168). This reflexive stance is critical to emancipatory practices if activists are to avoid reproducing processes of domination through the imposition of critical consciousness upon the participants.

The development of collective identifications and the emergence of collective actions

In concert with the conflict theory that is associated with critical social science, activists aim to promote the development of collective and oppositional identifications amongst oppressed people (Groch, 1994). The emergence of collective identifications amongst oppressed populations is based on the assumption that individuals within these populations share common identities and experiences. For example, activist social workers and researchers refer to these populations as unified categories such as 'the poor' (Fals-Borda, 1987; DeMaria, 1993), 'women' (Mies, 1983) or 'Guatemalan women' (Lykes, 1988). It is further assumed that on the basis of this shared identification oppressed people will be able to tell the truth of others within the same category or at least tell the truth more faithfully than a professional worker or researcher.

For activists, it is important that the oppressed not only recognize their shared identifications but that these identifications are also oppositional (see Fraser, 1989, p. 171). Groch (1994) defines oppositional consciousness as 'a consciousness that defines their [the oppressed] situation as unjust and subject to change through collective action' (p. 371). Through awareness of their opposition to dominant interests, it is envisaged that the oppressed will recognize their fundamental struggle against dominant interests (Corrigan and Leonard, 1978, p. 123; Moreau, 1990, p. 64). The development of collective and oppositional identity reflects a critical understanding of the social totality and the dialectical struggle between oppressor and oppressed on which society is based. This transformed self-understanding is central to engagement in the process of social transformation.

For many activists, particularly those who favour a revolutionary approach to activist practice, this process of collective and oppositional identification is seen as a precursor to the development of collective actions led by the oppressed. The role of the activist worker is not to lead the struggle for change but to facilitate the development of capacities amongst oppressed people to become protagonists in the 'advancement of their society and in defence of their own class and group interests' (Fals-Borda, 1987, p. 330). In consequence, activists commonly promote client-directed or 'user-led' processes at the levels of analysis and action (Ward and Mullender, 1991, p. 28; see also Sarri and Sarri, 1992).

Although activist social workers aim to foster the capacity of the oppressed to act in their own collective interests, it is envisaged that the society as a whole will benefit from the processes of transformation. Indeed, it is the frequent claim of activist authors that the various systems of oppression, particularly capitalism, patriarchy or imperialism, whilst having devastating consequences for oppressed people, have dehumanizing effects for all (Galper, 1980, p. 25; Dominelli and McLeod, 1989, p. 69). In this sense, the interests of the oppressed are universal concerns. This is evident in Marcuse's (1955) assertion that:

> the proletariat's interests are essentially universal. The proletariat has neither property nor profit to defend. Its one concern, the abolition of the prevailing mode of labour, is the concern of society as a whole. This is expressed in the fact that the communist revolution, in contrast to all previous revolutions, can leave no social group in bondage because there is no class below the proletariat. (p. 291)

Thus, while the social change agenda of activist social workers is orientated towards the alleviation of the misery suffered by oppressed peoples, it is considered that, in the longer term, social transformation will benefit the entire society.

Activist social work practice promotes the leadership of the oppressed in processes of social change. In accordance with standpoint epistemology, activists frequently regard the disadvantaged as better placed to understand the operations of society than those who benefit from the society (Marcuse, 1955; Harding, 1987). In part this is because it is assumed that the oppressed will offer a more inclusive leadership style than members of the elite (see Hartsock, 1990, p. 172). In addition, it would seem that participant leadership in the processes of change can lead to outcomes which are more responsive to the needs of oppressed people than professionally driven models of assessment and intervention (Sarri and Sarri, 1992; Mathrani, 1993).

The role of the worker

In this final section, I will discuss the role of the social worker both in the activist practice process and in broader processes of change. The increasing embrace of an egalitarian ethos in activist social work has led to the endorsement of participant led approaches to change. The emphasis on equity in the process of social change means that the worker is often excluded from the central role they might otherwise have played in both orthodox approaches to practice and in some models of activism (see Alinsky, 1969). Rather than adopt a position of leadership, then, the role of the activist is to facilitate the liberation of the voices and the energies of the oppressed for the processes of change. This is understood to involve the transfer of power from the worker to the participant. Some of the strategies for the transfer of power discussed in previous sections, include: the refusal of professional power and authority; the articulation of a shared knowledge base amongst the oppressed founded on their lived experience of disadvantage; and the facilitation of the recognition amongst the oppressed of their shared identity and their collective interests in change.

Although activists frequently insist that workers must seek to redistribute power, it is also recognized that the capacity of the worker to do so is often highly constrained. In accordance with the critical social science paradigm, the power of both workers and participants is assessed according to their location within the social structure. Hence, it is recognized that whatever actions the practitioner may take to redistribute power in the practice context, the basic structural inequities remain and are reflected in their relationship to their client (see Schrijvers, 1991, p. 166; Carniol, 1992, pp. 8–9). A view common amongst activist social workers is that this difference constrains the capacity of social workers to contribute to radical social change. For example, Hudson (1989) describes the problems of power that face feminist social workers:

> It would be easy, for example, for individual woman social workers to work with a women's group with the best of intentions and yet sometimes quite unwittingly, perpetuate power imbalances and thereby constrain the autonomous development and strength of the group. (pp. 82–3)

The activist approach to the analysis of power suggests that the power differences between workers are both immutable and oppressive. This conceptualization of power in the worker–client relationship has led some practitioners to conclude that the most empowering action a worker can take is to minimize their involvement with oppressed people; that is, to transfer skills and knowledge as efficiently as possible and exit themselves from the lives of service users (see Middleman and Goldberg, 1974).

A further area of concern for activist social workers is the extent to which social workers, particularly those working 'within' the system, can engage in radical change activity (see Carniol, 1992, p. 16; Fook, 1993, p. 68). The expectations of social service organizations and clients about the individualistic forms of help social workers will offer and the extensive workloads carried by many social workers limit opportunities for the kinds of progressive social change envisaged by activist social work theorists. Also, Carniol (1992, p. 17) points out that, the hierarchical and bureaucratic structures of many welfare agencies promote non-egalitarian practice processes. Carniol (1992) states, 'in a larger system that persists in its top-down, vertical social relations, these experiments in democracy and freedom find themselves racing against time' (p. 17). Furthermore, it would seem that the limited power of the social worker and their clients in many social work practice contexts, and within the society generally, limits possibilities for social workers to initiate radical change.

Despite these apparent limitations, many activist social workers suggest that the ambivalent position of the activist worker, that is as an agent of the ruling class whilst also a protagonist for change, offers them a significant opportunity to engage with the dialectic struggle between oppressor and oppressed. Leonard (1975) claims:

> elements of social work have always demonstrated a degree of ambivalence to the bourgeois values to which it is especially exposed by its class position. This ambivalence is one source from which radical practice can develop. (p. 49)

Thus, although radicals continue to insist on the class privilege experienced by many social workers, this does not mean that the social worker cannot engage in social change practice. Activist social workers frequently argue that the contradictory character of social work practice must be recognized if social workers are to contribute to progressive social transformation (see Leonard, 1975, p. 55; Hanmer, 1977, p. 93; Hudson, 1989, p. 70). The ambivalent position of the worker does imply that the social worker will need to make a concerted commitment to change activity, if his/her practice is not merely to further middle class interests. In particular, this means that workers must eschew their own class interests in favour of the marginalized. Indeed, Freire (discussed in Maguire, 1987) suggests that the liberatory worker must commit 'class suicide' (p. 68).

The goal of fundamental social transformation demands, then, that activist practice is not simply an approach to social work practice, but rather it is a way of life (Mullaly, 1993, p. 200). Activist practice demands that the worker is willing to live out a different set of values from the hierarchical and ultimately unjust ones that predominate in social welfare bureaucracies, teaching institutions and society more generally (DeMaria, 1993, pp. 51–2; Dominelli, 1995, p. 135). Activist social work processes involve approaches to practice which go beyond, and often contradict, that which social welfare organizations expect of social work practitioners. For many, activist social work requires congruence between personal and work practices. For instance, Galper (1980, p. 12) suggests that radicals bring greater consistency to their lives by integrating political commitments and their work practice. Moreover, this frequently involves political activity outside that associated with one's social work practice. For example, activist social workers frequently stress the importance of building coalitions with radical change organizations such as advocacy bodies and progressive unions (see Corrigan and Leonard, 1978; Mullaly, 1993, ch. 10).

Conclusion

In this chapter I have outlined the theoretical impulses that shape the past of activist social work and also define its present. Despite the enormous diversity within the critical canon, I have identified some of the pivotal assumptions about processes of power, identity and change through which critical practice theory is developed. This rich heritage has, in many respects, served activism well; it has enabled the reorientation of official practice discourses away from a focus on the individual towards an incorporation of broader concerns, at least in some practice approaches. Indeed, over the past three decades critical ideas have claimed a legitimate space in some arenas of professional social work training, as witnessed by the incorporation of these ideas in social work and social policy core texts. However, cracks are beginning to appear in the facade not only because of the dramatic political transformations upon us, but also because contemporary theoretical critiques and practice research are raising challenges about the relevance of critical practice theory for sustaining vision and practice in the local contexts where social workers are situated. Gibson-Graham (1996) asserts that if social structure 'takes up the available social space, there's no room for anything else . . . If [it] functions as a unity, it cannot be partially replaced' (p. 263). In the next chapter, I will demonstrate how the work of Foucault and radical poststructural feminists can be used to reveal and reconstruct the assumptions of critical social work.

3 Foucault, Feminism and the Politics of Emancipation

Critical practice approaches have fared ambivalently in contemporary welfare states. On the one hand, to the surprise of many critical social workers, there has been some official endorsement of what were formerly regarded as radical causes (Langan, 1998). For example, the importance of practice partnerships between social workers and service users is enshrined in child welfare legislation in the United Kingdom (the Children Act, 1989), New Zealand (the Children, Young Persons and Their Families Act, 1989) and in some states of Australia (the Victorian Children and Young Persons Act, 1989). On the other hand, the rise of the new right and an orientation towards risk management practice provides a hostile terrain for progressive social work.

In an epoch characterized by dramatic transformations in the organization and delivery of welfare services, the inroads made by the range of 'post' theories such as poststructuralism, post-Fordism and postmodernism into the social sciences and humanities are seen by many social workers as unnecessary and unwelcome. Despite the recent emergence of debate about the relevance of these contemporary theories within the social work literature, their influence on social work, particularly day to day practice and policy making, is limited. Fawcett (1998) contends that:

> a reluctance to theorize, an oral tradition and a generalized reliance on 'common sense' may account for this relative lack of influence. The complexity of some of the material involved and the difficulty in relating theory to practice could also be contributing features. (p. 264)

It may well be that aspects of social work 'culture', especially the long-standing ambivalence about practice theory, contribute to an indifference towards post-structuralism. In the title of their paper 'Oh no! Not more isms', Featherstone and Fawcett (1995) capture the weariness amongst social workers towards theory, particularly theories that do not appear immediately relevant to practice.

While social workers across many practice fields have been hesitant to engage with poststructural ideas, critical social work authors are amongst the most hostile critics of these contemporary developments. For while some embrace poststructural and postmodern ideas as 'unambiguously progressive' forces (Moore and Wallace, discussed in Leonard, 1996, p. 7), many are alarmed at the retreat from universal notions of justice, equity and radical change these ideas imply (see Dixon, 1993; Hewitt, 1993; Taylor-Gooby, 1994; Fals-Borda, 1994; Kenny, 1994; Reason, 1994; McDermott, 1996). Activists such as Lisa MacDonald (1996) lament the growing influence of postmodernism on social theory, for, in her view, 'it provides the perfect rationalisation not to fight. It absolves you' (p. 51).

Yet there is more to the reticence towards poststructuralism than can be explained by reference to social work 'culture' or to differences of opinion about change orientated work. In its challenges to humanism, poststructuralism strikes at the very foundations of modern social work, whether 'orthodox' or 'radical'. Post-structuralism challenges the humanist claim that through rational thought and action human societies can transform themselves. This is a momentous contest for modern social work, which has pursued 'the beautiful (aesthetics), the good (ethics) and the true (science) as it attempts to bring about a pleasing quality of life and a just society using the insights of the social sciences' (Howe, 1994, p. 518). While post-structuralism provides a general contest to the underpinnings of social work, it offers a pointed challenge to activist practice. Poststructural theories call into question the authoritarianism that lies, often unrecognized, in emancipatory practice theories.

In this chapter, I begin an exploration about what, if anything, the profoundly destabilizing impulses of critical poststructuralism can offer social work. Here, my goal is to overview the key concepts of critical poststructural theory as represented in the work of Foucault and the radical poststructural feminists. I will focus particularly on their approaches to the concepts of power and subjectivity (identity), and I will outline the implications of their work for rethinking and diversifying emancipatory political practices. This will provide the basis for the further exploration, in later chapters, of the contributions that poststructural theories can make to reworking social work in an era of uncertainty.

Poststructuralism: an overview

The term 'poststructuralism' refers to a broad band of theoretical projects developed in the social sciences and humanities over the course of the twentieth century (Weedon, 1987). There is little that unifies poststructural theories, and because of the considerable differences amongst poststructuralists it is generally more useful to discuss the work of individual thinkers. Notwithstanding these variations, the linguistic work of de Saussure has provided an important base for poststructural theories (Weedon, 1987, pp. 22–5). De Saussure emphasized the productive charac-ter of language; from this viewpoint, language constitutes those entities it describes (Rojek et al., 1988, p. 120). Furthermore, de Saussure theorized that language is a system of signs in which the signifier (the sound or written image) and a signified (the meaning) are in an arbitrary relation to one another, though this relationship is fixed in language (Weedon, 1987, p. 23). For instance, the term 'woman' is made possible through its contrast with other terms such as 'man' or 'girl', and even though this term is assigned it is assumed to refer to something real; hence the meaning of the term 'woman' is assumed to be unchanging from context to context.

Whilst acknowledging their debt to de Saussure, poststructuralists also reject some of the key notions of his work. Whereas de Saussure emphasized that the relation between the signifier and the signified is assigned rather than essential, poststructuralists take this notion further to emphasize that *all* meaning is unstable (Weedon, 1987, p. 25). For poststructuralists, meaning is constructed through discourses, which are always historically and contextually situated, and in any one context a number of discourses operate thus making possible competing inter-pretations of entities. For example, a 'social worker' may also be identified as 'helper', 'victim', 'oppressor' according to the interpretative possibilities that are available within any particular context. Poststructuralists are concerned to apprehend the processes through which social objects are produced in language, particularly the processes through which certain truths are claimed whilst others are marginalized. Because meaning, including the meaning of identity, is established through competing discourses, language becomes for poststructuralists a major site of struggle (Weedon, 1987, p. 33).

'Poststructuralists are concerned to move away from notions of "essential" meanings or beliefs in a fixed, singular, logical order' (Featherstone and Fawcett, 1995, p. 27). Rather than continue the search for 'the Truth' of what social work 'is', it can lead instead to the recognition that there is no such 'thing' as 'social work' and that the term refers to a broad range of locally situated practices. The evaluation of whether social work is 'orthodox' or 'radical' proceeds not by reference to universal definitions of what counts as activist or otherwise, but rather from a consideration of the effects of practice and policy making processes within specific sites.

The notion of discourse

Poststructural theorists prioritize the role of language in constituting social reality. The assumption is that there is no way of directly experiencing the social world; rather, one can only know 'reality' through language. Parton (1994a) defines the notion of discourse in the following way:

> Discourses are structures of knowledge, claims and practices through which we understand, explain and decide things. In constituting agents they also define obligations and determine the distribution of responsibilities and authorities for different categories of persons such as parents, children, social workers, doctors, lawyers and so on . . . They are frameworks or grids of social organization that make some social actions possible while precluding others. (p. 13)

By fixing norms and truths, discourses shape what can be written, said and even thought within a particular context (McHoul and Grace, 1991, p. 31). Furthermore, discourses have a material existence in that they do not simply construct ideas but also the 'field of objects' through which the social world is experienced (Foucault, 1977, p. 199). According to this view, there is no reality outside discourse (Foucault, 1981b, p. 67). This is not to say that language entirely produces experiences such as poverty and domestic violence but that these experiences can only be understood through language. Discourse fundamentally shapes these experiences in that discourse facilitates understanding about and action towards them.

Despite the antagonism expressed by some social work theorists towards poststructuralism, language is central to much of the change activity in which practitioners and policy workers are involved. For instance, feminist social workers have challenged the language practices through which family violence is understood. Activists have contested the silences about experiences of family abuse and have initiated campaigns for the public naming of such violence. From a poststructural perspective, the value of the activist practices described here is not that they have exposed the 'Truth'; but, rather, through generating new meanings, activists have increased the possibilities for understanding and action available to those who experience family violence and for those who work with them.

Foucault and the 'rules' of discourse

Foucault contends that there are four elements to the formation of discourses. My purpose in outlining these rules is to further demonstrate how Foucault's notion of discourse can be useful for rethinking some of the assumptions about social 'reality' and social change on which social work, particularly progressive practice, depends.

First, discourses are produced by specific 'rules' and procedures which make it possible for 'certain statements but not others to occur at particular times, places and institutional locations' (Fairclough, 1992, p. 40; see also Foucault, 1981b, p. 52). Discourses make some things sayable whilst marginalizing other claims. For instance, the possibilities available to social workers for understanding 'family violence' are different now than they were at the end of the Second World War. In addition, the coherence of discourse depends on the suppression of differences (Featherstone and Fawcett, 1995, p. 27). For example, critical practice discourses frequently refer to 'workers' and 'service users' as though each identity group is homogeneous and entirely distinct, thus neglecting the differences within each category and the commonalities across them.

Second, discourses and power are interconnected; as Foucault (1991a) claims, 'power and knowledge directly imply one another' (p. 27). Foucault's work asserts the impossibility of objective knowledge as he points out that all knowledge 'is defined by power relations' (Leonard, 1994, p. 12; see also Foucault, 1980d, pp. 131–2). Rather than evaluate whether particular claims were 'true' or 'false', Foucault is concerned to understand the processes through which truth claims become possible and particular individuals come to be seen as capable of speaking that truth.

In common with the critique made by many critical social workers, Foucault has pointed out that the truth status of modern social sciences has enabled human service professionals to exercise disciplinary power in relation to marginalized populations (see Foucault, 1981a, 1991e). Regimes of truth can operate, also, through popular discourses. For example, political and religious doctrines produce truth claims and procedures for differentiating between what is true and what is false. As Foucault (1981b) notes:

Doctrine binds individuals to certain types of enunciation and consequently forbids them all others; but it uses, in return, certain types of enunciation to bind individuals amongst themselves, and differentiate them by that very fact from all others. (p. 64)

For Foucault, processes of exclusion and marginalization operate not only by delimiting the number of people who have access to certain 'Truths' (as in professional discourses) but also by establishing a strict regime of what counts as Truth. Even emancipatory political doctrines operate according to an economy of truths, which can, ironically, further the exclusion of alternative perspectives. For instance, in the process of making something visible, such as through consciousness raising, something else is rendered invisible, such as other truth claims (Healy and Peile, 1995; Leonard, 1996; Rojek et al., 1988). As truth and power are linked, from a Foucauldian perspective it becomes necessary to consider not only the effects of professional discourse but also how subjugated knowledges can also be suppressed via the forms of knowledge such as critical knowledge and lived experience that activists advocate.

Third, discourses are discontinuous and contradictory. This means that in every context there are a number of discourses operating, which may be overlapping, distinct or discontinuous, and understanding and action in context will be shaped by a combination of discourses (Foucault, 1981b). By emphasizing the complex, conflictual and contextual interactions of discourse, Foucault (1980d) challenges the Hegelian notion of the unfolding social totality central to the critical theories informing progressive social work discourses. The discourses shaping knowledge can vary dramatically from context to context and between historical epochs. For example, the discourses of social work or medicine of a century ago bear little resemblance to their contemporary forms. Even so, social workers are no more 'free' now than they were in a previous historical epoch; rather, they have *different* possibilities for action.

A fourth 'rule' of discourse is that rather than seek the deep truths or meanings of discourses, Foucault (1981b, p. 67) insists on a principle of exteriority. By this Foucault means that one must consider the concrete operations of discourse; that is, to ask what are the effects of discourses, or what do they produce. For it is in these operations, in the practical effects of discourse, that the form and limits of the discourse are exposed. For example, even though many critical discourses promote democratic practice relations, these practice theories can, paradoxically, promote authoritarian relationships in so far as the critical 'Truth' of the activist remains unquestionable.

Deconstruction

In contrast to modern social science discourses which are concerned with uncovering the truth about social conditions, poststructural thinkers, such as Foucault and Derrida, seek to apprehend the processes through which truth claims are made. The strategy of deconstruction, articulated in the work of Derrida (1991), is amongst the best known poststructural methods for 'undoing' modern truth claims. I will briefly outline this approach here because of its importance to the political action undertaken by poststructuralists, such as the radical poststructural feminists who use these methods to destabilize patriarchial social practices (Pringle, 1995).

In modern discourses, truth is made possible only through oppositions or contrasts such as the following: man not woman; presence not absence; identity not difference (Gatens, 1991, p. 112). Deconstruction is intended to expose and undo the oppositions through which 'reality' is represented in modern social thought. Derrida views these oppositions as deeply problematic because:

- Dualisms ignore the diversities within categories as well as the commonalities amongst opposed categories. For example, the opposition between man and woman fails to acknowledge the diversity within gender categories and the likenesses across them.
- The dualistic structure establishes a hierarchial structure through which the first term is privileged over the second. For example, in psychoanalytic discourses 'man' is associated with presence and 'woman' is associated with absence (Gatens, 1992, p. 134).
- The privilege of the first term is maintained by devaluing the second term. For example, the meaning of the term 'structural' is dependent on its contrast to its opposite notion of 'local', even though in critical social work theory at least, the value of the former relies on the devaluing of the latter.

Deconstruction is aimed at uncovering the binary oppositions through which social reality is understood. Through this structure particular identities and processes are privileged whilst others are marginalized. For example, Gatens (1996) contends that the apparently neutral term of 'citizen' increasingly referred to in social and political discourses is defined in masculine terms. Thus, the status of women as citizens is dependent on their capacity to approximate the bodies, capacities and activities of white, middle class, heterosexual and able-bodied males. The expression of differences from this masculine ideal confines many women to the status of Other or less than a 'citizen'.

The first step of deconstruction exposes the oppositions through which entities are defined and reverses them, so that what was devalued is revalued. The second stage is focused on finding a way in between the dualisms and then breaking them open (B. Davies, 1994, p. 39), so that a full spectrum of positions can be identified. For example, in contrast to the dualism between straight and gay that can be found in homophobic and gay and lesbian liberatory literature alike, a deconstructive strategy could help to articulate a broad range of sexualities between and beyond these categories. As a political tool, deconstruction is not aimed at displacing an old truth in favour of a new one. Instead, the intention is to displace oppositions so that a range of truths is possible (Pringle, 1995, p. 199).

For social workers, deconstruction is useful for undermining and reworking some of the fundamental oppositions of contemporary practice discourses, including: orthodox/radical, conservative/communitarian, social control/social care, and casework/social action, and may even assist social workers to rethink the opposition between public service and market place that is of increasing concern for social work.

Contemporarily, contest is being made to these oppositions, particularly from within conventional practice contexts, such as statutory settings (Wise, 1990; Healy, 1998) and casework practice (Fook, 1993). To use a deconstructive strategy is not to uncritically endorse the flip side of the oppositions described; rather, it is to suggest that by exposing and tearing apart the oppositions that have become an unquestioned part of the critical social work landscape, it is possible to diversify what counts as radical activity within and directed towards contemporary welfare states.

Having outlined poststructural notions about discourse and deconstruction, let us now turn to a consideration of how these understandings are used to conceptualize notions of power, identity and change in the work of Foucault and the radical poststructural feminists.

Power: a Foucauldian approach

Foucault specifically rejects a 'juridico-discursive' model of power on which both liberal and revolutionary theories of power have been based (Sawicki, 1991, p. 52). For Foucault this model, which sees power as the possession of individuals and a force that is imposed, is inadequate for comprehending the operations of power through the local practices associated with 'our bodies, our existence, our everyday lives' in the modern era (Foucault, 1978, p. 70). Although Foucault does not seek to develop a theory of power, a number of principles for the analysis of power are enunciated in his work. Sawicki (1991, p. 21) summarizes the elements of Foucault's approach to power in the following way:

1. Power is exercised rather than possessed.
2. Power is not primarily repressive, but productive.
3. Power is analysed as coming from the bottom up.

This means that, firstly, in the modern epoch power can no longer be seen purely as the possession of individuals or the state; rather, power is everywhere. Foucault (1978) asserts that, 'Power acts through the smallest elements: the family, sexual relations, but also residential relations, neighbourhoods etc. . . . we always find power as something which "runs through" it, that acts, that brings about effects' (p. 59). Instead of understanding power through an analysis of the state or an over-arching social structure, Foucault directs attention to how it is exercised within specific contexts of action. In other words, the focus is less on identifying what or who is the oppressor or the oppressed in accordance with a general overarching principle; what is important is to understand the practices through which power is exercised and locally sustained. Whilst refusing the idea that individuals possess power, Foucault's work does, nonetheless, allow that the historical and contextual location of individuals shapes the kinds of power they can exercise. Bordo (1993) asserts that, 'It [power] is held by no-one: but people and groups are positioned differently within it' (p. 191).

A second claim made by Foucault is that power is not only repressive, but also productive. Foucault (1980d) points out that:

> If power were never anything but repressive, if it never did anything but to say no, do you really think one would be brought to obey it? What makes power hold good, what makes it accepted, is simply the fact that it doesn't only weigh on us as a force that says no, but that it traverses and produces things, it induces pleasure, forms of knowledge, produces discourse. (p. 119)

According to Foucault, power is productive in that it constitutes things, such as discourses, knowledges and 'identity'. An important part of Foucault's thesis is that far from ignoring the individual, power is exercised through the individual as it categorizes the individual, attaches itself to his/her identity, imposing a law of truth on him/her (Foucault, 1982, p. 781).

Foucault has argued that the social sciences and the helping professions have played a vital role in providing a bridge between the individual and 'the efficient management of "men and things"' (Foucault, 1981a, p. 25; L. McNay, 1994, p. 115). These sciences contribute to contemporary modes of government-ality by proving methods for observation of, and intervention into, the most minute and intimate details of individual lives. In modern societies, the informa-tion elicited through the individualizing methods of the human sciences informs systems of surveillance (see Foucault, 1981a, 1991a). A major point of Foucault's critique of the human service professions is that through their 'caring' interventions, helping professionals make it possible for the state to manage and discipline its citizens (see Foucault, 1981a, 1991a). This point, that the human services provide a conduit for state control, has been long recognized by critical social welfare thinkers.

Yet, Foucault's analysis also suggests that it is too simplistic to view the operations of the human services purely in terms of the imposition of state power onto the individual. Foucault contends that people willingly participate in modern forms of power because power acts not only to subjugate them but to produce their sense of self, to induce pleasure or to enhance their individual capacities. Put simply, there is no 'self' without power. Foucault (1991a, p. 139) refers to the 'micro-physics of power' to describe the contemporary practices, such as forms of surveillance and timetables, to which individuals willingly submit in order to produce a specific kind of self, body or soul. Bartky (1988) uses Foucault's insights to argue that the disciplinary practices to which many adult women submit their bodies in contemporary Western cultures, such as dietary, fitness and appearance regimes, subjugate by developing competencies and not simply by taking power away. These individualizing forms of power are linked to totalizing power in so far as they contribute to the production of a certain kind of population: one which is both more docile and useful to the modern state.

This view of power as both repressive and productive provides a useful way of explaining the complex operations of power between service providers and service users in contemporary welfare states. For while it is indeed true that social control is an important dimension of contemporary social service work, this notion cannot explain the operations of power that fall outside a unilateral relationship of control (Gordon, 1988). In highlighting the oppressive dimensions of social work practice, critical social work theorists have failed to observe the ambivalent and, sometimes, positive dimensions of human services activity within local contexts. As Wise (1990) illustrates: 'What many people who write about the "stigma" of social work don't seem to realise is many clients love having a social worker and kick up a great deal of fuss if they can't get one' (p. 242). In promoting a view of power as something that operates through rather than upon individuals, Foucault's work encourages social workers to recognize the multiple possibilities for power in local practice contexts (see Healy, 1999).

Third, in contrast to the deductive approach to analysis adopted by critical social scientists, Foucault insists on an ascending order of analysis. Repeatedly, Foucault (1978, 1991e) points to the analytic inadequacy of attempts to deduce these relations of power from the analysis of superstructures because these accounts fail to grasp the multiple and differentiated operations of the modern technologies of power. Instead, Foucault advocates research that begins within specific contexts of social practice. According to Foucault (1980e), one should conduct

> an ascending analysis of power, starting, that is, from its infinitesimal mechanisms, which each have their own history, their own trajectory, their own techniques and tactics, and then see how these mechanisms of power have been – and continue to be – invested by ever more general mechanisms and by forms of global domination. (p. 99)

Foucault does not deny the existence of oppressive social structures, such as capitalism or patriarchy (indeed, he frequently refers to the notion of capitalism in his own work). What he does refuse, however, is to accord them priority in explaining local phenomena. The superstructure does not produce local power relations; rather, it is the local relations that enable global phenomena of power. Foucault's work encourages social workers to look to the rich data of everyday practice to understand how social practices are sustained and can be challenged.

From identity to subjectivity: the role of discourse

Poststructural theorists reject the humanist notion of identity, which suggests that one's identity is unified and constant. For Foucault (1981b, p. 65) the notion of the stable, human subject ignores the role of discourse in constituting the self. In preference to the term 'identity', poststructuralists refer instead to subjectivity to denote 'the conscious and unconscious thoughts and emotions of the individual, her sense of herself and her ways of understanding her relation to the world' (Weedon, 1987: p. 32). Poststructuralists reject the view that individuals have pre-social identity or essence such as that of 'woman' or 'proletariat'. Rather, according to them, one's subjectivity is produced through discourses. B. Davies (1991) asserts that:

We can only ever speak ourselves or be spoken into existence within the terms of available discourses . . . our patterns of desire that we took to be fundamental indicators of our essential selves (such as the desire for freedom or autonomy or for moral rightness) signify little more than the discourses, and the subject positions made available within them, to which we may have access. (p. 42)

According to this view, the identities which are ascribed to us, such as 'woman' or 'man', do not have a fixed meaning nor do they represent fundamental essences. One's sense of self is produced through discourses, which establish specific subject positions such as male/female, worker/client, middle class/working class. In certain contexts particular identity categories will come to the fore, whilst others are marginalized, and, as usually there are a number of discourses operating in each context, a number of identities will be relevant to the constitution of self in those contexts.

Modern human sciences and social movements have used identity categories as though they reflect the 'reality' or the 'essence' of a person. Indeed, critical practitioners advocate the use of identity categories as the basis of political action. By contrast, poststructural theories stress the instability of identifications. From a poststructural position one's sense of self is recognized as precarious, contradictory and reconstituted afresh each time we speak (Weedon, 1987, p. 33). As the discourses through which the self is constituted are often discontinuous and inconsistent, the various subjectivities that make up identity are likely to be experienced contradictorily (B. Davies, 1994, p. 43). For example, gender, race and class identities do not necessarily add up in the same direction and one identity may confer status, whilst another may contribute to disadvantage within a specific context. The practice of collective identification, common to many contemporary social movements, is called into question as poststructural theory highlights that shared identifications such as that of 'woman' or 'proletariat' may provide no basis for shared political interest whatsoever.

From this perspective, discourses and the subject positions that they make available to us or from which one is excluded very much affect the way we live. One direction for political practice is that of destabilizing discourses that continue oppression by excluding individuals from non-oppressive subject positions or those that confine individuals to a narrow range of possibilities. For instance, in some contemporary feminist discourses there has been a struggle to rename 'victims' of violence as 'survivors', for the latter category is claimed to more fully and positively represent the capacities and potential of individuals who have experienced violation.

Radical poststructural feminism

In the extensive interaction between 'post' theories and feminist thought, a variety of poststructural and postmodern feminist positions have emerged. I use the term 'radical poststructural feminism' to denote the work of contemporary feminist thinkers who use poststructural ideas to transform the operations of social and political discourses which maintain gender oppression. In this analysis, I draw primarily on the work of Hélène Cixous and a variety of feminist social theorists, particularly Gatens, Grosz and Yeatman. Radical poststructural feminists challenge the essentialist logic of modern social and politics discourses, including modern feminist practices. I contend that insights from this diverse body of work can lead social workers away from a search for an 'essence' about practice towards a recognition of its diversity and the importance of ongoing negotiation and reflexivity in relation to social work practices.

Amongst radical poststructural feminists there is considerable caution about the use of the term 'patriarchy' as an explanation of gender relations and oppression. It is not only the term 'patriarchy' but notions of the social whole which are problematic in that an analytic emphasis on a social totality leaves the local patriarchical practices underexplored (Pringle, 1995). In preference to 'patriarchy', radical poststructural feminists refer instead to patriarchal practices or phallocentricism. Wearing (1996) observes that:

> In most post-structural feminist analysis there is a shift from thinking about 'patriarchy', with its emphasis on male control of the structures of society, to the notion of 'phallocentrism', which denotes male control of language, symbols, definitions, discourses, sexuality, theory and logocentric thinking. (p. 39)

Radical poststructural feminists seek to expose and dismantle the phallocentric imagery through which many contemporary social and political discourses, including modern feminist practices, are constituted.

Radical poststructural feminists refuse the humanist notion of 'woman' as a pre-given and fixed social identity. The contraction of difference to a singular opposition man/woman, is, for Cixous, evidence of a reductive phallocentric logic. However, the term 'woman' may be used as a political identity; that is, as an identity strategically deployed for the purpose of struggle against patriarchal practices. Cixous (1994a) asserts that, 'as women we are at the obligatory mercy of simplifications. In order to defend women we are obliged to speak in the feminist terms of "man" and "woman"' (p. 201). While sometimes necessary, the formation of a political action around identities, such as those of 'women', 'working class', 'non-English speaking', must be subject to ongoing interrogation to recognize the contextual and negotiated character of these entities.

For Cixous (1994b, p. 100) the diversity of experiences and interests within one individual can never be adequately apprehended, let alone the joint interests of those situated within an identity category such as 'woman' or 'man'. This recognition of the diversity of identifications means that political representation is always provisional and incomplete. Radical poststructural feminism raises questions about the totalizing projects of modern feminism in so far as they suppress differences amongst women (Yeatman, 1993, 1998; Gatens, 1996). Reflecting on aboriginal women's critique of Australian feminist projects, Larbalestier (1998) writes:

> These critics clearly reject any commonality of experience or interests between 'black and white' women. Implicit in these critiques of feminism is a rejection of anglocentric

normative frameworks embedded in histories of displacement, dispossession, negative stereotyping and cultural stigma (p. 78).

Radical poststructural feminists recognize that gender cannot be isolated from the other ways in which one is positioned through discourse in terms of such things as race, class and ability or disability. Instead of reducing women's interests to one or an oppositional struggle between 'groups' of women, radical poststructural feminists promote an internal politics of contestation (Yeatman, 1993). As differences move centre-stage it is recognized that at times shared gender identity will confer no common basis for struggle (Ang, 1995, p. 68). At the very least, common identification can never be assumed and instead should be subject to 'continuing negotiation, self-reflection and questioning' (Larbalestier, 1998, p. 82).

The deconstructive project of radical poststructural feminism

The linguistic sphere is, for radical poststructural feminists, a prime site of battle. For Cixous, 'changes cannot be initiated outside of linguistic spheres. Transformation begins from the inside, when hidden hierarchical orderings are uncovered' (Conley, 1992, p. 38). For these feminists, the masculine bias of sociopolitical theories, including many modernist feminist projects, is not superficial but rather intrinsic to their structure (Grosz, 1990, p. 163; Gatens, 1992, p. 120). In destabilizing the core claims of these discourses, feminist thinkers aim to contribute to the celebration (rather than the suppression) of differences in the practices of the institutions of society, such as the civil sphere, education, welfare and economic exchange (Gatens, 1996, p. 98).

Radical poststructural feminists attack the latent patriarchal commitments that exist even within feminist discourses in so far as these discourses reinforce rather than explode the opposition between 'male' and 'female'. The acceptance of this dualistic structure, although repressing the complex experiences and multiple capacities of both men and women, is particularly oppressive for women. Feminist philosophers, Gatens (1992, 1996), Grosz (1989, 1990) and Lloyd (1986) have repeatedly demonstrated that the terms associated with mastery and presence, such as 'mind', 'reason', 'logos' are defined in the masculine whilst 'passivity', 'chaos', 'irrationality' are associated with the feminine. However, rather than revalue the term 'woman', poststructural feminists turn their attention to deconstructing the opposition between 'man' and 'woman' so that the diversity within each category and the commonality across them can be spoken (Wearing, 1996, p. 39). Rather than a term denoting a fixed essence, 'woman' is understood as a fluid and open ended category.

Like Foucault, Cixous is critical of Hegel's work. In her quest to challenge closure to differences Cixous (1981a) is particularly critical of the dialectic method which has been central to critical social science theories. Cixous critiques the notion of the dialectic because it privileges mastery over difference and multiplicity (Conley, 1992, p. 38). In the dialectic, all struggle is reduced to two opposing forces which are, ultimately, collapsed into one. Cixous calls for the dialect to be exceeded; for activists to refuse a synthesis and instead to embrace differences and respect for otherness (Conley, 1992, p. 38). Thus rather than seeking unity, Cixous aims to encourage 'a polyphony of voices' (Conley, 1992, p. 30).

Radical poststructural feminism can be used to challenge aspects of critical social work discourses. In particular the attempts to fix an essence of social work, as oppressive or anti-oppressive, can be attacked on the grounds that it ignores the historical and local contexts of social work activity and the importance of negotiation and self-reflexive action within specific practice sites (Larbalestier, 1998). The search to unify social work around a common core, be it 'radical' or 'orthodox', has contributed to the construction of numerous oppositions about practice processes. These dualisms, such as that between care and control, have allowed critical social work discourses to proceed as though some forms of practice and practice sites are innately emancipatory, while others contain few or no possibilities for progressive practice. These oppositions gloss over the difficulty and yet the necessity of the ongoing interrogation of the possibilities and limitations of critical practice within contexts of action.

The body: Cixous, poststructural feminism and 'writing the feminine body'

The destabilizing work of the radical poststructural feminists is intended to make way for social practices that value difference, diversity and complexity. Drawing on the work of Lacan, the radical poststructural feminists turn to the body as a site for alternate knowledge building and action. Radical poststructural feminists stress that the body is not only biological, it is also a cultural artefact. Grosz (1994) summarizes that:

> The body is regarded as the political, social, and cultural object par excellence, not a product of a raw, passive nature that is civilized, overlaid, polished by culture. Thus, body and culture do not exist in hierarchical relation, with body as the raw material on which culture is inscribed. Rather discursive processes and biology complexly interact such that the body is a cultural interweaving and production of nature. (p. 18)

Grosz's view is that the body is produced not only through biology, but also through cultural processes which are inscribed upon the body.

Poststructural feminists use the notion of cultural inscription to theorize bodily differences. The social and historical discursive practices to which male and female bodies are subjected contributes to differences that, although not universal across societies nor entirely consistent within them, tend to follow patterns within cultures. Importantly, these differences and capacities are not simply mediated through consciousness but rather inscribed on the body, and this influences the shape and the desires of the body. Gatens (1992) warns against reifying these differences as though they represent fundamental essences; rather, she argues that the body must be granted a 'history' (p. 130). For example, it is often the case that men and women have different capacities for nurture and care due to the cultural practices which situate women in these roles and relieve (or exclude) men from them. Yet, it is recognized that while bodies are typically fashioned in very specific ways, there is nothing essential about male and female bodies. Gatens (1992) points out that certain types of male and female bodies have more in common with one another, such as the bodies of elite athletes, than others within the same gender categories.

From the notion that differences have been devalued in the discourses of modernity, Cixous argues for the insertion of diversity in language. As part of this project, Cixous advocates *écriture féminine*: writing the female body. This process of writing from the female body is intended to challenge the construction of centre (masculine) and margins (others) in discourse. Rather than simply replace one unity or essence with another, the intention is to create ways of writing in which differences are understood outside the binary opposition between presence and absence. In referring to this process as *écriture féminine*, Cixous uses the term 'feminine' to denote difference and diversity. This equation is for Cixous only relevant in this current historical epoch in which dualistic thinking and phallocentricism have converged so that woman is constituted as the 'absent' Other, the marginal (Gatens, 1992, p. 134). The use of male and female are temporary devices, as Conley (1992) asserts: 'Although still used for historical reasons, "masculine" and "feminine" will hopefully, she [Cixous] argues, be replaced soon by others, by colour adjectives, for example' (p. 40).

The purpose of *écriture féminine* is not for women to write for all women, for this can again amount to mastery over others (Gatens, 1992, p. 134). It is, indeed, to give up the claim to speak for others and instead to open discourses to diversity. Rather than reinforce an opposition between male and female, this project aims to challenge 'the masculine monopoly on the construction of femininity, the female body and woman' (Gatens, 1992, p. 134) and in so doing to introduce possibilities for democratic dialogue and contestation across differences. Only by returning the feminine to language is it possible to end the oppositions which deny a place in language for those who are Other to the white, middle class, heterosexual and able-bodied male (Gatens, 1991, p. 118).

The vision of Cixous's project is that of a heterogeneous society. This society does not accord with the eye of the master, but rather 'a myriad of little eyes or pupils (pupilles), everywhere' (Conley, 1992, p. 27). Through encouraging the writing of differences, Cixous aims to destabilize phallocentric discourses which, in their search for unity or essence, are intolerant of difference.

In turning attention to bodily differences, radical poststructural theory can expose the gender dualisms that continue, often unrecognized, in progressive social work approaches. Many critical discourses, including feminist practice theories, have reinforced an opposition between the structural (meaning big and important) and local (referring to small-scale practices with individuals, groups and communities). Ironically, through this schema, in which the structural is privileged as the place where the real work of emancipation and resistance takes place, the practices of front line service delivery, typically undertaken by women, are devalued as sites for theorizing and transformation. By contrast, acknowledging a spectrum of transformative activity profoundly challenges the deeply gendered assumptions of contemporary critical practice theories and makes possible the emergence of diverse activisms in social work.

Moreover, Cixous's notion of the *écriture féminine* has relevance to rethinking the processes through which social work practice theories are developed. It can challenge authoritarian approaches which base the analysis of practice in the grand narratives of modernity whilst remaining impervious to, indeed dismissive of, the uncertainties, complexities and irrationalities of practice. The principle of *écriture féminine* to use what is marginal to challenge the centre can be employed to use that which is marginal in modern practice theory, that is the diverse practices and locations of social work, to tear apart essentialist claims of social work theory. This does not mean an anything goes approach to practice theory. Rather, it means to critically engage *with* the diversity of social work practices to apprehend what social work 'is' and what it can be.

Rethinking politics: principles for action

Poststructuralism strikes at the core of modern theories, including the critical theories, on which many emancipatory movements and progressive social work theories have drawn. Notwithstanding the diversity, and disagreements, amongst the critical poststructural thinkers discussed in this book, their work does have some shared implications for political practice. The work of Foucault and the radical poststructural feminists promotes heterogeneous political practices that are subject to ongoing interrogation and negotiation within sites of practice. In the remainder of the chapter, I will investigate some directions in which the theories discussed here can take emancipatory political action. This will form the basis of the next chapter, where I will outline the implications for the core assumptions of critical social work practices.

Towards a politics of detail

The work of Foucault and radical poststructural feminists gives priority to local contexts and social practices as the sites of analysis and action. These thinkers 'resist any tendency to totalize what they regard as complex and multifaceted' (Kenway, 1992, p. 124). The totalizing discourses of modernity have tended to devalue the extent to which historical and local contexts, such as organizational contexts, shape and constrain political activity. Thus, these discourses produce universal strategies for change that have questionable utility in specific social contexts. For example, as I will discuss further in Chapter 5, much of the discussion about service user participation in social work has focused on the minimization of the statutory and organizational obligations many workers bear, if indeed these constraints are acknowledged at all! Moreover, the focus on the social totality found in critical discourses can lead to political alienation by consistently devaluing local changes in contrast to the goal of complete transformation (Gibson-Graham, 1995).

One direction in which the poststructural theories discussed in this chapter lead is towards a 'politics of detail' in which the understanding of power, identity and processes of change begins in the analysis of the everyday social practices

(Bennett, 1998). This focus on detail promotes engagement with local aspirations and possibilities for change and sensitivity to the immediate barriers to transformation. As an illustration, Smiley (discussed in Pringle, 1995) suggests that 'rather than imposing on "women" the identities of potential overthrowers of the patriarchal order, it is better to start with the practice questions of empowerment and disempowerment' (p. 210). This approach promotes a detailed analysis of the local practices that sustain oppression as a basis for understanding how these practices might be resisted and transformed. Poststructuralism contributes to a revaluing of the local practices of social work, which typically occur with individuals, groups and communities, as sites of information and transformation.

Interrogating and reworking notions of change

Poststructuralists are suspicious of modern claims about progress, particularly the assertion that rational thought is the precursor to effective change strategies. From a poststructural perspective the ideal of moving forward through rationality tends to legitimate scientific and rational ways of knowing. The equation of progress with moving 'forward' rather than 'differently' devalues action that does not conform to a singular idea of progress. This contributes to blindness about the constraining effects of practices that fit a progressive ideal, and also to an inability to acknowledge those forms of progress that fall outside established definitions of this term. For example, these discourses have marginalized the critical potential of certain contexts of practice with the consequence that little is known about 'progressive' practices in 'conventional' settings such as hospitals, prisons and child protection agencies.

A further issue is that the emphasis on rationality can neglect other ways of knowing, such as bodily and emotional knowledge. The processes of consciousness raising, commonly promoted in activist practice models, provides an illustration of the potential for activist practices to silence non-rational forms of knowing. Consciousness raising processes ignore the plethora of ways in which bodily and irrational or emotional knowledge impede change or make it possible. For example, as I will discuss further in Chapter 6, in a critical practice context in which I was involved, the participants' commitment to a feminist discourse helped them to engage with values of 'independence' and 'survival' but did so at the cost of suppressing the ways in which they also remained 'dependent' and 'victimized' within some contexts of their lives.

In their commitment to singular, linear and rational notions of progress, activists participate, paradoxically, in the 'continuing renewal of existing arrangements of power and domination' (Rojek et al., 1988, p. 134). In contrast, critical poststructural theory rejects these singular notions of progress, and leads instead to the diversification of what counts as 'truth' and, thus, to what counts as significant change. Through the ongoing interrogation and deconstruction of discourse, poststructural theory leads to the multiplication of 'what is considered true, rational and valid' (Grosz, 1990, p. 167). The importance for social workers of the rejection of singular notions of progress is that it can lead away from attempts to fix an essence of social work and instead to make visible a heterogeneity of progressive practice possibilities relevant to the diverse contexts in which social work occurs.

A focus on social practices rather than social identities

The poststructural work discussed in this chapter radically challenges the identity politics on which many modern social movements rely. First, Foucault suggests that the formation of identities is vital to the modern operations of discipline and surveillance. Modern power operates by binding individuals to identifications which, in turn, requires that individuals submit to power (such as the power of the school, the prison, the social services, the gym, the consciousness raising group or even the beauty clinic) in order to maintain a coherent sense of self. From this perspective, the practices of identity politics exemplified by the forming of collective identities such as 'woman', 'gay' or 'differently able' can reinforce the modern operations of power. Judith Butler (1995) contests, feminist strategies seek to unify women around the identity of 'woman' thus:

> Surely there is caution offered here, that in the very struggle toward enfranchisement and democratization, we might adopt the very models of domination by which we were oppressed, not realizing that one way that domination works is through the regulation and production of subjects. (p. 48)

To embrace an identification is, then, to constitute oneself through the very terms that make surveillance and disciplining possible.

Secondly, some authors, such as Yeatman (1993, 1995, 1997) and Tapper (1993) have challenged the embrace of identity in so far as this practice fails to provide a basis for positive engagement with politics and leads, instead, to a politics of rancour and hatred. The politics of *ressentiment* is based on the view that the way in which one is constituted through discourse as 'man' or 'woman', 'straight' or 'gay', 'anglo' or 'non-anglo' predetermines one's access to power and, significantly, to the status of 'oppressor' or 'oppressed'. Two important claims are made. The first is that the status of 'oppressor' and 'oppressed' are fixed so that those situated on the left hand side of these dualisms are, by their very existence, responsible for the oppressed status of the other. The second thought is that those situated on the right side have little or no access to power and that powerlessness is proof of one's goodness and the other's evil (Tapper, 1993, p. 134).

The politics of *ressentiment* is not transformative because it pre-empts investigation into how subject positions of 'oppressor' and 'oppressed' are constituted and how social practices of oppression are locally sustained and hence how they might be contested (Yeatman, 1997). It means that ultimately individuals are the passive victims of their identifications. Those with access to power are considered to have little interest in the transformation of social relations, while the powerless are represented as incapable of accessing or using power for their own empowerment (Tapper, 1993, p. 134; Pringle, 1995, p. 207). This limits political action to the critique of the powerful, rather than to the understanding and transformation of power relations so as to enhance the humanity and accountability with which power is exercised.

The poststructural work discussed in this chapter points to the many non-democratic and non-emancipatory ends to which the notion of 'identity' has been put in modern societies and political practices. In contrast to the embrace of identity practised by many contemporary social movements, Foucault (1982) promotes the ongoing reinvention of the self as a strategy for transgressing the kinds of individualizing practices imposed on populations in the modern epoch. Perhaps progressive social workers cannot afford to eschew notions of 'oppressor' and 'oppressed' because of the usefulness of these terms in making visible social inequities that might otherwise appear to be a natural state of affairs. However, the insights of 'post' encourage activists to resist ontologizing these statuses, that is making them the entire and inescapable definition of individuals and groups, and instead to reorientate our energies to understanding how these subject relations are locally developed and how they can be resisted and transformed within the local contexts of practice and service users' lives.

From collective identities to provisional coalitions

Whilst poststructuralists refuse the notion of an essential self as the foundation for shared struggle, collective action remains possible. However, the 'we' of shared political activity is always a provisional category and maintains only in so far as common concerns can be identified (Foucault, 1991c, p. 385). If there can be said to be a core to poststructural politics it lies in the ongoing recognition of difference and so leads to the impossibility of one voice that speaks for all. In contrast, to many contemporary critical movements, poststructuralism challenges the stand-point position that the marginal status of identities confers a more total understanding of the 'truth'. Thus according to L. McNay (1994):

> The oppositional truths articulated from below have no greater claim to 'reality' than the official truth, but they have a resistant or progressive function insofar as they hinder the 'domination of truth' by those who govern. (p. 137)

For poststructuralists there can be no Truth, only truths. While the voices of marginalized people can challenge the Truth claims of professional, and even political, discourses, no voice is innocent of the operations of power. Through advocating an internal politics of contestation, poststructural theorists, such as Foucault and the radical poststructural feminists, support the creation of a kind of plurivocality so that diverse voices can be heard, interrogated and represented. Politics, then, does not involve a lifelong commitment to a political cause or identification but to an embrace of dynamic and diverse engagements.

Towards open ended, dialogic change practices

In their work, Foucault and the radical poststructural feminists express a profound scepticism towards the narratives of modernity. Poststructuralists challenge attempts to impose order on social 'realities' and practices, which they regard as inherently fragmented and inconstant. Indeed, the visions of a new social order which have guided many modern social movements are considered to be dominatory because they evade the dynamism of subjectivity, power and context (Foucault, 1991f). Despite the enormous variation in their work, Foucault and the radical poststructural feminists contend that the danger of emancipatory philosophies lies less in their content than their often unacknowledged commitment to Truth. Their will to impose a truth on others, even if it is perceived to be an emancipatory truth, leads to a closure to other truth claims.

In a dramatic revision of the role of theory and critique, the poststructuralists discussed in this chapter do not seek to describe the Truth of the world and certainly there can be few pretensions to providing a plan of action (Foucault, 1991e). Philosophy is necessary in so far as it interrogates what is. However, its role is as an instrument to be taken up and transformed in the course of action. The kinds of open ended approaches to theorizing suggested here expose the authoritarianism that is inherent to practice theories which have sought to proclaim the truth and lead the way. By proposing a more open ended approach to philosophy, the work of critical 'post' theorists can contribute to more democratic approaches to building social work practice theories based on respect for the local sites of practice as different, not inferior, sites for understanding critical social work practices.

Conclusion

Social work is diverse, and rather than attempt to fix an essence of practice, activists might do better to acknowledge its variability. By destabilizing the truth claims of the grand narratives of modernity, on which orthodox and critical approaches to practice have relied, poststructuralism can contribute to the reinvention and diversification of activist practice approaches. Poststructural theorists fashion a more modest role for theory. Democratic possibilities for building theories about social work practices emerge as it is recognized that neither 'theory' nor 'practice' can tell us the whole truth but together they can further understanding and action in the negotiated truths and heterogeneity of social work practices. The further exploration of these possibilities is the subject of the next chapter.

4   Critical Social Work Responses to 'Post' Theories

During the last decades of the twentieth century, a range of 'post' theories transformed many fields of the humanities and the social sciences. Social workers have been reluctant interlocutors with these theoretical developments; however, during the 1990s a burgeoning body of literature emerged contesting, or attesting to, the merits of these perspectives for practice. Even though in the light of recent poststructural critique, the opposition between 'conventional' and 'activist' should be regarded with some suspicion, my primary focus will be on critical social workers' responses to these contemporary theoretical developments. With this emphasis in mind, I will outline three major orientations adopted by social workers towards post theories. These responses can be summarized as: rejection of these post theories as regressive; acceptance of aspects that reinforce extant critical social work theories; and critical engagement with these perspectives in efforts to rethink and diversify critical practice processes.

Throughout much of the chapter I will focus on the third perspective, which uses poststructural theory to destabilize social work discourses and to emphasize the contextuality, diversity and complexity of local practices of change. I will outline how, in its emphasis on context, poststructural theory can assist the dismantling and diversification of the core critical practice concepts. But, first, I will begin with a general outline of the responses to these contemporary ideas.

Response one: reservations about poststructuralism as a counter-revolutionary force

Many social workers are sceptical about whether post theories can make any useful contribution to advancing critical practice. Instead of assisting critical social workers in their search for a critical centre to practice, poststructural theory leads to the promotion of uncertainty, diversity and complexity. It is this focus on ambiguity, so appealing in many areas of social science and humanities and even within some domains of social work, that has proven problematic for progressive authors both within social work and outside it. Until recently, the dominant response of critical social workers was to cite the various forms of post theories as counter-revolutionary forces.

Many activists condemn poststructural theories as grossly ignorant of the patterns of oppression that transcend localities and historical epochs (Hartsock, 1990). To these authors, poststructural perspectives appear particularly troublesome in this historical epoch when the forces of globalization are intervening so oppressively in the lives of the most marginalized. Leonard (1995) observes that:

> Alongside a progressive politics of difference, and carrying more weight, another politics exists – the politics of governments and multinational corporations engaged in a struggle to impose upon the world, regardless of diverse cultures and populations, a single global economy dedicated to the logic of the market and largely indifferent to the social burdens for the most powerless, of attendant massive structural change. (p. 16)

Critical thinkers are reluctant to forgo a notion of the social whole while it continues to provide a useful framework for understanding the 'local' experiences of the poor and dispossessed. Taking into account the oppressive impact of contemporary transformations, critical social workers are advised, at the very least, to proceed with great caution in adopting a politics that privileges difference and locality.

Second, critical authors are hesitant to embrace the poststructural notion of fragmented and multiple identities while the categories of class, gender and race continue to represent virulent social divisions (Walby, 1992, p. 35). For example, critical social theorists express concern that the notion of fragmented and shifted identities denies 'the historical tenacity and material longevity of oppressive orders and structures' (Ang, 1995, p. 67). Some authors contend that the retreat from identity weakens contemporary progressive struggles. Hartsock (1990) asks:

> Why is it that just at the moment when so many of us who have been silenced begin to demand the right to name ourselves, to act as subjects rather than objects of history, that just then the concept of subjecthood becomes problematic? (p. 163)

From this perspective, Foucault's call for the decentring of the subject in modern analyses must be regarded with some scepticism by those social actors such as women, children, indigenous people and the insane, who never were the centre of Enlightenment thought (Sawicki, 1991, p. 106).

Third, critical authors contest whether progressive political practices can be founded on a notion of diversity. There is concern that the celebration of difference will lead not to justice but to the uncritical endorsement of differences produced by fundamental social and economic inequalities. For example, while the emphasis on difference may increase respect for the rights of teenage mothers, it can also obscure the social conditions that structure this choice (Healy and Peile, 1995). In addition, some question whether difference and uncertainty provide an adequate basis for progressive contest in the policy making contexts. Taylor-Gooby (1993) asserts that in a climate of retreat from public welfare provision, the poorest and most marginal groups 'will fail to attract the appropriate attention if the key themes of policy are seen as difference, diversity and choice' (p. 19).

Even amongst critical social theorists receptive to some dimensions of poststructural thought, there is concern about the failure of contemporary theorists to delineate the limits to the 'celebration' of differences. As L. McNay (1994) points out, 'Foucault clearly makes value judgements about what constitutes progressive political behaviour and what constitutes an abuse of power or domination of truth, yet he fails to make these assumptions explicit' (p. 141). Similarly, Cixous does not celebrate racist or patriarchal values even though these could be considered part of a spectrum of difference. An articulation of the normative framework embedded within critical poststructural theories is necessary to understand the marginalizations and exclusions that these perspectives can promote.

Fourth, activists contend that poststructural theories lack strategies relevant to contemporary political struggles. Many progressive authors recoil at Foucault's subordination of 'the state' in his analyses of power and practices of change. As far as many progressive social analysts are concerned: 'Foucault was "OK" – but he had no theory of the state . . . his conception of the micro-physics of power allowed no way in which little struggles might be connected to form the basis for a society-wide struggle with revolutionary potential' (Bennett, 1998 p. 63). Similarly, many activists question the utility of the strategies offered by poststructuralists, most of which focus on the linguistic sphere, for offering effective interventions into the material 'realities' of racism, sexism and poverty. For instance Hartsock (1990) observes, 'the point is to change the world, not simply to redescribe ourselves or reinterpret the world yet again' (p. 172).

It is relevant to ask, as radicals have done, whether social workers can afford to embrace a perspective that fails to offer clear alternatives at a time when progressive welfare practices have been so undermined by a succession of conservative governments throughout the Western world. Ellermann (1998) remarks that, 'Once we set out along the deconstructive path down which discourse analysis beckons, there seems to be no firm ground on which to stand and no absolute truths to which we can cling' (p. 35). Without the certainties and identities that modern critical social theories have provided for us, for whom and by what means can activists fight for justice?

Finally, despite its promotion of diversity, poststructural theory offers little towards the reconstruction of emancipatory political processes. For instance, the emphasis on locality is promoted, it seems, in the absence of strategies to contest the domination of local elites and local truth claims. This is problematic in so far as the local processes can be as non-democratic as the processes of identity politics that poststructuralists contest. Hence, the poststructural vision of heterogeneous political practices is fundamentally flawed in so far as it fails to acknowledge the privileges and marginalizations that can occur even within local contexts of 'dialogue'.

The irony of poststructuralism is that in its promotion of a non-dogmatic stance, it fails to address its own potential for rigidity (Peile and McCouat, 1997). There is nothing to prevent the assumptions of the poststructuralist discourse, such as the emphasis on heterogeneity, locality and complexity, from becoming truth claims in themselves. Indeed, despite their antagonism toward metanarratives and grand theory, poststructuralist theorists rely on strict 'disciplinary truth apparatuses'; that is, conventions through which truth is established and sustained (Foucault, quoted in Barrett, 1992, p. 215). Moreover, these apparatuses are effectively closed, as the esoteric character of much 'post' theorizing puts it beyond the reach of the diverse communities it claims to celebrate. Bordo's (1990) criticism of postmodern philosophy is thus similarly applicable to poststructural theorizing, as she states,

'We deceive ourselves if we believe that postmodern theory is attending to the "problem of difference" so long as so many concrete others are excluded from the conversation' (p. 140).

Response two: embrace of poststructural critique of the human services

Alongside the antipathy expressed by many progressive social workers towards 'post' theories, some authors have used the poststructural analyses of human sciences to extend critical understanding of contemporary welfare practices. One area of affinity between Foucault (1981a, 1991a) and critical social work is the recognition that welfare practices are implicated in the processes of social control (see Rojek et al., 1988; Howe, 1994; Leonard, 1994). Foucault's researches emphasize that in the modern era 'matters of values, justice, right and wrong have been superseded by concern with the "norm" and deviation from it' (p. 132). The human service occupations, including medicine, law, education and 'social work', are orientated towards the normalization of deviant populations.

Yet Foucault's work also extends well established radical perspectives on the controlling dimensions of care work by demonstrating *how* the human services contribute to the subordination of marginalized populations. Leonard (1994) suggests that a Foucauldian history of social work would show the subtle operations of control that operate through welfare processes which bring 'patriarchal bourgeois reason, objectivity, method and organization to bear on the irrationality, subjectivity, chaos, and disorganization of the casualties amongst the subject classes' (p. 21). Notably, this emphasis on rationality can be detected in both orthodox and critical social work discourses. The claim is that in its blind faith in the truth claims of modernity, social work has played a central role, alongside all other human services, such as medicine, law, nursing, education and the therapies, in the practices of surveillance and disciplining.

Foucault's critique of the oppressive aspects of welfare activity is not altogether different from that developed within the critical social work canon. However, Foucault's work does challenge the opposition that has emerged in the critical literature, which champions the emancipatory potential of some techniques of social work (usually non-statutory, community action forms) whilst depicting others as conduits for state control (particularly statutory or individual work modes). For Foucault there is no escape from power. Practice cannot be disconnected from modern systems of power, which pervade everywhere. While critical practice is possible it is always shaped by the historical and local contexts in which social work practices are embedded.

Challenging the activist embrace of Foucault

Despite the proliferation of critical social work writing endorsing Foucault's criticisms of the modern human services, I consider that practitioners should be cautious in approaching this aspect of his work. To adopt Foucault's analysis as the complete explanation of the operations of contemporary social work is to miss his call to the investigation of local practice sites. Foucault's historical critique was intended to incorporate the entire scope of the human services field, including the work of judges, teachers, psychiatrists and medical practitioners. Critical social workers, then, must interrogate the usefulness of his insights for engaging with both the specifics and the diversity of social work practices. I take particular issue with the application of Foucault's general critique of positivist scientific foundations of human services to social work, as illustrated in Leonard's (1994) remark that:

> A professional discourse such as that of social work is based on an assumption of expert knowledge as an increasingly close approximation to the truth about what exists in the objective world – our diagnosis, assessment, interpretation – and because of this excludes, with differing degrees of rigidity, outside knowledge. (p. 22)

Notwithstanding the lucidity of Foucault's critique of positivism, its direct application to understanding and transforming contemporary social work practices is flawed for a number of reasons.

In contrast to many human service professions, social work cannot be said to hold a uniform knowledge base. Many social work theorists acknowledge the permeability, unevenness and the reactionary character of social work knowledge (see, for example, Rojek et al., 1988; Howe, 1994; Opie, 1995). For example, in her study of social workers in aged care, Opie (1995) found that social workers were less able than other human service professionals to delineate clear areas of technical or professional knowledge and skill. The variability of social work knowledge is evidence of the influence of a range of paradigms, *other than positivism*, on knowledge development. For more than three decades, the positivist paradigm has been the subject of heated debate amongst social workers (Peile, 1988; Atherton, 1993). During this time, interpretivism (which is strongly relativist) and critical perspectives have had considerable influence on the field (see Langan, 1998). In this way, social work knowledge is markedly different from many other human service occupations, such as psychology and medicine, whose knowledge foundations remain strongly positivist.

To point to the precariousness of social work knowledge is not to deny that social workers wield power through their knowledge, including power in relation to service users. I am suggesting, however, that Foucault's critique of positivism is limited for apprehending the operations of power/knowledge in social work practices that are avowedly anti-positivist, anti-expert and anti-technical. The failure to engage critically with other approaches to knowledge in social work is problematic because knowledge, even the knowledge gained through lived experience, is never innocent of the operations of power (Scott, 1992).

By limiting the use of poststructural theory to those aspects that reinforce well established critical social work perspectives, activists may miss the opportunities this body of work provides for rethinking social work. What I propose, then, is that progressive social workers move beyond the conditional acceptance of critical poststructural theories to a fuller engagement with the more troublesome and disruptive aspects of this body of work. It is to this challenge that I now turn.

Response three: poststructural theory and social work processes

A third response that has gained momentum in the 1990s is one endorsing the opportunities that 'post' theories provide for transcending rationalist assumptions of modern discourses of practice and policy making (see Opie, 1988; Lowe, 1990; Gorman, 1993; Pardeck et al., 1994; Pozatek, 1994; Laird, 1995). From this perspective, poststructuralism is used to deconstruct claims to a 'core' or 'essence' of social work and to move instead towards practice theories that engage with the complexity and contextual diversity of social work practices.

This approach claims that poststructural theory enables a more productive engagement with the variety of welfare practices than has been possible within the critical tradition alone. This is because the insights of poststructural theory invite us to recognize that 'social work', like all other entities, is constituted through discourses. Hence, just as entities vary from context to context, so too the nature of what social work 'is' will change accordingly. Critical social work theories have tended to down play the importance of context as is evident, for example, in the paucity of activist literature addressing progressive practice possibilities in conventional practice contexts, such as hospitals or bureaucracies, or in contexts involving the use of statutory power. By drawing attention to the productive power of discourse, poststructural theory invites critical social workers to locate their understandings within the historical and local contexts of practice.

This recognition of context is crucial because social work, whether orthodox or critical, cannot evade the historical context in which its practices, like the practices of all human service professions, are embedded. In all Western countries, the human services have contributed to the practices of colonization and dispossession. The liberatory claims of critical social workers are bound to be regarded with suspicion by those whose experience of welfare practices has been anything but liberatory! This distrust is not erased merely because social workers claim to adopt a progressive outlook. In her critique of contemporary critical practice literature, Larbalestier (1998) asserts:

> For indigenous Australians the notions of a 'beneficent state' working for their 'best interests' is at the very least a representation to be contested. As welfare clients they are all too familiar with the various forms of encouragement and coercion to change their ways of being in the world to more 'socially adaptive' and 'purposive directions' . . . [which were] integral to Australia's assimilation policies aimed at the *eradication* of indigenous cultural identities. (p. 78)

Critical practice is possible, but recognition of the historical and local contexts of social work practice demands greater modesty in claims about what can be achieved.

Attention to historical context is important also for drawing critical social workers' attention to the shifts, over time, in the uses and effects of critical practice strategies. In contemporary societies, many of the techniques aimed at shaping and directing the conduct of individuals, such as community consultation and community education, were initially developed in a range of non-government organizations and have since been colonized by government services (Bennett, 1998, p. 76). Recognition of the shifting contexts of social work action should motivate critical social workers beyond complacency about the innately critical character of any practice approach.

Poststructural perspectives emphasize the open and multi-faceted character of texts and narratives (Opie, 1988, p. 4). All claims to truth, including the claims made by critical social work theorists to understand the true origins of problems faced by service users, are exposed to interrogation and negotiation. From a poststructural perspective, then, social work should be less concerned with un-covering causes and explanations through scientific means, than with focusing on the 'text, narrative and artistry' of practice (Parton and Marshall, 1998, p. 247). For instance, narrative therapy, a practice approach drawing on poststructural ideas, involves social workers and service users in creating new and meaningful narratives which are intended to extend possibilities for understanding and action. In addition, poststructural theory draws attention to the intolerance of differences that lie at the heart of social work practices, including critical practice approaches. For example, consciousness raising practices have tended to discount the alternate claims of subordinate populations as the workings of the 'unconscious' or 'false conscious-ness'. By contrast, in recognizing the multiplicity of truth claims, poststructuralism can contribute to new and more respectful ways of encountering differences. I want now to turn to a consideration of the implications of poststructural theory for representing the core entities of critical social work, particularly power, identity and change.

Representations of practice

In its focus on the representations of practice, poststructural theory draws attention to the discourses through which activist social work is constituted (see Rojek et al., 1988). For critical social theories do not exist outside relations of power, as a revelation of what was there all the time, but are produced through them. Thus, the representations of critical discourse must be examined not just for the claims they make, but also for the kinds of subjectivities, social objects and power relations they make possible.

Despite the many heated debates amongst critical social workers, the core understandings of activist practice have remained hermetically sealed from contest. For instance, a wide range of activist practice theories are premised on the claim that the original causes of oppression lie in the social structure, even though there is considerable disagreement as to whether these structures are primarily patriarchal, capitalist, imperialist or a combination of all of these. Indeed, the claims of activist practice discourses are so far beyond question that critical social work theorists charge those who fail to adopt them with contributing to the oppression of service users. One way in which activists have strengthened the moral appeal of their claims is by representing them as analogous to the 'real' needs of the poor. This is an unethical and arrogant practice in so far as critical practice perspectives are no more derived from the engagement with the 'others' whose interests they are claimed to represent than are the orthodox theories they contest. Rather, the origins of these critical social work claims, like the assertions of conventional practice theory, lie in the grand theories of modernity.

The insights of poststructural theory can increase the self-reflexivity of activist practitioners by encouraging the ongoing interrogation of the processes through which some truth claims are produced while others are suppressed (Rojek et al., 1988, p. 137). For example, a poststructural critique could focus on how the representations of the relations between service users make certain differences visible (such as class differences) whilst obscuring others (such as the local operations of power and knowledge and the changes to these relations over time). To be sure, there are dangers inherent in the destabilizing impulses of poststructural discourses. Many activists fear the slide into an endless relativism that these perspectives imply, as Dixon (1993) remarks: 'In the relativism of the argument that we are all different but equal flows a certain ambivalence for politics – which is premised on inequalities' (p. 26). Yet, in unsettling the truth claims that have become an unspoken and unquestioned orthodoxy of critical social work practice theories, poststructural perspectives can contribute to more open ended approaches to practice in action and theory-building.

Power

Poststructural theory challenges the adequacy of critical approaches for explaining the local operations of power through 'our bodies, our existence, our everyday lives' (Foucault, 1978, p. 70). Foucault's claim that power and knowledge are linked undermines critical social work perspectives which situate power in overarching social structures. He (1980d) insists:

> Truth is a thing of this world; it is produced only by virtue of multiple forms of constraint. And it induces regular effects of power. Each society has its own regime of truth, its 'general politics of truth'; that is, the types of discourse which it accepts as true; the mechanisms and instances which enable one to distinguish true from false statements, the means by which each is sanctioned; and the techniques and procedures accorded value in the acquisition of truth; the status of those charged with saying what counts as true. (p. 131)

From this perspective, activists are invited to redirect their analyses. An understanding of the superstructures is insufficient for understanding how power relations are sustained and transgressed through the power–knowledge relations of practice.

The poststructural work of Foucault suggests that activist discourses, like all discursive practices, do not exist apart from power; rather they are fully invested with it. Leonard (1996) acknowledges that:

> The appeal to science as a justification for professional, bureaucratic or revolutionary practice, tends to solidify power in the hands of intellectuals and state functionaries and denies it to the mass of the oppressed and dispossessed whose welfare has been claimed to be one of the central rationales of scientific advance in the West. (pp. 11–12)

Activists are encouraged to turn their attention to the forms of power, including the exclusionary effects, that their discourses produce. For example, the claims of the revolutionary can subjugate by dismissing alternate claims of subordinate populations through, for example, portraying them as false consciousness.

In addition, Foucault's work draws attention to the repressive and the productive aspects of power. While it threatens core assumptions of critical practice discourses, this claim is important also for articulating the forms of power, particularly worker power, on which critical practices rely. Practice processes such as raising consciousness, initiating collective involvement and struggle do not occur in the absence of power. Thus, rather than a surrender of power, what activist practice discourses demand is a *different* use of power from that usually associated with professional practices. Foucault's emphasis on the micro-physics of power suggests that local relations of power are not merely an effect of the structural. This understanding makes possible a fuller articulation of the range of power relations that emerge within local practice contexts, and in so doing can help to extend and diversify understandings of critical practice processes.

Identity

Poststructural theory, particularly the work of radical poststructural feminists, draws attention to the oppositions through which identity is represented in critical practice discourses. In the critical social science school, power is regarded as 'coercive/oppressive and identity is structured in a hierarchy in which one subject position is seen as dominant over the others' (Gibson-Graham, 1995, p. 175). In critical social work discourses, these oppositions[1] include:

middle class/working class
the privileged/the poor
technical knowledge/lived experience
voice/silence
researcher/researched
worker/client
powerful/powerless

Within these representations the social worker is situated on the left hand of the dichotomy whilst the service user is on the right. Although in their practice activists may seek to reverse or transcend these dualisms, the dichotomies themselves remain central to activist analysis. For example, in her discussion of feminist community work, Dixon (1993) contends that 'I think, at base, we need to hold onto a major duality: the powerful and the powerless' (p. 26).

---

1 In developing this model of the dualistic representations of worker and service user identities, I draw on the work of radical poststructural feminist Hélène Cixous. In her work, Cixous (1981b, p. 90) outlines a series of dualisms through which masculinity and femininity are constituted in modern discourses.

Critical social work representations have made important contributions to the rethinking of practice in so far as they have encouraged workers to adopt a stance of humility and self-reflexivity. Yet, these dualistic representations also risk some very serious simplifications. Fine (1994) warns, 'If poststructuralism has taught us anything, it is to beware the frozen identities . . . to suspect the binary, to worry the clear distinctions' (p. 80).

Rather than acknowledge and celebrate diversity, the oppositional categories of social work reduce a range of differences to just two positions: 'worker' and 'service user'. The reduction of differences is constraining for both sides. For example, in being positioned outside power, the service user is confined to a politics of *ressentiment* rather than engaging in positive political action based on a recognition of their capacity to exercise power. The assumption of powerlessness can lead to forms of paternalism and authoritarianism in so far as it is assumed that individuals are without power and require the power of the other to protect them or to enlighten them (Yeatman, 1997; Langan, 1998).

In addition, these representations imply that contrasting identities will lead, necessarily, to unilateral and oppressive power relationships between 'social workers' and 'service users'. For instance, Burke and Harrison (1998) claim that: 'A white male social worker brings to the situation a dynamic that will reproduce the patterns of oppression to which black women are subjected in the wider society' (p. 235). This assumption does not allow for local variations in power relationships. Perhaps, more importantly though, it pre-empts investigation into how local social practices of oppression are produced and sustained (Yeatman, 1997). In other words, although an analysis beginning within broad social structures can tell us much about social patterns of inequality, it fails to inform us about how these patterns might be resisted and transformed within specific contexts of action.

Similarly, the portrayal of social workers as 'powerful' and as 'experts' is questionable in so far as it obscures other ways in which these individuals are positioned through discourses, in relation to categories such as gender, race, sexuality and lived experiences. The oppositional categories through which critical social work theories, including feminist discourses, constitute practice identities are inadequate because, as Gatens (1998) points out, the position of the powerful and authoritative figure in modern discourses is inhabited by a very specific kind of subject: 'the white, able-bodied, heterosexual, middle-class man' (p. 7). Critical discourses are limited in their representation of the diverse ways in which social workers, many of whom are women, are able to occupy the categories of authority and power assigned to them. Indeed, Gatens (1990) goes so far as to question whether these categories adequately apprehend the experiences of the privileged men for whom they were originally intended.

Change

Finally, poststructural theory calls into question the linear notions of progress on which modern forms of social work, whether conservative or orthodox, have relied. Poststructural theory, particularly the work of radical poststructural feminists, invites the revaluing of those forms of knowledge that have been marginalized in modern discourses, such as the non-logical, irrational and emotional forms of knowledge. Poststructuralism can be used to destabilize the rationalist claims of critical discourse which imply that if one gets the analysis right the correct practices will follow.

Critical social workers' faith in rationalism is evident, for example, in Mullaly's (1993) assertion that 'the individual living in poverty would be treated in a punitive or remedial manner by a conservative social worker but would be treated as a victim of an oppressive social order by a Marxist social worker' (p. 44). To claim that a particular analysis will necessarily effect certain practices is extraordinarily naive to inconstancies of human action and to the considerable evidence in contemporary history of the very non-liberatory processes that are sustained and even prosper in the context of emancipatory claims. Indeed, the twentieth century has been littered with examples of the use of utopian ideals to justify oppressive social practices (Lyotard, 1984; Leonard, 1996, p. 11). Within local practice contexts, critical discourses can lead to the suppression of different perspectives, even amongst those whose interests critical social workers claim to champion. As I will examine further in Chapter 6, consciousness raising processes can contribute to a narrow form of change in which members of the oppressed population learn to speak differently about their experiences whilst the social practices in which they participate remain unchanged.

Foucault's work further problematizes emancipatory strategies on the grounds that they are implicated in processes of surveillance and disciplining practices (see Foucault, 1980c, 1981a, 1991f). For instance, Foucault suggests that contemporary practices associated with sexuality, such as the proliferation of discourses about this topic, do not liberate sexuality but rather make it the subject of public obsession (Foucault, 1981a, p. 44). According to this insight, then, it is not sufficient to subscribe to a set of 'emancipatory' strategies; one must also interrogate the local effects of these practices.

In its promotion of locality and complexity, poststructuralism can draw attention to the everyday practices of social work as sites of analysis and action. The importance of this redirection is reflected in Lane's (1990) observations of feminist community work:

> Whilst universal 'truths' and 'guidelines for practice' may be comforting . . . the challenge for community work theory/practice is embrace, rather than deplore, the uncertainty of a 'ceaseless critical engagement' with the day by day experiences of the women with whom we work. (p. 179)

The insights of poststructural theory can destabilize the dualisms which privilege rational thought and structural change in progressive practices. In its unabashed celebration of differences, poststructural theory draws attention to the authoritarianism at work in utopian ideals. It is through these destabilizing impulses that poststructuralism makes possible new forms of activist social work that engage with the diversity of context, knowledge and aspirations of the service workers and service users involved in the practices of social work.

Grounding the debate in practice

Social workers have, quite rightly, criticized the arcane language and esoteric nature of much 'post' theorizing (Leonard, 1997). A dialogue between 'post' theories and the practices of social work is not as yet well developed. It is my intention over the next two chapters to show how a dialogue could be developed between these two arenas. In the following chapters I will ground the discussion of contemporary theories within contexts of social work practice. My intention is to extend critical social work practices by:

- outlining the possibilities and the limits of critical practice approaches for understanding activist practices in a broad range of practice contexts;
- analysing the adequacy of structural approaches to power for apprehending the operations of power within activist practice processes;
- examining the perception and function of 'identity' within activist practice processes, particularly how these representations can become more complex over the course of practice;
- interrogating the liberatory and constraining effects of activist change programmes within specific contexts of practice. In other words, I will consider not only the emancipatory effects but also what and who is suppressed through current approaches to critical practices.

A discourse analysis approach

In concert with the poststructural emphasis on the productive character of language, I will use a discourse analysis approach to investigate critical practice processes. Discourse analysis illuminates the processes through which discourses constitute and constrain social relationships, practices and institutions. Although critical social workers have used discourse analysis methods to critically review social work practice theories, the use of these methods to investigate social work processes is a largely uncharted terrain. Discourse analysis can enrich progressive social work practices by demonstrating how the language practices through which organizations, theorists, practitioners and service users express their understanding of social work also shape the kinds of practices that occur (see Healy and Mulholland, 1998).

In this research I will use the practices of social work to speak with and speak back to critical social work practice theories. In order to address my overriding research concerns with the destabilizing and reworking critical practice theories, as I turn to the investigation of specific practice contexts, I use discourse analysis to investigate the language through which:

- critical social workers delineate what social work, particularly activist practice, 'is';
- workers and service users construct and express their understanding of social work within particular contexts of action.

My claim is that the critical analyses of practice have been limited in so far as their reliance on grand theory has obscured the complexities and contingencies within local practice contexts. I aim to counter this trend by basing my analysis of social work within specific sites of action. The discourse analysis methods will allow me to access the local complexities that, all too often, lie concealed beneath the certainties of critical practice theories and to use these alternate perspectives from practice to unsettle the contemporary representations of what social work 'is' and what it can be. In many of the practice excerpts I draw on conversation analysis conventions, to mark the tone and pace of the interactions recorded. In the appendix I include a legend of the conventions used.

Investigating what social work 'is'

Through situating my investigations within specific practice contexts, my intention is to assess the potential and the limits of poststructural insights for transforming critical practice understandings and action. In accordance with the poststructural respect for the local and the ad hoc, my researches are not orientated toward finding out the truth about social work; but, rather, to develop practice theories that are sufficiently open-ended to engage with the diversity of social work across practice contexts.

In this investigation I will consider both 'orthodox' and 'activist' practice settings. In investigating conventional practice contexts, I will focus on the uses and limits of critical notions of power for extending participatory processes in statutory social work. This focus is important for many social work positions which, particularly in front-line service delivery, involve statutory functions. Yet, critical social workers have contributed little to understanding how workers might exercise this power differently, other than to advise practitioners to minimize their use of it.

As my interest is primarily in understanding and reworking critical social work perspectives, I will focus mainly on an analysis of the operations of power, identity and change within a context of activist practice. This context, which I will refer to as the 'young women's anti-violence project', was a community based campaign drawing on a range of critical practice perspectives, including feminism, critical community work and participatory action research. My research derives from the two years in which I was involved as a social worker and researcher with the project.

My interest in this project arose from experience as a social worker in a youth service where I became aware of the extraordinary levels of violence in the lives of homeless young women, particularly amongst young mothers. Initially, I had discussed the idea of a project concerning young women's experiences of domestic violence with young women involved in a range of social services and with the professionals working with them. The young women whom I consulted pointed out that 'domestic violence' was not a term that they applied to their experiences of violence for a range of reasons including: their youth (for them, domestic violence was something that happened to older people); their involvement in 'unconventional' and unstable relationships; the range of people, other than partners, who were responsible for the violence they had experienced. As a result of these discussions, the project centred instead on a broad scope of violence to which young women, particularly homeless and parenting women, are vulnerable.

The campaign began with a core group consisting of two project workers (myself and a co-worker) and seven young women between the ages of 17 and 24 years, all of whom were (or had been) teenage mothers with between one and four children each; most had experienced homelessness, all were in a low income bracket and all identified that they had been subjected to violence, such as sexual assault, child abuse and domestic violence. All the young women in the core group identified as Anglo Australians, though in the various public meetings and in the ongoing work of the group, young women from a broad range of ethnic communities have been involved with the project. Over the course of the first year a total of 31 young women and many professionals were involved in the project through interviews or participation in a public forum held by the group. In the second year the project developed into a peer support and advocacy network, which has ongoing contact with young women and young mothers.

With the participants' permission I recorded the development of the project through: audio-taping some of the group meetings and public action undertaken by the group; field notes on the content of the meetings and other action undertaken by the group; the maintenance of written records of my reflections on the project as well as those of my co-facilitator and the young women who participated in the core group. I also recorded comments about the campaign from people who had a more marginal role within it, such as professionals or young women who had attended one of the public meetings held by the project group. At the conclusion of the first year of the project I conducted interviews with the young women who had participated in the project to gain further insights from their reflections on the effects of the project.

Researching as a practitioner

By situating myself as a practitioner in one of the practice contexts under investigation, my intention was to make explicit connections between the theory, practice and research dimensions of social work. These connections have been lost or minimized as the practices of social work have been viewed, all too often, as inconsequential to social work theorizing, including critical practice theorizing. As Fook (1996) observes 'Might it be that the people whose discourse we accept in setting the terms of the debate [about theory and practice] are not those who experience the practice of social work?' (p. xiii).

As a practitioner, I was able to recognize more different perspectives than would, perhaps, be possible if I had made only my role as theorist or researcher explicit. In particular, my identifications across practice, research and theory building increased my sensitivity to the 'othering' practices on which critical social work theories are based. The term 'othering' is used to describe a process by which the diverse characteristics within a population are reduced or ignored altogether. Denzin (quoted in Fine, 1994, p. 79) notes that critical approaches to the study of power tend to:

> create self (colonizer) and other (colonized) as dichotomous categories, oppositions
> defined out of clearly defined cultural, ethnic, racial and gendered differences. Such

treatments (after Derrida and Bakhtin) fail to treat the complexities and contradictions that define membership in each category. (p. 79)

Critical social work theories rely on this process of othering in their depictions of practice identities and practice relationships. In contrast, by positioning myself within the practice contexts, I intend to contest these othering practices by highlighting the complex interweavings of practitioners' and service users' histories and identities that can occur, particularly in long term practice processes.

The inclusion of myself within the practice research gaze did not mean that I could ignore the structural inequities that also constituted the relations between workers and service users. However, it did mean that I was constantly confronted with the complexities and contradictions within the practice context, which all too often have been ignored in critical social work theories. By beginning the research and theorizing from the vantage point of practice, I intend to draw attention to how critical practice theorizing might proceed differently if it were located at least in part within local contexts of action, rather than being situated, almost exclusively, in the grand theories of modernity.

Conclusion

In this chapter, I have outlined three orientations to poststructural theory adopted by critical social work authors. I have focused in some detail on the exploration of what, if anything, the destabilizing influences of poststructural theory can offer for extending the understanding of critical social work processes. In the next two chapters, I will examine these ideas further in contexts of social work practice.

5   Rethinking Professional Power and Identity

Power and identity are central concerns of critical social work theory. Critical approaches have emphasized the political nature of social work and represented social workers and service users as opposites in terms of experience, interests and access to power. For activists there is a fundamental contradiction between the broad intention of social work, to help and to empower, and the power wielded by professional social workers. Critical authors have highlighted the privileged access to power that arises from the class and professional status of social workers, and these thinkers link this advantage to the ongoing oppression of service users (see Ward and Mullender, 1991; Andrews, 1992). Critical social work discussions about collaboration between workers and participants are dominated by the goal of increasing equality in practice. Worker power is represented as anathema to the dialogic and egalitarian practice preferred by critical workers. As a consequence, critical practice theory is replete with strategies for reducing or, indeed, eliminating the power wielded by workers in the lives of service users.

In contrast to critical social work, poststructural theories emphasize the discursive constitution of power. The critical poststructural work of Foucault and Cixous tears apart the foundational assumptions of critical social work as it draws attention to the fine detail of the operations of power and identity which have been missing from structural accounts. Foucault's insistence that 'power is everywhere' strikes at the heart of the distinction critical social workers make between themselves and orthodox social workers. Foucault's work suggests that it is futile to differentiate between controlling and non-controlling forms of social work on a number of grounds. Firstly, in many contexts of practice, overt social control is an inevitable and irreducible dimension of practice. The recognition of the inescapable nature of the social control exercised by human service workers redirects critical practice theorizing towards an exploration of how this power might be made increasingly accountable and just to those subject to it. Second, Foucault insists that power/ knowledge operates through all discourses, including activist ones. Critical discourses are fully implicated in the practices of power and control in so far as these discourses impose specific Truths upon others (see Foucault, 1980c; Conley, 1992). Critical social workers cannot distance themselves from control but they can, at least, acknowledge the forms of control that function via their practice discourses. Critical poststructural theory ruptures the foundations of critical social work and opens the canon to a number of challenges which will be examined in this chapter including:

- development of critical approaches to the exercise of power and authority;
- recognition of the productivity of worker power for activist practice;
- attending to differences within the category of 'powerful worker'.

Before turning to an examination of these challenges, let us overview the notion of worker power in critical practice theory.

Representations of worker power and identity

Critical practice theories seek to make visible the links between overarching social structures and local relations of power and identity. In Chapter 4, it was argued that critical practice theories depict social workers and service users as opposites with different positions within social structures and distinct political interests. Critical approaches draw attention to the oppressive dimensions of social work practice, particularly the inequitable and exploitative character of the relationships between the human service workers and clients of the welfare state.

Critical authors have identified three main sources through which workers access power. Firstly, power is conferred via the middle class status of the worker. Critical authors have emphasized that the class differences between professional human service workers and service users ensure inequity in the practice context (see E. Wilson, 1977; Andrews, 1992). Moreover, the vested interest of professional workers in the maintainence of the status quo compromises their capacity to commit to social transformation (Fox Piven and Cloward, 1993).

A second source of power is the statutory authority conferred upon social workers as agents of the welfare state. Radical welfare theorists have long contested the view of welfare work as a benign and caring activity and, instead, they have emphasized the social control dimensions of state funded care (Corrigan and Leonard, 1978; Leonard, 1994). For them, a primary function of state welfare activity is to quell dissent in the context of mass inequity (see Fox Piven and Cloward, 1993). The statutory functions undertaken by social workers are one expression of their primary allegiance to the state, its laws and norms, rather than to the best interests of service users.

A third source of power derives from the professional status of the worker. Even though social workers do not always have access to statutory authority they remain powerful because of their professional identity. The relationship between workers and service users is steeped in inequality which arises from the prestige accorded to the expert voice of the social worker compared to the non-expert and marginal voices of service users. Moreover, critical authors contend that despite a rhetoric of equity and participation, professionals are usually reluctant to shed power and privilege necessary to achieving more equitable relations (Shemmings and Shemmings, 1995).

Critical authors persistently assert that the power relations between workers and service users are unilateral, hierarchical and inequitable. Professional power is understood to be inevitably disabling for service users. The workers' access to legitimated power and knowledge is conveyed by their privileged location in the social structure and is immutable and unchanging from context to context. Even though workers may experience specific forms of oppression, such as those associated with gender, race, (dis)ability or sexuality, this does not erase the oppressor status conferred by their professional identity (Healy, 1999). Critical practice strategies encourage the redistribution of power in the practice context; however, it is recognized that the power differences between workers and service users cannot be eradicated altogether. Many critical theorists consider that the capacity of human service workers to contribute to radical social change is, at best, contradictory and partial. Indeed, it is frequently advocated that the interests of service users are to be served by the minimization and, ultimately, the complete withdrawal of social workers from the lives of the oppressed (see Middleman and Goldberg, 1974; Hudson, 1989).

Rethinking social control

In critical practice theory, power is represented as a possession of individuals and groups who hold privileged positions within overarching social structures. In emphasizing the political nature of social work practice, critical social workers have represented workers and service users dualistically: as the 'powerful' and the 'powerless'. Critical poststructural theory challenges these representations.

For Foucault (1980b, p. 52), power is ubiquitous. Foucault rejects a view that power is attached to identities, such as the identity of the 'professional social worker'. Rather, power operates through discourses and practices that are specific to particular institutional locations. Like critical social work theorists, Foucault (1991e) recognizes that human service workers do enact power in relation to others, particularly subordinated populations. However, in contrast to critical social workers, critical poststructural theorists recognize that power is inherent in all relationships (Yeatman, 1997). Furthermore, Foucault's analyses suggest that social control is present in all human services work, including ostensibly radical practice approaches. For even though social control may take different forms across practice contexts, the lesson of poststructuralism is that there is no escape from it (White, 1997). Recognizing the inevitability of social control releases critical social work to engage differently with this issue than has been possible within the critical tradition alone.

Critical poststructural theory can alert practitioners to the forms of control that operate through liberatory frameworks. This is important to overcoming particular elisions within contemporary critical theory about the operations of power and identity in social work. Wise (1990), a feminist social worker, critiques much of the writing within this tradition on the grounds that it is

> often couched in abstract theoretical terms with little reference to the everyday realities of practice, and they seem unwilling to deal with the inevitable aspects of social control in feminist social work, preferring instead to see it only as a tool of empowerment for women. (p. 239)

The inability to address the social control dimensions of social work is not confined to feminist social work. Indeed, amongst activist social workers there has been little discussion of the operations of power, let alone social control, within critical social work practices. If activists recognize the presence of worker power in their practice, they view it as an aberration of their intention to empower and to liberate.

Given the negative view of power that pervades much critical social work theory, it is perhaps unsurprising that authors within this canon have been remarkably subdued in their contribution to practice theory for contexts where the use of authority is an explicit and irreducible dimension of human service work. The practice strategies offered by critical social work theorists focus almost entirely on minimizing and, where possible, eliminating the control that social workers exercise in service users' lives (see Spicker, 1990; Ban, 1992; Dalrymple and Burke, 1995). Notwithstanding the importance of the contributions made by critical authors, they have avoided the rethinking of power and social control necessary for a more productive engagement to occur between critical practice theory and the overt social control functions that many social workers bear. Hence, it is no surprise that many strategies and notions promoted within critical practice theory, such as ideals of 'partnership' and 'participation', remain of minimal applicability to statutory and conventional practice contexts (Healy, 1998; Bricker-Jenkins et al., 1991).

The poststructural recognition of the inescapability of power, including the exercise of social control, offers a profound challenge to the core assumptions of critical social work. It means that even as activists seek to strengthen the emancipatory side of social work they do so *in full knowledge* of the control that workers exercise. It demands a full and ongoing recognition of the inequality that fundamentally structures social work interactions, whether radical or orthodox, whilst also allowing that other relationships of power and identity may coexist and develop over time. Let us now turn to an investigation of how these ideas can be applied to practice settings involving the explicit exercise of power.

Practice illustration: social control in statutory child protection work

Social workers in statutory settings are required to undertake professional assessment and decision-making. Often, these decisions have enormous implications for service users' lives. In child protection contexts, the social worker's role involves assessment and decision-making about whether parents and other care-givers are 'fit' to maintain guardianship of children. Although other actors, such as the courts and medical personnel, play important roles in this process, the judgements of social workers are also integral to it.

The critical child welfare literature is replete with criticisms of assessment and decision-making roles undertaken by social workers in statutory social work. Critical authors argue that social workers' engagement in professional assessment reflects and reproduces an inequitable and hierarchical practice relationship (see Mittler, 1995; Shemmings and Shemmings, 1995). The validity of social workers' judgements are also contested on the grounds that assessments reflect middle class values which have little relevance to the lives of service users (see Ryburn, 1991a; Calder, 1995). Some social work authors critique the inequity of the relationship between service worker and service user and advocate instead the formation of 'partnerships' between human service workers and service users (Thoburn et al., 1995, p. 33). Partnership requires the transcendence of professional boundaries and the recognition that the knowledge possessed by service users is as valid, if not more valid, than knowledge of the worker (Mittler,1995; Shemmings and Shemmings, 1995).

At the heart of the criticisms raised by progressive social workers is a concern about the exercise of social control entailed in such activity. Yet, the seemingly endless critique of social control amongst critical welfare theorists has done little to address the urgent questions of how critical perspectives may inform statutory child protection practice, other than to advise workers to minimize the power differentials in the practice context. In contrast, a more productive interaction between activist ideals and statutory social work can be facilitated, as the work of 'post' theorists encourages recognition of both the inevitability of control and also the local constraints which shape the relationship between social workers and service users. This perspective demands that critical social workers situate their theorizing within the unavoidable obligation faced by statutory workers to use legal force if necessary to ensure minimum standards of well-being for the most vulnerable members (Stevenson, 1996; see also Wise, 1990; Clark, 1998). Practice insights can be drawn from critical social theory to recognize the impact of social and economic systems on service users' lives and to demand sensitivity to the cultural differences in the formation of assessments. However, this is very different to suggesting, as critical social work theorists have done, that judgements should not be made.

Secondly, critical poststructural theory challenges critical practitioners to recognize the limits of ideals about the kind of relationship workers and service users should establish. For example, critical thinkers advocate the transcendence of professional boundaries in favour of a more mutual and less hierarchical relationship with service users, even within statutory social work (Ban, 1992; Mittler, 1995). By contrast, critical poststructural theory draws attention to the problematic of grafting a standard for relationships without due regard for the specific demands made on both worker and service user within local practice contexts. Certainly, the intensity of long term statutory work can contribute to a less formal relationship than is typically associated with professional work (Wise, 1990). However, the directive that workers *should* reduce the distance between themselves and service users can deprive workers of a much needed resource; namely the capacity to stand both within and outside various systems, such as family systems and alternate care systems, in order to negotiate a minimum standard of care for those members of our society who are most vulnerable to abuse and neglect (see Dingwall et al., 1983; Killén, 1996). The imposition of a relationship 'ideal' impedes workers in the difficult task of exercising power in ways that are maximally effective and just. Moreover, unless the ideal of partnership is carefully negotiated it can lead also to confusion for service users about the nature of their relationship with human service workers (Healy and Young Mothers for Young Women, 1996).

Thirdly, critical poststructural theory can be used to illuminate those operations of power that have been suppressed within critical social work accounts of statutory practice. In particular, the poststructural theory discussed in this book draws attention to the multiple operations and effects of worker power even within statutory contexts. Critical poststructural insights can be invoked to challenge representations of the service users as the powerless victims of statutory authority. This point is emphasized by Gordon (1988) who, in her historical analysis of child welfare observes:

> It is a mistake to see the flow of initiative in these social control relationships in only one direction, from top to bottom, from professional to clients, from elite to subordinate. In fact, the clients were not usually passive but, rather, active in arguing for what they wanted. (p. 295)

To state that workers and service users exercise power is not to deny inequalities that endure between them, but rather to refuse to constantly situate service users as the passive victims of those exercising statutory power. Moreover, critical poststructural theory can challenge the emphasis within critical practice theory on the dominatory effects of statutory power by illuminating the multiple and, even, empowering effects that statutory authority can produce. Van-Krieken (1992) asserts that, 'what may be the imposition of control to one can be a way out of an untenable situation for another' (p. 141).

Critical commentators have chastised critical 'post' theorists for their esoteric language and concerns. Yet, ironically, this 'school' directs social workers to the very problems that have been evaded within critical social work theories; that is, towards a consideration of how statutory workers might practically apply the powers they inevitably wield in ways that are maximally 'humane, accountable and just' (Van Krieken, 1992, p. 145). The work of Campbell (1997), although not explicitly written from a critical poststructural stance, provides a practical illustration of one direction this may take activist practice theory; she asserts that:

> Active participation by family members requires professionals to demonstrate their willingness to inform and listen respectfully: to give full and frank information on their evidence of risk to the child, their interpretations of that evidence, and the resources and services they have to offer the family; and to hear what the family has to say about the evidence, their own views and interpretations and what resources they have at their disposal and feel that they need. (p. 8)

The emphasis here is not on the minimization of worker power; rather, Campbell provides strategies for increasing the transparency of decision-making and collaboration in full cognizance of the worker's statutory responsibilities. The application of critical poststructural theory to statutory social work does not involve a retreat to a liberal pluralist stance in which the workers' and service users' voices exist side by side in a power free conversation. On the contrary, critical poststructural theory draws us to an ongoing disclosure of the operations of power in practice and to the recognition that although statutory workers cannot avoid the use of power they can increase the accountability, humanity and justice with which this power is exercised.

The division of social work practice as critical or non-critical according to whether workers are involved in the overt exercise of social control is imprudent. This opposition has suppressed the emergence of critical practice theories that are responsive to social work practices in statutory settings and other settings involving the overt use of authority. As a consequence, the activities of many, perhaps the majority, of social workers are excluded from the critical canon, and critical practice theory is denied insights about power and resistance within conventional, particularly statutory, practice contexts. By contrast, a critical poststructuralist analysis of power can renew critical practice theory by recognizing the inevitability of social control in human services work. It challenges critical social workers to develop practice theories that can engage critically and productively with what social work 'is', rather than what the received wisdom of critical social science theory tells us it should be.

The productivity of worker power

An important way critical social workers differentiate themselves from orthodox practitioners is through their approach to power. Activists advocate the diminution of power differences between workers and service users, and through this shift they intend to advance the capacity of service users to direct change activity. The radical egalitarian stance is often championed by activists as one way of reducing the power imbalance between workers and service users. As differences, particularly differences in knowledge and skills, are correlated with inequity, the radical egalitarian stance promotes the redistribution of power through the sharing of knowledge, skills and tasks within the practice context (Phillips, 1991, p. 123).

The emphasis on shifting worker power and, ultimately, on the total removal of workers from practice contexts erroneously implies that the achievement of democratic and egalitarian relations involves the absence of worker power. Indeed, within the critical canon there has been little acknowledgement of the forms of power that activist practice theory promotes and requires. This unwillingness to acknowledge the use of power does not mean, however, that it is non-existent, only that it is not critically reflected upon (Kristeva, 1981, p. 141). Indeed, a cursory overview of the critical practice literature reveals the considerable use of power demanded of critical social workers. For example, activist workers and researchers are routinely involved in initiating practice projects and processes (Alder and Sandor, 1990; Reason, 1994); promoting participant involvement and leadership (Ward and Mullender, 1991); facilitating meetings (Mathrani, 1993); raising consciousness and promoting activist attitudes (Corrigan and Leonard, 1978; Dominelli and McLeod, 1989; Moreau, 1990; Dixon, 1993; Finn, 1994); imparting technical information and skills (Sarri and Sarri, 1992); and even initiating the sharing of power itself (Thorpe, 1992; Finn, 1994). The actions of the worker *are* powerful as they dramatically shape what workers and service users do and even think in the practice context. These practices are also potentially powerful in so far as it is anticipated that these strategies will spark large-scale social transformation.

Critical social work has tended to conflate worker power with the authoritarian use of power. This depiction has detracted from critical attention to the *different* use of power that activist practice entails. Leaving aside the question of the discipline and surveillance of subordinate populations through critical social work practice (a question I will address in Chapter 6), here I will consider the forms of worker power which critical practice discourses produce and on which they are reliant. In order to illuminate these specific operations of power, let us now turn to the examination of worker power in an activist practice context.

Practice illustration: young women's anti-violence project

In this section, I will refer to a context of activist practice to illustrate the exercise of worker power *within* critical social work. I will refer to this context as the young women's anti-violence project. The project began as a participatory action research project involving a core group of young mothers in analysing their own and other young women's experiences of violence (see Chapter 4 for a description of the practice context). The project developed into a peer support and advocacy network which involves young women in offering individual support and political advocacy for young women, especially in relation to social disadvantage, violence and discrimination. Also the group is involved in political action and advocacy, ranging from consultancy with government departments through to direct action. In developing the network, workers and participants have drawn on a selection of activist practice models including participatory action research, feminist practice principles and structural social work.

I was involved as a project worker over a two-year period. With the permission of my co-worker and project participants, I regularly collected audio-tapes of group meetings and public action undertaken by the group. I also maintained field notes drawing on my own experiences as well as that of other workers and project participants. My intention in grounding this analysis of power within a practice context is to show the complexities around worker power that were evident there; it is not suggested that analyses of other practice contexts would reveal similar operations of power. However, I contend that the exercise of worker power witnessed in the practice context is not an aberration of critical practice theory, but rather a product of it. By demonstrating the power extant within a context of practice, I aim to stimulate critical reflection on the forms of power that critical practice approaches produce and on which they rely.

In this analysis, I will focus on the operations of power in the practice context, with attention to:

- the overt use of power by workers;
- the implicit use of power by workers;
- participants' ambivalence about the use of worker power.

The overt use of power

I use the term 'overt power' to refer to those forms of power that explicitly demonstrated the different roles and responsibilities of the workers. Despite the power sharing stance embraced by activist social workers, a detailed analysis of the activist practice revealed instances of the overt use of power by my co-worker and me. Power was exercised for the maintenance of the project focus and for facilitating the achievement of agreed project goals. Worker power was exercised for numerous purposes including: fostering critical reflection on young women's experience of violence; involving the participants in structuring and directing each of the project meetings; facilitating involvement of all participants, not only the most articulate and outgoing, during the project meetings, challenging narrow definitions of violence and, thus, encouraging articulation of the diversity of violence experienced by the young women. Moreover, the exercise of this power differed from the hierarchical and authoritarian power relations typically associated with professional practice (Simon, 1990, p. 30). Instead, an egalitarian ethos was evident through, for example, the use of proposals rather than directives, expressed hesitancy in the use of power, explicit invitations to participants to challenge us and the frequent recognition in the workers' talk that the knowledge and capacities of the participants were key resources for change.

Let us now consider one illustration of this different exercise of power in the practice context. The example, which we will examine in this section, involves the workers' use of technical knowledge in the practice context. We can contrast the exercise of technical knowledge shown in this illustration with the scathing critique of technical knowledge found in the activist literature. Activists invite human service workers to abandon a desire for their practice of technical expertise on the grounds that such knowledge inevitably predominates over the knowledge 'derived from experience, commonsense and citizenship' (Andrews, 1992, p. 37; Gaventa, 1993, p. 22). On the face of it, Foucault's work supports the critique made by activists in so far as he repeatedly pointed to domination by expert voices and the suppression of other voices (see Foucault, 1980a, 1991a). Nonetheless, Foucault's recognition of the relationship of power and knowledge is not confined to technical knowledge. Foucault's work demonstrates that all knowledge including technical, revolutionary, and even knowledge gained from 'experience' is fully implicated in the operations of power (see Scott, 1992). Hence, while activists must always be aware of the silencing effects of technical discourses, the analysis of power/knowledge must not be confined to this. We must also attend to the local operations of technical knowledge and its interactions with other forms of knowledge. Specifically, we should explore whether this knowledge operates to suppress or reveal subordinate voices within specific contexts of action.

The following excerpt involves such an exploration as it focuses on the use of technical knowledge in an activist practice project. This excerpt was taken from the first stage of the project and demonstrates the young women and workers working collaboratively to achieve an analysis of the young women's stories of violence. The group had taken a decision to use some qualitative research strategies to analyse the 'data' of their life stories. The following excerpt provides one illustration of the interaction between 'technical' knowledge about qualitative research strategies held by the workers and the lived experiences of participants in the practice context. It is taken from a discussion two months after the project began. Prior to this meeting, the young women had spent eight meetings critically reflecting on and documenting their experiences of violence. In preparing to involve other young women in the project, the group engaged in a preliminary analysis of the themes that emerged from previous discussions. In this transcript, I have retained some conversation markers to indicate the tone of the interaction and a full key to these conventions is included in the appendix. In brief, the conventions used in the following excerpt are: round brackets ( ) indicate that the transcript was not entirely clear and that I have made an interpretation of what was said, or if the brackets are empty it means that I was unable to make any interpretation of the information; square brackets [ ] include contextual information that should help the reader make sense of the conversation; CAPITAL letters indicate force of emphasis of speech. This excerpt begins with the identification of one of the common themes in the young women's experiences of violence:

Leah: The common thing is our age. I mean in a lot of people . . . these things, A LOT of the people are talking about are bigger problems because of our age.

Melissa: Yeh, I've got that here [on the notes taken from earlier meetings]. 'Cos the fact that we are young mothers.

Worker 1: Okay, age is another thing.

Melissa: I've got immaturity and not knowing how to handle a relationship.

Worker 2: Age is common in all of them. The childhood, like the relationship between your violence and your childhood is fairly common too, is it?

Annette: I don't know if age is though because it happens to a lot of women that are . . .

Worker 2: But we are only talking about here, your experience. I mean one of things about your age is that (is was one of the things that was common) when you were children and as young adults.

Jo: Maybe because we haven't had real love. Like getting beaten up by (your father). Kind of like, you're saying, he doesn't love you by doing that, and maybe by having children, you know, a child can love a parent un-conditionally. I don't know if that's got anything to do with it?

Worker 1: Because you weren't loved as a child you've got to find love somewhere?

Jo: They need you there and

Annette: Are you saying we all went through this because of the age groups we are in?

Worker 2: No, I was thinking that a couple of times people said, particularly when we were talking about the experiences of violence that you've had [that these experiences] have affected your ability to choose being a young parent. Even though you ARE parenting, you would not necessarily have planned that for yourself. AND somehow that your experiences of violence contributed to that. Do you think age . . . do you think your experiences of violence as a child contributed to your experience as a young adult?

Melissa: I think, myself, 'cos my father belted up his kids with canes and I always thought it was quite normal, quite alright to belt your kids like that and the SLANGING matches and the rest of it.

In this excerpt, the qualitative research discourse introduced and facilitated by my co-worker and me was mixed with the discourse of the young women's stories. Far from a clear cut distinction or the dominance of technical over lived experiences, in our talk together the reference to technical knowledge and the analysis of the information recorded from previous meetings was interspersed with ongoing story telling by the young women about their experiences.

In contrast to authoritarian professional relationships, in this practice context, my co-worker and I appear to privilege the everyday world of the young women, through, for example, the frequent reference to the young women's experiences even during the 'technical' dimensions of the process. For example, in the analysis we would emphasize those aspects of the young women's talk that related specifically to the analytic task ('Okay, so age is another thing'). On occasion, the use of the young women's talk was used to 'discipline' them in the sense that these terms were used to draw them back to the task at hand when they appeared to depart from that purpose (Annette states 'it happens to a lot of women', to which the worker responds 'But we are only talking about here, your experience'; later also the worker states: 'I was thinking that a couple of times people said . . .'). The esteem accorded the young women's experiences as a site of truth in this context was recognized by the participants as illustrated via their ongoing story telling throughout the analysis process (for example, 'Maybe because we haven't had real love', and 'I think 'cos my father belted up his kids'). This analysis differed from orthodox practitioner-led practices in that the young women would continually update, confirm and sometimes challenge reflections that they had made earlier about their experiences.

Even in the exercise of power, my co-worker and I constantly referred to the young women's knowledge. However, the site is more complex than simply a shift from one site of truth to another. Attention to the way in which the young women's knowledge was used in the process suggests that movement towards the participants' knowledge as a site of truth is not a simple reversal of the dichotomy between technical knowledge and lived experience. In particular, my co-worker and I used the young women's knowledge in an active way, both to affirm the young women's views and extend the analysis (see for example 'No, I was thinking a couple of times people said . . .') and even to discipline them to conform to the agreed focus of the project. Thus, worker power was exercised both through technical knowledge and lived experiences, and, yet, this power was used to reveal subordinated voices rather than to suppress them.

In summary, then, although technical knowledge was employed in the practice context, it was not used in opposition to other forms of knowledge, particularly lived experience. Indeed, in the articulation and facilitation of technical discourses the relevance of the participants' lived experience was constantly emphasized. In this context, the technical knowledge of the workers was used as resource for enabling the young women to voice their experiences. Further, worker power operated through the lived knowledge of the participants as this knowledge was used by the workers as a base from which to exercise power in relation to the participants. This suggests that technical and expert forms of knowledge are more complex in local operations than the activist critique of professional and technical knowledge has allowed. Rather than delineate between certain forms of knowledge as necessarily linked to power and others to liberation, it is important thus to understand how these forms of knowledge function within local contexts of practice.

The implicit use of power

The activist critique of worker power has focused almost exclusively on the overt and authoritarian use of professional power, to the neglect of other operations of power. The neglect of the implicit dimensions of activist practice has suppressed recognition of the subtle exercise of worker power towards the achievement of such things as group cohesion, collective focus and, even, the participants' ownership of the social change process (see Lane, 1990; Healy and Walsh, 1997). It is these implicit operations of power in the context of the young women's anti-violence project that are the focus of this section.

Even a superficial observation of the young women's anti-violence project would suggest that the practice context was remarkably different from authoritarian or traditional professional practice settings. The tone of the project meetings was casual, as indicated by a high level of slang language and the recognition of the young women's voices as a site of truth in the practice context. In many ways, the practice context was similar to informal conversation, yet a detailed examination of the talk revealed specific features which departed from everyday talk. In contrast to the features of casual talk, identified by Sacks et al. (1978), the talk amongst workers and participants demonstrated:

- *A preference for self-selection.* Participants and workers would initiate speaking turns and seize turns for themselves, rather than offer turns to others or wait to be offered a speaking turn.
- *An intense pressure for conversational space.* In other words, participants were literally bursting to tell their stories, with the consequence that there was little opportunity for extended conversational space for either participants or workers. For instance, even brief gaps in conversation would be taken as a chance to start talking and there was frequent occurrences of dual story telling (that is, a number of unrelated stories being told at once).
- *Decentralization of the turn-taking process.* Although, in the initial meetings, workers did take a role in facilitating the turn-taking, as the process progressed no one played a central role in directing conversational turns. This decentralization is consistent with the power sharing ethos of activist social work.

Yet, despite the conversational features of the general meetings, which suggest an intense and chaotic environment, over the course of the project it was apparent that a high degree of order was achieved, at least on some occasions. Indeed, the order is evidenced by the accomplishments of the group over the first year including that: each participant obtained numerous opportunities for extended conversational turns in which to tell and critically analyse their experiences; the group documented and analysed their experiences of violence; the group developed and began to implement public action strategies in relation to young women and violence.

The group did achieve sufficient order to achieve the project goals. Yet, this order was achieved with minimal overt direction from either workers or participants. Although my co-worker and I played an integral role in the achievement of the activist process and outcomes, the democratic and egalitarian ethos on which the project was based constrained our access to, and exercise of, power. Our use of power included the inconspicuous forms similar to those used in conventional social work, such as the implicit and explicit expressions of support for the participants' talk. However, the use of implicit power also derived from the strategies promoted by critical practice theorists. To consider how activist discourses produce and rely on worker power, let us now turn to an examination of the use of 'action-reflection' strategies in the young women's anti-violence project.

The notion of action-reflection was initially developed in the work of Freire (1972), a radical educational theorist, and this strategy has since been endorsed by critical practice theorists (see Leonard, 1975; Dominelli and McLeod, 1989; Finn, 1994). Through these action-reflection cycles, workers involve participants in identifying the links between personal experiences and social context, particularly noting how social and economic structures contribute to personal pain and marginalization. The action-reflection process is intended to stimulate the oppressed to critical social action towards the transformation of the circumstances that perpetuate their vulnerability.

Through the implementation of action-reflection processes, workers intend to shape the consciousness of workers; however, the use of worker power that this process entails is usually ignored. Returning to the young women's anti-violence project, I will now consider how my co-worker and I exercised power through the implementation of action-reflection processes. My co-worker and I suggested the action-reflection process at selected meetings in the first phase of the project (when participants indicated that they wished to critically reflect on their experiences). However, the participants later used these cycles themselves to structure discussion within the project meetings and outside them, for example in discussion with other young women. Although the action-reflection structure was rarely discussed, a detailed examination of group meetings revealed just how powerful these cycles were in regulating the group interaction. When this process was introduced (by the workers), pauses *in talk* were at least triple those present at any other time and gaps *after talk* were at least double those present in other meetings throughout the entire project. These increases in silence during the action-reflection cycles were particularly supportive of critical reflection on individual experiences, since speakers did not need to compete with others for conversational space, and so could pause to collect their thoughts without such conversational breaks being seized by others as an opportunity to begin to tell their own stories or to divert the conversation away from the original speaker's talk. So as my co-worker and I initiated and supported an action-reflection process within the project meetings we exerted a powerful though often implicit effect on what was said and done there.

Attention to the social actions involved in the action-reflection cycles also confirms the participants' greater orientation to each other's talk, through, for example, listening attentively, referring back to the speaker's previous illustrations, and this occurs more than at other times during the project. One illustration of this is taken from a discussion about one young woman's experience of sexual abuse. Again in this excerpt some markers are incorporated to convey the tone of the talk and the emotions evident in the young women's talk: capitals indicate force of talk; ↑ ↑ depicts high pitch; > > indicates speed in talk. A full list of conversation conventions is included in the appendix. For the purposes of demonstrating the specific analytic concern at hand, 'pauses' are gaps of over 0.5 seconds and 'extended pauses' are gaps over 2.0 seconds, while commas indicate pauses under 0.5 seconds. This excerpt begins with one participant, 'Brooke', discussing her continuing contact with the relative who had abused her.

> Brooke: I'm still FORCED to talk with 'im at my mother's ↑house↑, 'cause she rings him up [PAUSE] an, umm, cause he's married and 'e's got a kid now, and I'm FORCED to get on the phone and talk to him, an he's STILL [PAUSE] you know, > he's thirty-five now or something >, and he's still on the phone, he get on the phone and goes 'hi honey, how are you?' [PAUSE] and I just go 'ohh hi', and he goes 'ohh, y:ou know I had ta get married I couldn't wait for you forever' and sayin' all this sorta sleazy stuff to me on the phone NOW [PAUSE] but, > I can't say anything >, cause my mum's right behind me [EXTENDED PAUSE]
>
> Annette: has your mum got an extension? [PAUSE]
>
> Brooke: ahh yeh,
>
> Melissa: get her on the phone,
>
> Brooke: she doesn't wanna know she won't listen, she
>
> Philippa: she doesn't [wanna know
>
> Sonia: she doesn't] know,
>
> Brooke: ohh, she knows, she definitely knows,
>
> Philippa: but she doesn't wanna acknowledge it.

In this excerpt there is evidence of opportunities for pausing and of focuses on one participant's talk, and these opportunities were much more extensive than at any other time during the group meetings. The participants demonstrate their attention through relevant questioning and suggesting helpful acts ('has your mum got an extension?'; 'get her on the phone'), and through supporting Brooke's talk ('she doesn't wanna know').

In the context of the intense motivation to talk amongst the participants, this orientation towards another's talk is quite remarkable and was assisted by workers' use of power to initiate the action-reflection cycles. In contrast to the activist critique of the use of power to reinforce professional power and status, in this practice context, the use of power was integral to effect a *transfer* of power. Indeed, the hierarchical relations of power that are said to characterize orthodox social work settings are less evident; indeed, in this excerpt a number of the participants themselves were involved in facilitating the telling and analysis of one another's experiences rather than acting only as speakers of their experience. In more politically conservative approaches to practice, the actions of questioning and support are often expressed only by the worker (see Sands, 1988). The recognition that activist practice discourses produce power and, further, that this power can be an oppressive and constraining force, contests the largely negative view of worker power articulated amongst critical social workers.

Participant ambivalence about the use of power

The presence of worker power, which the analysis revealed, was also recognized by the participants within this project and in their experiences of other activist practice contexts. In other words, even if activist workers wish to suppress the articulation of the power they use, it does not necessarily go unrecognized by those subject to it. One participant pointed out in a discussion with me outside the project meetings that:

> I think social workers saying, 'I'm giving you all the power' is bullshit, because you know you're going to them for a reason so why give up everything? There is obviously a reason you're going to them, you're going to them for their knowledge or something.

The young women who participated in the project were ambivalent about the use of power in this practice context and beyond it. From the outset, participants were keen to assert their independence and authority in the practice context. There were many instances of participants resisting the power exercised by my co-worker and me, through, for example, the mild derision of us and overt statements of independence when we offered support.

Yet, the participants also identified that some forms of worker support and direction were required to maximize their involvement and, ultimately, their self-direction of the group. In particular, the young women mandated the use of worker power to maintain the focus of project meetings and the overall goals of the project developed by the young women. For example, early in the project one young woman complained that the group was 'going off track', and throughout the project participants frequently asserted that an important part of the workers' role was to support the group focus. The following statement was made at the end of first year of the project. When asked about the workers' role, one participant asserted that the workers' role was basically to keep them 'on track':

> because we tend to sort've go off, raving on, 'cause we're all talking, you know, we know each other now, heheh, it's blah blah blah.

Ironically, according to this young woman, as the project progressed, the importance of the workers' role in maintaining direction increased ('we know each other now'). This 'different' role played by my co-worker and me allowed the young women some freedom to focus on their own experiences and interests without jeopardizing the achievement of collective project goals. Notably, some participants were adamant that their participation would have been enhanced by greater direction from the workers.

While most participants emphasized the importance of worker power to facilitate aspects of the young women's anti-violence project, two participants increasingly expressed overt opposition to the use of worker power in any form in the practice context. As the process progressed and the participants' critical knowledge extended, these two participants expressed dissatisfaction about the distance between the expressed goals of critical practice, namely 'co-participation' between workers and service users, and the evidence of the continuing presence of worker power in the process. The following excerpt is taken at an advanced stage of the project, during a discussion about the ongoing transfer of responsibility of the management of the project from the workers to the participants:

> Worker 2: you said yes Annette, what do you mean? What would you like to do more of?
>
> Annette: just to have more say over the decisions, just to be able ta, say, practical little things, ya know, that to make me feel like an EQUAL, it just still feels a bit like teacher/student, you know.

These criticisms were taken seriously by all participants, including my co-worker and me, and they generated considerable discussion about the ongoing inequities in the project and about the possibilities for working towards greater equity. Yet, through these criticisms, this participant also expresses an understanding that in this context there *is* some degree of equity between workers and participants. The young woman's rebuke that it 'still feels a little bit like teacher/student' indicates that she recognizes that, in this context, there are attempts to overcome power asymmetries. Indeed, in a more authoritarian environment, the notion of 'teacher/student' and its concomitant inequities would not be seen as a criticism. Moreover, the upfront manner in which the criticism is expressed suggests an environment in which criticism is, at the very least, tolerated and it would seem, even invited (as the comment is initiated by the worker's question: 'what do you mean?').

In the practice context, the tension between accepting participants' independence and exercising power to support the process was, at times, confusing for both my co-worker and me. There was a constant tension for my co-worker and me between yielding power and using power effectively towards maximizing the participation involvement and control (see also Schrijvers, 1991). These tensions were not an aberration of activist practice theory but rather arose from the contradictions between the stated ideals of activist practice, particularly the explicit claim that workers should refuse power, and the implications of activist strategies, which explicitly and implicitly demanded the use of power. Unless these tensions are recognized they can have deleterious effects in the practice contexts. The imposition of singular or impossibly high standards of practice can lead to disillusionment and blame (Phillips, 1991). For example, the ideal of total equity can obscure trans-formations that are different from this goal. This is seen in the previous illustration, where the participant emphasizes the continuing discrepancies between workers and participants whilst leaving unacknowledged how the process differs from traditional 'teacher/student' relationships. In addition, a radical egalitarian position effectively insulates practice theory from critique and reform, as the failure to reach critical visions of total equity does not lead to a reconsideration of these ideals; rather, it can result in the reproach of local actors for falling short of these ideals.

Power and productivity: some tensions in managing egalitarianism

The sustained critique of worker power has suppressed articulation of the tensions around the operations of power within the activist practice contexts. In reviewing the tensions around the use of worker power within activist practice discourses, it can be said that the relationship between worker power and participation is a complex one. Although worker power will be enacted differently across practice contexts, I contend that the use of power is imperative to activist practice approaches. Once egalitarian practice relations are recognized as an accomplishment of power rather than as arising from the absence of it, we are compelled to address ourselves to the productive exercise of worker power within activist practices.

Differences within the category of 'powerful worker'

In this chapter, I have examined some uses of power in social work practice. I have argued that critical poststructuralism can open the critical canon to conventional practice settings, particularly those involving the use of statutory authority, and to the forms of power that are produced within activist practice theory. There is a third important contribution that the critical poststructural work of Foucault and French feminist theorists can make, and that is towards the illumination of the instabilities extant within the category of 'professional worker'. In these final sections of the analysis of worker power in activist theory I will address two challenges that critical poststructural theory makes to the notion of the 'powerful worker'. The first of these challenges is the recognition that while human services are implicated in the exercise of social control, the enactment of power varies across forms of human service work. Secondly, French feminist theory demands a critical examination of how differences amongst workers, particularly corporeal variations, shape workers' access to and experience of power. Let us now turn to an exploration of these challenges.

Social work and the 'problem' of professional expertise

Critical social workers and critical poststructural theorists, particularly Foucault (1991a), share a view of the power wielded by human service professionals as a malevolent force. The widespread critique of professional power found in both these literatures has tended to conflate power and professional power such that distinctions in the enactment of power amongst human services have been rendered invisible. The critique of worker power is intended to empower service users to recognize the knowledge and capacities they have gained through lived experience. Towards this end, practice strategies are aimed at disabusing service users of their esteem for professional expertise. Activist practice strategies for the empowerment of service users rest on the assumption that service users recognize professional knowledge as hegemonic and further that they hold various forms of professional activity in similarly high esteem. Hence, activist strategies for challenging professional knowledge are not differentiated according to context or the type of professional practice with which the service user is engaged. In this section, I will analyse how the critique of worker power which emerged over the course of the young women's anti-violence project impacted on the power relations between workers and service users in this practice context.

In contrast to critical assumptions about service user subservience to professional knowledge, from the outset of the project the young women appeared to evaluate the 'technical knowledge' of social and community workers differently from that of many other professionals. The participants' view of the effectiveness of social welfare professionals relied less on workers' technical merit and more on their capacity to relate to the young women; this capacity was strongly connected to perceptions of the workers' lived experiences rather than their technical expertise. Ironically, the technical knowledge of the social worker was viewed ambivalently and, indeed, it was often a source of ridicule. From the first phase of the project, the view of social workers as naive and lacking lived experience of disadvantage was ubiquitous in the talk of the young women, and this critique intensified over the course of the project. Many of the young women had little difficulty in positively evaluating their knowledge in comparison to that of human service workers, as one young woman stated:

> I know how to put a social worker down, you just tell them they have no idea of what they're talking about because they haven't been there and done it. So, I tell them, 'don't give me any of that textbook psychology crap'.

The representation of service users as deferential to human service workers (see Andrews, 1992) neglects the lucid critique of welfare knowledge that can also be held by service users. This, of course, does not mean that service users are unafraid of social welfare personnel or that they are uniformly critical of social workers. Rather, it is suggested here that the perceived relational character of social work leaves its practitioners more open than those in many other occupations to critique on the basis of a dissonance between relevant and actual expertise.

The critique of professionalism that activists promote and that was implemented in the young women's anti-violence project had different and more devastating implications for social welfare personnel than for other human service professionals. It was remarkable that even in the later phases of the project, as the young women developed a profound and scathing critique of social workers, they appeared to maintain respect for other professionals, particularly those whom they regarded as holding a distinct technical knowledge base necessary to undertake their professional work. In their discussions about a range of professionals, including midwives, teachers, doctors, the young women rarely raised the issue of the lived experience. Moreover, the young women were more tolerant of elitist, dismissive and other forms of authoritarian behaviour from these professionals because they perceived that these human services workers had something 'technical' to offer them, such as birthing or medical services.

The emphasis on the professional identity as the site of power in practice relations has occluded the importance of non-worker identities on the kinds of power and knowledge social workers convey in practice. Yet, in the young women's anti-violence project, the non-worker identities of my co-worker and me, particularly in relation to such things as parenting status, age and interests, was integral to the expertise we were seen to hold. For example, the parenting (and non-parenting) status of my co-worker and me was at least as important, if not more so, in the young women's evaluation of our knowledge.

At one level, this emphasis on lived experience is resonant with the formation of relationships beyond 'worker' and 'participant' identities. At the same time, however, this emphasis, particularly when lived knowledge becomes an unquestionable site of truth, can have effects which are non dialogic. Just as professional knowledge has served to subjugate other non-professional knowledge, to merely shift the site of truth to lived experience can be to ignore the complexities of this lived knowledge also. In the practice context of the young women's anti-violence project, the priority accorded to lived experience contributed to a superficial analysis of the knowledge and capacities of my co-worker and me. The possibility for oversimplification arises because certain kinds of lived knowledge are obvious; for example, it can be assumed that people share common knowledge because of their gender, race or parenting identities. Yet, other forms of knowledge, such as the historical knowledge from class background and past experiences, are not always obvious nor are they necessarily appropriate to disclose in the practice context. Even so, these forms of knowledge can also inform the workers' practices.

This sense of commonality was important to my co-worker and me. Indeed, even though my co-worker and I differed from the young women participants in that, for example, neither of us had been teenage parents, we saw ourselves as personally connected to the struggles confronting the young women. Our sense of commonality with young women, particularly our own experiences of marginalization and violation, although different from that of the participants, provided an important motivation to work alongside the young women for change. The importance of commonality as a point of connection and motivation for practice is suppressed in activist practice theory via the oppositional representations of the powerful worker and powerless client.

The critique of professionalism promoted through critical practice theory is limited in so far as it neglects the considerable differences in the kinds of power/knowledge relationships that emerge in distinct forms of human service work. The specific kinds of work social workers do, which involves relational, intimate and sometimes highly practical life concerns, makes their expertise more open to challenge and more dependent on non-worker identities than that of professionals whose terrain is more clearly delineated to specific technical tasks. A critical dialogue between workers and service users demands that professional knowledge, like all knowledge, can be interrogated and questioned. However, the failure to differentiate amongst the forms of power/knowledge that emerge in specific forms of human services work has led to practice strategies which promote inordinate criticisms of social welfare personnel whilst leaving other more overtly technical forms of human services work unscathed and perhaps even elevated in the eyes of service users. Although critical poststructuralists such as Foucault share the activists' critique of human service professions, their concern with the 'local' operations of power and identity potentially directs activists towards recognition of distinctions amongst human service professions such as those identified in this section.

Differences and power

The depiction of the 'powerful worker' has suppressed discussion of differences across professions in the exercise of power. Very often the notions of power central to socio-political discourse are written in masculine terms (see Lloyd, 1986, 1989; Gatens, 1992). These representations are imported into activist theory with little recognition of the complexities that define membership in the categories of 'power' and 'identity' to which activists refer. This is seen vividly in the conflation of power and 'social worker' identity in critical social work, which has glossed over differences amongst workers, such as sexual differences, class differences and racial differences, even though these variations impact on how individual workers occupy the category of 'powerful worker'. The representation of the disembodied, powerful worker is present even in the work of feminist social workers in the dualisms of the 'powerful' and 'powerless' on which they rely (see Dominelli and McLeod, 1989, p. 62; E. Wilson, 1977, p. 8).

Feminist poststructural theory explodes the unity of the identity categories on which activist theory draws by illuminating the corporeal (that is, the body) in processes of identification and power (see Grosz, 1994). Poststructural feminist theorists recognize the body as a signifier enabling certain kinds of actions and prohibiting others. The body is the site of historical and lived knowledge and thus it offers both resources and vulnerabilities within the practice context. Gatens (1996) observes that:

> The present capacities of female bodies are, by and large, very different to the present capacities of male bodies. It is important to create a means of articulating the historical realities without thereby reifying these differences. (p. 69)

The body of the worker, then, is not incidental to the kinds of knowledge they bring to practice and the forms of power they can exercise. At the same time, however, critical poststructural theory recognizes that the operations of power and identity are unstable across contexts and, hence, a necessary equation between specific identities and power is not tenable. It is suggested, rather, that the universal depiction of workers as powerful is limited in so far as it neglects the significant bodily differences amongst them. The representations of worker power in unitary terms has precluded reflection on corporeality in individual workers' access to and exercise of professional power.

The phallocentricism of critical practice theory is evident in the forms of power that are represented. Critical approaches have critiqued workers for the overt and authoritarian use of power and for failing to address the overt power differences between themselves and service users. The taken for granted assumptions about the authoritarian and hierarchical exercise of power are phallocentric in so far as these characteristics are often, though not always, absent from women's speech even amongst women in professional roles. Repeatedly, in the discourse analysis literature gendered differences in communicative speech patterns are observed (see Fishman, 1983; Goodwin, 1988; Tannen, 1991; Holmes, 1995; West, 1995). Most significantly, it has been identified that in both informal and professional contexts, female speech tends towards more egalitarian forms than the talk of men (Holmes, 1995). To identify these gender differences in communication patterns is not to suggest that these patterns are essential. Certainly, there are many individual exceptions. However, the pervasiveness of these patterns across contexts and cross-culturally does call for an examination of the assumptions about power and authority on which activist theory draws.

The research evidence about gender differences in talk raises the question of why so much of the analysis of power in social work has emphasized hierarchy and authority, even though this is unlikely to be the preferred speech pattern of females, who, after all, constitute the majority of practising social workers. It also raises the further question of why critical practice theory has failed to acknowledge the importance of the communication patterns typically associated with female speech, such as indicators of active listening, hesitancy in the use of imperatives and the encouragement of feedback in achieving egalitarian relations (see Fishman, 1983; Goodwin, 1988; Holmes, 1995; West, 1995). In activism, as elsewhere, the important though often implicit conversational work that women often do is left unacknowledged, and where it is recognized it is viewed as support or help but certainly not as power. These phallocentric assumptions have meant that the bodily resources that impact on worker's enactment and experience of power remain unspoken in activist practice discourses. Let us now turn to an illustration of the presence of these gender differences in the workers' use of power in the young women's anti-violence project.

Practice illustration: difference and the exercise of power

An overview of worker–participant collaboration in the young women's anti-violence project indicates that the talk of my co-worker and me was consistent with some of the typical features of women's talk. West (1995, p. 122) identifies two features frequently present in women's talk that, notably, can support the establishment of egalitarian practice relations in both professional and non-professional contexts. The first feature is the minimization of status differences; and a stress on connectedness between speaker and hearer (see also Fishman, 1983; Goodwin, 1988; Holmes, 1995). For example, in offering directives to others, female speakers will typically employ 'mitigated directives' (West, 1995, p. 119; see also Goodwin, 1988; Holmes, 1995). The term 'mitigated directives' refers to the downgrading of the authoritativeness of the speaker by, for example, the use of proposals and questions rather than commands to the hearer. A second difference observed by West (1995) is that women speakers frequently seek to reduce power differences by stressing their connection to their audience. Thus, for example, rather than issue a command to the hearer, women speakers frequently include themselves in the directive through the use of terms such as 'let's' or 'shall we' (West, 1995, pp. 122–3). The following excerpt from the project provides some illustrations of the workers' use of the communication features identified by West (1995); it is taken from the beginning of a group meeting only a few weeks after the project began:

Worker 1:	Okay, well, what we're going to do today was the next thing on the list [notes from previous meetings]. Everyone in the group has indicated that they've had one or the other of those experiences, like social violence, means you know, feeling intimidated, afraid in social places or in your own home. So Jo gave the example of not being able to wash her hair with both eyes closed
Young women:	heheheh
Worker 1:	an example I can identify with!
Young women:	heheheh
Worker 1:	Leah gave the example of umm when you came home an' there was some, there was a roadblock or something like that
Leah:	ohh that was a siege up the road
Worker 1:	yep

The speech patterns illustrated here are consistent with the characteristics of women's talk as discussed by West (1995), yet they are also effective for increasing the symmetry of the relationships between workers and service users. The reference to life examples of the young women ('So Jo gave the example . . .' and 'Leah gave the example . . .') is consistent also with the value placed on the elevation of lived experience as site of knowledge in activist practice models. In other words, in this discussion I use their experience rather than refer to a technical or professional register to direct the group (Bogoch, 1994, p. 71). Moreover, even in the overt exercise of power I stress my connection with the group members ('an example I can identify with'). In the practice context, these strategies contributed to increased equity between workers and service users, for even though, initially, there was a high degree of compliance with the workers' suggestions, over the course of the project the young women increasingly offered alternatives to our suggestions and were able to challenge the power exercised by us (see Healy and Walsh, 1997). The capacity of the young women to offer such challenges is an accomplishment of the participatory practice relations that were achieved over time between workers and service users.

Difference and worker vulnerability

In this analysis, I have argued that bodily knowledge of the worker has been an untapped resource for activist practice theory. Similarly, I contend that the representations of the 'powerful worker' have elided the vulnerabilities of workers. The frequent portrayal of social workers as self-assured, arrogant and accustomed to believing that they 'can determine the best interests of others'(Ryburn, 1991b, p. 11; see also Moreau, 1979; Andrews, 1992) ignores difficulties workers can experience in the exercise of power; especially for workers who are Other to the white, middle class, high status professional from whom the critical depictions of professional identity derive.

In contrast to the conflation of professional identity and hierarchical forms of power in much of the activist literature, it is often the case that the speech of men and women as professionals is differently received by their audience. For example, there is considerable discourse analytic evidence to indicate that female speakers often have reduced access to the hierarchical and unquestionable forms of authority than male speakers in established positions of authority (see Goodwin, 1988; West, 1984, 1995). It would appear that even as women adopt a professional status, this does not necessarily undo their construction as inferior Other to the 'white, Protestant, male' (West, 1984, p. 64).

Women professionals, especially in non-technical occupations, are frequently subject to the questioning of their professional competence. Thus, the activist imperative on the critique of professional power takes on a further complexity. For surely there is a danger that when this imperative is directed primarily at female social welfare workers it risks making a virtue out of some very deeply embedded sexist assumptions about women in the public sphere. Unless activists differentiate between the questioning of professional hegemony and challenges towards professional competence, their approaches may inadvertently support sexist and unjust assumptions about the lesser competence of female professionals, and perhaps even support the hegemony of male and high status professionals. Indeed, the critique of professionalism that emerged over the course of the project was focused almost exclusively on welfare professionals with little apparent effect for a range of other human service professionals, such as doctors or lawyers.

Activist practices are orientated towards the achievement of justice for the oppressed. Yet, ironically, the unitary images of identity and power can have paradoxical effects in so far as they ignore differences amongst those they claim to represent. The notion of the 'powerful worker' has suppressed discussion about the impact of the corporeal on the exercise of worker power. The imperative towards giving away claims to power, potency and competency neglects the possibility that, for those who are Other to the white, middle class male, such claims are often dismissed before the gift was made. In addition, the directive to give up power also ignores the possibility that for some activists, particularly white, middle class males, a perception of power, potency and competency may remain regardless of their overt attempts to give up their position of power.

Rethinking power in activist social work

Critical poststructural theory can be used to destabilize the depictions of worker power promoted in activist practice approaches. While critical poststructural thinkers, particularly Foucault (1991a), share activist concerns about the domination exacted upon subordinate populations via human service work, they also invite the interrogation of worker power in practice. In this chapter I have shown how the insights of critical poststructural theorists bid social workers towards:

- the development of practice modes that engage productively with the power and social control inherent to social work activity, particularly statutory work. The emphasis, then, is not the refusal of power, for such an ambition is an absurdity in many contexts of practice, but rather towards analysis of how worker power can be made more humane and accountable;
- the recognition that achievement of activist practice does not involve an absence of power, but rather its highly specific use;
- an acknowledgement that worker power is not always enacted overtly and, often, the most powerful actions occur without service users' or workers' recognition that power has been exercised;
- a rupturing of the unitary depictions of the disembodied, powerful and authoritarian worker towards a recognition of the impact of the corporeal on the resources and vulnerabilities that workers may bring in the enactment of power in the practice context.

Despite the uses of poststructural theories for rethinking worker power and identity in activist practices, which I have outlined here, I do not suggest that insights provided by critical social science should be cast aside altogether. For instance, the recognition within critical social work of the controlling dimensions of social work remains as important, if not more so, for critical practice in the contexts of increasingly minimalist and managerialized welfare states. Yet at this point in the history of critical social work, the insights of Foucault and radical poststructural feminists can redirect activists towards more open and contextually sensitive approaches to understanding and transforming relations of power and identity in social work practices.

6 Liberation or Regulation: Interrogating the Practices of Change

Activist social workers promote the participation of the oppressed in processes of change. Critical practice strategies are intended to equip the marginalized with the skills, knowledge and power necessary to understand and act on their collective interests (see Tandon, 1981, p. 24; Fals-Borda, 1987, p. 330). The practices of consciousness raising and collective action are viewed as instruments of liberation. In this chapter, I critically examine these representations by investigating the operations of power and identity that were effected amongst the participants and upon them in the course of the young women's anti-violence campaign. By situating this analysis within a practice context, I intend to stimulate the reader to critically review the effects of critical practice strategies within their own contexts of practice. I will begin with an overview of the challenges critical 'post' theories pose to the tenets underpinning activist practice strategies.

Interrogating critical practices

Foucault's emphasis on power/knowledge can be used to highlight the processes through which the truth claims of critical practices are established and what and whom these critical truths include or exclude (see Kristeva, 1981; Davies, 1994). For Foucault (1980d) 'The political question, to sum up, is not error, illusions, alienated consciousness; it is truth itself' (p. 133). In contrast to the liberatory claims of activists, critical practice processes, such as consciousness raising, can be shown to instate new though no less fixed standards of truth telling than those central to orthodox practice discourses. When the claims made by oppressed populations do not adhere to critical truths they are dismissed as 'raw' or 'unformed' (see Hall, 1981, p. 12) or as evidence of false consciousness. Yeatman (1997) refers to consciousness raising processes as 'a totalizing politics which can be made over to particular kinds of blackmail and personal tyranny' (p. 146). The form this 'blackmail' takes can be anything from a patronizing tolerance of voices of difference to the active exclusion of those who fail to adopt critical perspectives.

The insights of poststructural theory draw attention to the historical and local contexts in which the practices of social workers, like the practices of all human service professions, are embedded. The recognition of the contextual embeddedness of social work practices has profound implications for the liberatory aspirations of activist social workers. Larbalestier (1998) asserts that:

> Assisting people to change their lifestyles, to rethink their priorities and options may be particularly fraught in countries with histories of colonialism and migration like Australia, North America and the United Kingdom. In these countries, 'norms of truth', as well as exhibiting class-based differences, may have culturally specific meanings . . . and be embedded in histories of exploitation and oppressive policies. (p. 71)

The insights of critical poststructural theory problematize the ambition, present in orthodox and radical modalities, to assist people to 'change their lifestyles' and 'rethink their priorities'. In thinking that the critical truths we proclaim as activists are in some way more pure and enlightened, outside the forces of the history and local contexts that shape our activities, we doom ourselves to repeat the mistakes we see in the practices of our forebears. Thus, for activists, the insights of critical poststructural theories demand caution in our claims and more self-reflexivity about the local effects of our liberatory intentions.

In addition to challenging the premises of consciousness raising activity, poststructural theory can help us to diversify activism beyond the oppositional and collective approaches advocated within critical practice theories (see Fraser, 1989; Ellsworth, 1992; Groch, 1994). These oppositional identifications and processes are premised on the idea that the world can be divided into 'villains' and 'victims' according to an individual's fixed location within the social superstructures of capitalism, patriarchy, imperialism and so forth. In encouraging respect for the diversity of local contexts of experience, the work of critical poststructural theorists can usefully point to the disempowering effects of the constant prioritization of the social whole in the conceptualization of identity and, hence, action for change. Feminist theorist Rosemary Pringle (1995) writes that: 'without ignoring continuing inequalities, I believe it is important to identify tactical successes and not imprison women in a permanent no-win situation' (p. 205). Whilst continuing to recognize entrenched patterns of domination, critical poststructural perspectives can assist activists to recover local aspirations and activities as sites of radical social transformation (Pringle, 1995, p. 207).

The insights of critical poststructural theories can draw attention to the intolerance of differences that lies at the heart of oppositional and collective approaches to activism. Oppositional politics is orientated towards the annihilation of the Others, be that another person or idea, rather than towards facilitating critical engagement across differences. Foucault (1991c) laments:

> Polemic defines alliances, recruits partisans, unites interests or opinions, represents a party; it establishes the other as an enemy, an upholder of opposed interests, against which one must fight until the moment the enemy is defeated and either surrenders or disappears. (pp. 382–3)

The reliance on polemics suppresses the emergence of the complex understandings and innovative responses required to address contemporary social issues. Foucault (1991c) asks, 'Has anyone ever seen a new idea come out of a polemic?' (p. 383).

The work of poststructural theorists favours pragmatic approaches to activism relevant to the diverse local contexts in which practice occurs. Rather than premise activism on universal plans, postsructural theorists construct action in relation to local resources and local aspirations for change. Thus, for example, it is recognized that there will be differences between activist practices enacted in small community agencies and those that emerge in bureaucratic, authoritarian or privatized environments. The work of poststructural theorists invites social workers to reclaim and speak back to activist theories in defining and reworking what it means to be change agents in the diverse contexts of contemporary social work practices.

Let us now turn to an evaluation of critical change processes in action. In the following section, I will examine the consciousness raising processes. Initially, I will consider the assumptions on which these practices are based. These assumptions are, firstly, that participants, as oppressed people, lack critical consciousness about their experiences and, secondly, that consciousness raising strategies are innocent of the operations of power. Here, I will analyse these assumptions in relation to the young women who participated in the anti-violence project.

The 'unconscientized' participant

Consciousness raising processes derive from the idea that the oppressed dwell in a 'culture of silence' (Fox and Compton, quoted in Maguire, 1987, p. 48). The process of consciousness raising, advocated in a broad spectrum of critical practice theories, is intended to equip the oppressed with the insights required to effect positive and radical change. A number of researchers, using both socialist and feminist perspectives, have argued that young mothers tend to accept conservative ideas about the family and motherhood (S. Taylor, 1986, p. 383; Cameron, 1992, p. 57). This apparent adherence to traditional values asserting the naturalness of domesticity and motherhood is interpreted by critical researchers as 'instrumental in shaping the decision of the women to continue with an unplanned pregnancy' (Cameron, 1992, p. 61; see also J. Wilson, 1989, p. 24). Moreover, it is claimed that these traditional ideas do not serve the best interests of young mothers: as J. Wilson (1989) points out, 'it is ironic that these young women often share the values of their strongest critics' (p. 20). As the absence of critical perspectives amongst young women is well documented in the activist literature, consciousness raising processes were pertinent to activist practice with the young mothers who participated in the young women's anti-violence project.

Yet, in contrast to the ubiquitous image of the unconscientized young parent, from the outset of the project it was apparent that all the participants had some exposure to critical concepts; that is, to ideas that drew connections between individual experiences and structural injustices. A major source of these critical perspectives was the young women's contact with human service workers. All members of the project group had previously attended young parents' services where workers tended to incorporate critical approaches into their practice. The prevalence of critical perspectives amongst the service workers who were involved with these young women is evidence of the increasing legitimacy amongst social workers of formerly marginal ideas (Langan, 1998).

The young women also accessed critical ideas through popular culture. Indeed, rather than a patriarchal monolith, the artefacts of popular culture, such as magazine and television programmes, presented a mixture of discourses, including feminist concepts. Notwithstanding the extremely negative portrayals of single parents in the media, the participants were able to identify media role models of successful single parents. A case in point is the popular American sitcom 'Murphy Brown', in which the lead character is a single mother, albeit a very privileged one! The young women saw parallels between the discriminatory treatment they received as low-income and homeless single parents and that shown to Murphy Brown. For example, in demonstrating the pervasiveness of the discrimination experienced by single parents, one young woman observed: 'Look at all the fuss they kicked up about Murphy Brown havin' a child outta wedlock, I mean that was ridiculous.'

The focus of the project was the exploration of the links between gender and violence in the lives of young mothers. Hence, critical reflections on gender formed a basis of the consciousness raising process. From the outset, there was consensus amongst participants about the importance of gender in explaining the life circumstances of high profile women, like female members of the royal family and media personalities. Yet there was considerable variation amongst the young women in the extent to which they found critical perspectives meaningful for explaining their own life experiences. Although there was evidence of the deep conservatism identified by critical authors, only one participant consistently rejected the relevance of critical perspectives for her. The following illustration is taken from the second project meeting, when, as part of the consciousness raising process, my co-worker and I asked the participants to consider how their gender identity shaped their childhood experiences. One young woman, Philippa, was emphatic in her response:

> we all had the same sort of upbringing, we were all equal, we done [sic] the same sorta things my brother was allowed, ya know, there was never, 'oh that's a girls thing to do', it was always equal.

Amongst all the participants, Philippa most closely resembled the unconscientized position frequently discussed in the feminist literature about young mothers (see S. Taylor, 1986; J. Wilson, 1989; Cameron, 1992). Yet Philippa's apparent lack of critical insight could not be attributed to her lack of exposure to critical perspectives, particularly feminist perspectives. For prior to the young mothers' anti-violence project and throughout it, Philippa was exposed to these ideas. Unlike many of the other participants, Philippa's experiences of violence were limited to childhood abuse, something to which she and her brother were exposed, it seems, in equivalent measure. Thus, in the context of her life experiences, Philippa did not consider that gender identity was a primary factor in determining her vulnerability to violence.

Yet, also, from the outset, some of the participants demonstrated an understanding and integration of critical perspectives. The following excerpt, taken from the fourth meeting of the project group, occurred during a discussion about participants' perceptions of the pressures on them to maintain relationships, even violent relationships, at all costs.

> Annette: but that's community pressure too, with this young parent, you know, HOW you're such a bloody, won't shut your legs and stuff like this
> Worker 1: yes

Annette:	that mentality
Worker 1:	yes
Annette:	to keep ya in a marriage, because you feel legitimate, when you're married
Worker 1:	yeh
Annette:	and that's the wrong reason to get married.

The presence of a number of critical concepts in this statement, such as 'community pressure', 'mentality' and 'legitimacy', suggest that the young woman possesses at least some critical understandings of her personal experiences. Through her reference to these terms, this young woman denaturalizes some of the features of social life, such as the 'naturalness' of marriage, which may otherwise be taken for granted. As this interaction occurred in the initial stage of the project, it can be assumed that this young woman had prior access to critical discourses.

In contrast to the outright rejection of critical perspectives, expressed by Philippa, and to the embrace of them, demonstrated by Annette, a far more common position amongst the project participants was considerable inconsistency in the linking of personal experience and critical perspectives. Doubtless, there was evidence of the deeply conservative views identified by critical authors (see J. Wilson, 1989, p. 20; Cameron, 1992, p. 57); however, the proponents of these conservative views did, at other times, express perspectives that could be regarded as critical. Moreover, in some instances, these traditional views were strategically deployed by the young women to differentiate themselves from the prevalent negative representations about them (Moore, 1992, p. 6). The following excerpt occurred during a meeting three months after the project began during a discussion about the young women's experiences of violence and its aftermath for them.

Sonia:	I mean, a lot of young women think that having kids is the way out
Annette:	yeh exactly, the way to adulthood
Sonia:	IT'S A WAY OUT. But to some its not, but to some it IS, you know, I mean when, when I had Liam, my whole life just changed *(worker: hmm) (young women: yeh)* ya know, and I was GLAD for that, because I was, I mean, was down in the gutter really badly, and I picked myself because I had Liam to look after. *(young women: yeh)* but some women just, CAN'T do it, *(Worker: yes)* ya know, I mean some women go out there and think, ohh yeh, this is gonna change my life, *(Worker: hmm)* but it doesn't. And they're still down in the gutter, and they can't pick themselves up
Melissa:	and unfortunately they've got the child down there with 'em. *(group and worker: YES).*

One reading of this excerpt, consistent with critical social work ideas, highlights the conservatism conveyed in the young women's talk. Adherence to traditional motherhood ideals, such as that of self-sacrifice, is evident in the young women's insistence that, as 'good' mothers, they had prioritized the interests of their children. Sonia's remark 'I picked myself up because I had Liam to look after' is obviously affirmed by the other participants. A poststructural reading could contest this interpretation by drawing attention to the narratives of resistance that exist alongside the conservative perspectives advanced in the young women's talk. For instance, the young women invoke traditional concepts in order to show their differences from other, less deserving young women ('and they're still down in the gutter'; 'and unfortunately they've got the child down there with 'em'). In showing that they are different from this caricature, these young women are also demonstrating themselves to be deserving as parents ('my whole life just changed') and so challenge their exclusion from the category of 'good mother'.

Just as the young women used traditional notions of motherhood to contest the ideas that endure about them, so too they disputed the adequacy of identity categories such as those of 'young women', 'young mother' and 'victim' on which the critical consciousness raising process depended. Even in relation to the analysis of violence, the young women insisted that no single identity, including those associated with gender, was the most significant factor in explaining their vulnerability to abuse. For example, those young women who had been part of the street culture identified that, at times, they shared more in common with other homeless people than many others in the category of 'young woman'. For example, in the third meeting of the project, Annette described her experience of the homeless culture in this way:

> there was like, I think, like there was family, but then, it was like distant relationships or distant, you know, it was like there was a core group in the valley that, had been to jail, had been raped in homes an' NO-ONE became part of it regardless of whether you were a girlfriend or whatever. There was somethin' between these people that no-one else could ever be a part of.

In their discussions about childhood violence the young women earnestly highlighted that as children they shared a vulnerability to abuse with male children, particularly their brothers. The participants recognized differences between their brothers and themselves in relation to the specific types of abuses they had experienced. They were concerned, however, that a focus on gender, when isolated from other aspects of their experiences, would negate the violence to which they and their brothers had been subjected.

In contrast to the assumption that the oppressed, in this instance young mothers, lack critical consciousness, the participants in the young women's anti-violence project demonstrated some knowledge of critical perspectives from the outset. Amongst the participants there was considerable variation in the acceptance and use of these perspectives. While it may be that here was an unusually conscientized group of women, there is no evidence to support such a claim. Most had been exposed to social services, but activist social workers do not usually identify these as significant sites of transformed consciousness; indeed, quite the opposite. In addition, the young women disputed the search for a common identity focused on their gender for explaining their own and others' vulnerability to violence. Their dissent cannot be attributed to false consciousness but to disagreement with some aspects of the 'identity' categories that we, as activists, invoked in critically analysing their experiences with them.

Critical perspectives that categorize certain ideas as 'conservative' or 'radical', outside the context in which the utterances are made, pre-empt inquiry into the local interpretations and effects of them. In this way, universal understandings of what counts as critical or otherwise can devalue local acts of resistance (Fine and McPherson, 1992). For instance, here I have suggested that the young women's reference to traditional motherhood concepts is both an act of conformity and one of resistance. Poststructuralism destabilizes the critical truth claims on which consciousness raising strategies rest and so enhances respect for differences as a cornerstone of activist practices. Thus, while for women whose right to parent is not in question, it can be empowering to contest the connection between the identities of 'woman' and 'mother', for other women, whose parenting rights and adequacy are persistently questioned, the struggle is a different one. The insights of critical poststructural theories show us that if coalitions are to established across differences, then it is vital that activists are sensitive to the local and historical conditions in which action occurs. This does not mean an abandonment of critical perspectives altogether, but rather a recognition that the perspectives activists hold to be emancipatory for themselves may not have the same liberatory effects for those others with whom they work.

Critical consciousness: liberation and exclusion

In the activist social work literature, the consciousness raising process is represented as an instrument of liberation. In other words, it is seen as being outside the relations of domination associated with orthodox practice methods. Hence, the impact of these approaches on power relations amongst those subject to these processes is underexplored. Yet, Foucault (1980c, 1981b) draws us to such investigation in his insistence that the discourses of liberation are, like scientific and religious discourses, fully invested with power and it is inevitable that discourses will include and exclude particular voices. Using these Foucauldian insights, in this section I analyse how critical truth claims impacted on power relations amongst the young women over the course of the project meetings.

In order to demonstrate the profound influence of critical perspectives promoted in the practice context on power relations amongst the participants, I will contrast the experiences of two of the members: Leah and Philippa. There was considerable variation in the extent to which these young women's voices were heard and respected by other participants. A review of the audio-tapes from meetings across the project suggests that the differing speaking opportunities experienced by these women were an achievement of all the participants rather than entirely attributable to the characteristics of the individual women. The consciousness raising process was implicated in the exercise of power amongst the women and also in the establishment of positions of authority within the project group.

In the following excerpt, Annette uses critical ideas to challenge Philippa's non-critical stance. The example is taken from the second meeting of the project group, which focused on the social construction of gender. In general, the participants acknowledged the differences in the expectations placed upon male and female children and many also recognized that they reinforced these patterns in their parenting. This excerpt begins with Philippa's objection to these claims, drawing on reflections about her parenting:

Philippa: I just dress, I DRESS Jack, I fuss about him as much as I would if he were a girl though, whenever he needs a hair cut I take him straight down the hairdressers I REALLY FUSS, I don't think I'd be any more fussy if he was a girl,

Annette: but would you put him in pink though?

Philippa: he does wear pink

Annette: would you put 'im in a pink suit, a SOLELY PINK SUIT, not with any OTHER colour?

Philippa: no

Melissa: I wouldn't put a girl in pink either

Philippa: I don't particularly like pink, but if I found something pink I probably would though . . . it doesn't matter its not a problem, I mean you see guys walking around the streets now, with pink shirts, ↑I mean↑ pink shirt, purple jeans it doesn't matter.

The critical truths that were promoted by workers through the discussion, such as the belief that the children were unwittingly subjected to gender role stereotyping and that this was constraining, were also integral to the exercise of power amongst participants. These truths formed a disciplinary apparatus in that, through them, participants were empowered to evaluate the actions of others. In this excerpt, Annette is able to exercise the power of the interrogator as she repeatedly questions Philippa ('would you put him in pink', 'would you put 'im in a pink suit, a SOLELY PINK SUIT') and, in so doing, she was able to imply that Philippa engaged in gender socialization processes of which she was unaware.

Another way in which the consciousness raising process shaped the power relations was that the authority of individual participants was linked to their capacity to represent themselves in ways consistent with critical ideals. Throughout the project, Leah's position of authority was illustrated by participants' demonstrations of interest in her opinion and through explicit statements of support and even admiration for Leah. These actions were rarely initiated towards other participants. By contrast, Philippa's input was not sought or supported, and in fact she was often criticized by other participants for failing to demonstrate critical understanding. The following discourse sample provides an illustration of the contrasting ways in which Leah and Philippa were perceived as authorities; that is, as people whose opinion was worth hearing. This discourse excerpt occurred about four months after the project began during a discussion about welfare benefits to single parents:

Melissa: what's the difference between a family, mum and dad?

Annette: that's right

Melissa: they're on unemployment benefits and they've three children and more on the way, and they're on unemployment benefits?

Worker 1: well it might be something ABOUT our society's ideals about

[talk over]

Melissa: I mean what is the difference?

Leah: IT'S JUST FIGHTING AGAINST, WOMEN *(Worker 1: yes)* and SOLE parents *(Worker 1: yes)* there's nothing mo:more to it than that and do they care about

Annette: there's a lot of good sole parents out there, I think *(young women: yes)* that

	have got money they are trying to, *(Jo: hmm)* accomplish something, and have made a choice, when that choice was theirs to make
Leah:	YEH WELL THAT'S LIKE, yeh well, I FEEL, I feel, for myself, *(Worker 1: hmm)* I LEFT for my kids future, because, their father was treating them like *shit, (Worker: yes)* I thought I could do a better job on my own *(young women: yes)*, I don't have three kids through my own choice,
([talk over])	
Sonia:	You were married weren't you?
Leah:	yeh. I was, I was married.
Sonia:	well see that's the difference then.
Leah:	how?
Philippa:	bein' on the pension
(talk over)	
Leah:	I still don't see it as bein' any different
Philippa:	MY uncle's gettin, with this woman, she's pregnant, she's got now she's, on her FOURTH kid with four different fathers,
Jo:	that'd be dreadful
Philippa:	and she just keeps having another one, hopin that, that guy will stay with her.
group:	heheheh [talk over]
Worker 1:	I mean the answer's NOT to cut the pension though
Annette:	NO
[talk over]	
Philippa:	↑but she's a druggie and everything↑ I mean she's got
Annette:	she probably just because somebody gets a government handout (why) should they be judged anyway. I mean do people that are on, work allowance or whatever they call it now, UN:employment, it's to me, do they get, ya know, do they get put in a category, 'oh well we'll cut it off now because they haven't got a job after three months, that's it for them', YA KNOW.

From the beginning of the project Leah presented herself in ways congruent with an empowered and independent female subject, an ideal supported through the consciousness raising process. For example, in this excerpt, Leah argues that she is able to offer her children a 'better' future on her own. Furthermore, Leah bluntly rejects the suggestion put forward by Sonia that her marital status had any mediating influence on her right to parent ('I still don't see it as bein' any different'). Given the value placed on critical perspectives in the project, Leah's capacity to argue, and more importantly, present herself in ways compatible with critical discourses was a source of authority in the group. It is significant that Leah's independence is coupled with a strong attachment to a traditional motherhood ideal. Although highlighting her ability to cope on her own, she is keen to point out that she left her partner not so much for herself, but for her 'kids' future'. The importance of being seen to be 'good mothers' (by which the young women meant putting their children first) is a point to which all the participants continually returned throughout the project.

By contrast, the general lack of support for the 'non-critical' positions expressed by Philippa (and to some extent those expressed by Sonia) is evident. There were explicit rejections of both Sonia's and Philippa's positions by participants, most particularly by Leah and Annette. Indeed, there was a notable bluntness in the way in which Philippa's input was rejected. For instance, in response to Philippa's claim that she knew someone who had exploited the public welfare system, Annette exclaimed, 'just because somebody gets a government handout (why) should they be judged anyway?' From a critical perspective it was difficult to fault this position. However, the outright rejection of Philippa's views provide her with few face-saving opportunities to rethink her position without it appearing as total capitulation. While it is difficult to image activism without certainties, there is an irony that critical truths can also be used to effect relations of domination; that is, to subdue the voices and the experiences of those they are intended to liberate and with whom dialogue is sought.

Given the consistency and manner in which Philippa's perspectives were contested, it is little wonder, then, that Philippa increasingly felt alienated within the project. Philippa exited it prematurely, due primarily to the offer of a skills training programme. At a follow up interview, Philippa stated that although she gained some insight into social inequities through the project, she felt that these perspectives could not provide the answers to the questions that endured for her. In trying to come to terms with the violence she had experienced as a child, she had concluded that 'I just can't get any answers, no explanation or nothing, ya know'. Philippa was offended that her different experiences and interpretations had been marginalized in the process. The following excerpt indicates that Philippa felt anything but liberated by the critical reflection process:

> I was there, and they're all like male bashing and I'm thinking 'what am I IN here?' heheh, a bunch of feminists, they're all just MAN bashers, that's what it sounded like, I mean, I came home one night and I said to Russ [Philippa's partner] 'THEY'RE A BUNCH OF FEMINISTS' heheheh . . . you have to take a stand somewhere, but everything, EVERY LITTLE THING in their lives is 'oh men are just BASTARDS' ya know.

She later added that, at one point:

> I wanted to get up and say 'not all guys are bastards' but I would've been killed . . . I didn't feel I could say something, not about men (Worker 1: yeh) it was just like something people didn't want to hear.

Certainly, participants other than Philippa expressed ambivalence toward feminist perspectives, and they were similarly challenged within the project. However, it was the consistency of Philippa's rejection of the critical perspectives, particularly as these related to her own life, that contributed to her subjection to disciplinary power by other participants.

As these excerpts illustrate, the critical perspectives advanced through consciousness raising processes can become a site for the exercise of power amongst those subjected to them. Rahnema (1990) asserts that the notion of critical consciousness:

> implies that participants are not really equal and, therefore, the persons with a 'primitive' or 'semitransitive' consciousness have to learn from the few with a 'critically

transitive consciousness' before being able to make any meaningful contribution to the dialogue. (pp. 207–8)

It can be concluded that the critical perspectives promoted in the project context shaped what was said, and who counted as capable of speaking. This occurred through the affirmation of certain voices, and the marginalization of others, in this case those voices that didn't sing the critical 'tune' that emerged over the course of the project (Healy and Peile, 1995, p. 287; see also Lugones and Spelman, 1990).

Notwithstanding the liberatory potential of critical perspectives, they effected positions of authority within the group and they were used also as a basis for some participants to judge others. These critical perspectives became part of the disciplinary apparatus through which 'normality' and 'abnormality' and what is 'true' and 'untrue' were defined in the practice context (see Foucault, 1981a, 1991a). Importantly, these disciplinary apparatuses can be enacted even by those not formally identified with power (Foucault, 1991a, p. 201). Indeed, we see in the young women's anti-violence project that truth claims were used by both workers and participants to influence and reinforce power relations.

To be critical or not to be critical: tensions around critical perspectives in activism

In this analysis, it has been suggested that critical perspectives were integral to the operations of power amongst the participants in the project. Yet, this power was not necessarily experienced as domination. Even though participants came to the project with critical understandings it seemed that these ideas had been reinforced and expanded through the practice process. The critical perspectives advanced through the project enabled the participants to move, to varying extents, from a situation of self-blame to a recognition of the structural origins of their experience.

Some participants considered this critical awareness to have benefits for themselves and the many young women who have been involved in various aspects of the initial project and through the peer support and advocacy network that developed from it. As Annette asserted during a meeting three months after the project began:

> Ya know, like some of the issues that we've brought up, I think its just, UNBELIEVABLE, the links that you find with the community and the media that put so much pressure on us (Worker 1: yeh) you know, if they [other young mothers and young women] can just THINK ABOUT THAT, then they're not gonna come down so HARD on themselves, and thinking that they're a total failure in the world.

For some, the critical reflection process had usefully challenged self-blaming ideas, particularly in relation to their experiences of violence. Rather than facilitate a sense of themselves as victims, this redefinition appeared to contribute to a reduction away from a sense of personal culpability for the violence they had experienced and towards an understanding of the social conditions that contributed to their vulnerability. The project and the 'Young Mothers for Young Women' network that emerged from it provided a focal point for the young women to participate in public debate about representations of young women and patterns of violence (Healy and Walsh, 1997).

The critical reflection process translated, to some extent, to personal change in some of the young women's lives. In particular, most participants identified that the emphasis on equality and the denaturalization of violence had led them to question and challenge the violence they experienced. Only six weeks after the project began, one participant asserted that she had started to challenge silences around violence within her family:

Jo:	well actually the other day I talked about it [the violence] with my mum
Worker 1:	ohh ahh
Jo:	because she didn't know, REALLY what this [the anti-violence project] was about, an' I said, 'it's because Dad beat me up'
Worker 1:	hhh
Jo:	and she said 'Na, I wouldn't say he beat me/beat you up' and I said, 'mum, when someone raises their fist to you and punches you, they're beating you up'
Worker 1:	wow
Jo:	an' then she got upset so, I thought, that's enough for now
Annette:	I'll tell ya the rest tomorrow heheheh

My responses ('ohh ahh', 'wow') indicate strong approval for the young woman's claims about the changes she has made. Yet, despite the changes that had occurred for Jo, towards the completion of the project she also acknowledged the other aspects of her experience of violence (particularly sexual abuse) that remained unspoken in the private contexts of her life.

Another participant stated that the process had facilitated her decision to leave a violent relationship. During a discussion following the completion of the initial project report, almost six months after the project began, this participant made the following claim about it benefits:

Melissa:	it [the project] made me realize that I had to have some ↑changes↑ . . . getting rid of buggerlugs!
Worker 1:	> ohh how did it > How'd, How did that happen?
Melissa:	well just by REALLY looking at it, 'cause I never really sat back an' looked at it *(Worker 1: hmm)* ya know, an', sort've, The shit that was going on, So it made me sit back an' look at it, *(Worker 1: Okay)* and realize, I didn't have to put up with it. parentheses

From this young woman's viewpoint, the opportunity to 'sit back and look' at her situation, as much as the critical perspectives facilitated in the project, assisted her to leave an unsatisfactory situation.

Although the critical reflection process had effected positive change in the lives of the young women, there was evidence also of its constraining effects. In the previous section, I discussed the use of these perspectives to exercise dominatory power, even to silence, participants who did not speak with a critical voice. In addition, the privilege accorded to these critical ideas meant that participants were compelled to represent themselves in ways consistent with them.

Notwithstanding the important changes made by the young women, their public voice of defiance often contrasted with the silences that continued in other domains of their lives. The critical reflection process contributed to a dissonance between how these young women described their actions and how they continued to experience and to act in contexts of their lives beyond the project. These contrasts became particularly apparent as the participants moved to public action. For example, one young woman who had participated in a national radio interview about young women's experiences of violence became very concerned that her family might hear the broadcast. Indeed, while in this public context the young woman was able to speak at length about young women's experiences of violence, including her own, she revealed that she had not spoken to any members of her family, including those responsible for the violence against her, about these experiences.

The dissonance between public voice and private experience was especially evident in relation to the young women's ongoing vulnerability to violence. In concert with the ideal of the 'independent woman' that emerged in the talk of the young women, it would appear that there was an expectation amongst the participants that, regardless of their past experience, they would have sufficiently changed through the project to refuse violent treatment in their current contexts. Thus, the critical perspectives were implicated in a personal sense of failure for those participants who remained in violent relationships. For instance, outside the project meetings three participants separately raised with me their continuing but sporadic involvement with partners who were violent towards them. Yet within the meeting, these women like the other participants primarily discussed previous experiences of violence. About six months after the project began, I asked the young women about the potentially silencing effects of the desire to be perceived as non-victims:

Worker 1:	ya know, like if someone was in a violent situation, because you've all talked, or got out of this cycle of violence, then you suddenly start to realize you're back in it, would you feel like you failed?
Annette:	NO
Leah:	I would
Worker 1:	yeh
Leah:	'specially when you think you've come so far
Jo:	I think this is the place to COME if I got into that
Leah:	but the other thing is that I don't know if I'd WANNA come back.

In this excerpt, a diversity of opinion is expressed. Leah acknowledges her potential sense of failure ('specially when you think you've come so far'), yet is more successful than the other participants in presenting herself in a way that is consistent with the dual ideals of the independent woman and the competent parent. Although both Annette and Jo express a view that they wouldn't feel judged, participants who continued to experience violence were reluctant to discuss these experiences in the project group.

Whatever the uses of collective identification in forging energy and direction for action, some participants experienced difficulty in enacting aspects of this identification in their lives outside the project. This is not surprising, for as a collective, the young women had a common base from which to challenge their experiences of oppression. It is concerning, however, that in the project meetings the dissonance between the collective identifications of the participants, as survivors of violence, and the other subject positions they occupied simultaneously, such as victims of violence, was left unchallenged.

Oppositional and collective approaches to power and identity

Having outlined how the consciousness raising processes were implicated in the power relations amongst the participants, let us now turn to an examination of the effects of the second aspect of critical practice strategies, the development of oppositional and collective approaches to change. In Chapter 2, I outlined the premises of this aspect, so I will return only briefly to them here. The first premise underlying oppositional and collective approaches to social action is that oppressed people share common identifications, such as that of women, gays, indigenous people, and that in order to understand and act upon their oppression they should 'reclaim the identity that the dominant culture has taught them to despise' (Young, 1990, p. 166). The second plank is that, in accordance with conflict theory, one's identification is defined in opposition to others. Collective identification is based on a clear delineation of 'ally' and 'enemy' (see Morgen and Bookman, 1988, p. 9) in accordance with one's fixed position within overarching social structures, such as capitalism, patriarchy and imperialism. In the next section I will briefly overview the formation of oppositional and collective identifications in the course of the young women's anti-violence project. I will turn, then, to an examination of how the oppositional understandings and approaches to power and identity impacted on power relations and processes of change within the project group and in the public arena.

The forging of common identifications

In forging a foundation of collective understanding and action, the young women emphasized the shared knowledge that derived from their experiences as young mothers and survivors of violence. This lived knowledge was viewed as a vital foundation for outreach and action with other young women. In a discussion about how they would address the young mothers who attended the public forum organized by the project group, Leah stated:

> I think I'd like to say, well, sort a say, with the seven of us, all of us being young mothers, we can say that all of us had experienced, almost everything we've got down there [here Leah is referring to the abuse experienced by the participants and which was documented during the critical reflection process].

Frequently, the young women stressed the value of their lived experience ('we can say that all of us, had experienced . . .'). The young women contrasted their knowledge with that of professionals, particularly social service professionals, who were viewed as lacking the experiences necessary to connect with young mothers at the level of shared experience.

In accordance with the conflict position that underpins activist social work practices, the young women expressed their identities in opposition to those connected with power. For example, professionals (particularly police and social workers) and men were identified as oppressors. One illustration of the antipathy to those identified as 'oppressors' occurred during a discussion about who should be invited to a public forum about young women and violence. The following excerpt is taken from a discussion about how to respond in the event that the male partners of the young women attended the forum:

Worker 1: well, what if that happens? like should we set a boyfriends' group, or something?
Brooke: NO! they can fuck off!
Melissa: no
Sonia: no
Annette: no they had a couple turn up at the last speak out, and they said 'NO' it's not
Melissa: go and do some shopping go home, ya know, go home
Annette: it's not good, because some women won't talk *(Jo:yeh)* if a man's sitting there so maybe he could come back later, ya know
Jo: so when we go to groups we'll just say 'look, no partners'
Worker 1: yes
Annette: BRING 'EM AND THEY'RE DEAD,
Worker 1: heheh
Sonia: dead in the water.

The level of antagonism shown towards males in this excerpt (for example, 'they can fuck off' and 'bring 'em and they're dead') was typical of that shown towards those identified as 'powerful'. However, this dualistic and oppositional construction of identities was difficult to sustain because it required the suppression of identifications with these others, many of which were integral to how the young women defined themselves. Although the participants frequently referred to their shared experiences as young mothers, there were, nonetheless, important differences amongst them. These differences were rarely acknowledged in the project meetings and, instead, experiences of difference were usually raised in conversations outside our sessions together. In particular, the young women acknowledged variations amongst themselves according to such things as the type and extent of violence and other factors such as current living circumstances and family backgrounds.

Two illustrations of this sense of difference were provided by Philippa and Leah. The following interaction occurred during an interview subsequent to Philippa's premature exit from the project:

Worker 1: did you find that other people had the same sorts of experiences as you, did you feel less alone as a result of talking to other people or has that changed at all? (5 second silence)

Philippa: oh sort of, but still umm it was like totally different to everybody else
Worker 1:   yes, yes
Philippa: like they had, they didn't really have all the childhood (stuff) not that I
              heard anyway.

Philippa asserts that her experiences of violence, which mainly pertained to childhood abuse, were very different to the focus on adolescent and adult experiences of violence which became the focus of project meetings. Philippa's sense of difference is perhaps unsurprising given her marginalization within the project group. However, even those participants who appeared to experience high levels of inclusion also experienced themselves as different, as the following excerpt illustrates. This passage is taken from my field notes, in the fourth month of the project, and refers to a discussion between Leah and me:

> Leah and I went to [a] Youth Service to talk about the Young Women's Public Forum. Leah made some interesting comments about being a young mum. In particular, she talked about feeling 'different' to other young mums in the group. She felt that although she hadn't been well-off (in her childhood) she certainly hadn't experienced the poverty of others in the project. . . . At the same time Leah seems to feel very different to others her age who have not had children. Her boyfriend and his friends who are all Leah's age [early twenties] have never experienced anything like the responsibility of three kids.

In her discussions with me, Leah acknowledged her sense of difference both within the project group, in relation to other members, and beyond it, with her boyfriend and his friends. This is remarkable in that during the project meetings she frequently emphasized the unique knowledge that the participants, as young mothers, shared.

In some contexts, such as the project meetings and public forums, the claim of shared knowledge conferred legitimacy on the voices of the young women. Yet, these collective and oppositional identifications glossed over the diversity of experiences and identifications which were important to participants' sense of themselves. For although it is certainly true that the young women identified commonality amongst themselves and with other young women, there were other identifications that were of great importance to them. At times, the boundaries of identification shifted so that the young women appeared to have more in common with some young men or homeless people and even the media stars of American television sitcoms than with others in the category of 'young woman'. The forging of a collective identity did not make these other identifications less salient; but it did mean that they were suppressed in the project meetings.

The suppression of complex power relations

Consistent with critical practice approaches, the formation of collective and oppositional identifications was coupled with a conflictual view of power. Although this oppositional approach was useful for providing the project group with direction and motivation for change, it led also to an oversimplification of power relations in the practice context. The reliance on an opposition contributed to an emphasis on the dominance of those with access to formal power and a downplaying of the positive political capacity of those identified as powerless. In other words the understanding of power relations became polarized over the course of the project. The caricatures about power relations impeded the formation of coalitions with others outside the project group and constrained the development of understandings about the operations amongst participants and within their lives. In the next section, I will outline how the oppositional approaches to power limited the formation of complex understandings and actions amongst the project group.

Power as domination

In the emancipatory social movements to which contemporary critical forms of social work are linked, there is a tendency to collapse all forms of power together as domination (Yeatman, 1997). This negative approach to power pre-empts inquiry into the local operations of power, as it is necessary only for an individual to be identified as powerful for them to be seen also as an oppressor (Tapper, 1993). This is a significant weakness in terms of developing coalitions with the powerful in so far as there is little opportunity to differentiate between those forms of power that are productive for extending empowerment to participants and those forms that are used to further domination.

In the course of the young women's anti-violence project a critique of institutional forms of power, such as the power exercised by police and by social workers, became commonplace in the project meetings and the public forums. Although my co-worker and I supported many aspects of the young women's critique, we disagreed with the blanket statements about those perceived to be powerful. The following excerpt is taken from my field notes and it was recorded in my discussions with my co-worker immediately after the public forum, which was held by the project group almost five months after the project began:

> Robyn said it concerned her that we as workers were being lumped together with police ... Robyn felt the accusations, such as that made by Annette that workers were 100% bad, needed to be challenged.

The claims about the dominatory power of human service professionals were problematic in so far as they glossed over the significant variations that the young women had relayed in discussing their experiences of violence. The participants had been subjected to verbal, physical and sexual violence by the police, whereas their main complaints about human service workers, such as nurses, doctors, social workers and teachers, concerned the failure of these professionals to exercise power to protect young people in situations of violence. Moreover, the conflation of power as domination left little room to differentiate amongst human service professionals and police, who the young women identified as sources of support, and those who contributed to their marginalization and domination.

Speaking to the Other

The view of power as domination had constraining effects for the project group in their attempts to establish dialogue and to make claims upon the powerful for change. Even though all the participants had reported at least some positive experiences of human service workers, in the context of the project a polarization between the interests of professionals and service users became increasing ubiquitous in the young women's talk. The polarization contributed obstacles in developing coalitions with human service workers who were sympathetic to the concerns of the project participants.

An illustration of how the oppositional view infused the participants' approach to service workers occurred during the public forum on young women's experiences of violence. The project group anticipated that human service workers would accompany young women to the forum, so a series of questions was prepared for them. The following is the workers' response to a request that they identify how their work practices demonstrated prejudice towards young mothers. The workers' response to the question, which I quote in length here, suggests that although they were sympathetic to the young women's critique of human service workers, they differentiated themselves from it:

> The first question we found really difficult to answer, about prejudices. As workers we are all aware that every young parent faces prejudices and probably everyone here today would acknowledge that young parents have been treated really shitty by lots of people in the community who obviously 'have a problem'. I'm sure that most of you would agree today that the workers who have come here with you are positive workers and probably don't operate in the same way that some of the workers you've had bad experiences with do. As a group we found it difficult to word, if we had any prejudices or stereotypes obviously and we feel that obviously it would make you very ANGRY if I stood up here and started saying those things . . . It was easier for us to say that sometimes we've made assumptions about young women and young mothers when young parents come in. These assumptions don't necessarily have bad connections with them or anything like that, they're different to prejudices or stereotypes . . . And also to stand up here and say 'well I assume that all young mums are really BAD people, and that they're TERRIBLE MUMS', I'm just not gonna say that. Those are assumptions that other people might have, yes, young mothers have issues, but they're also very resourceful and can seek support when they need it. There's not always a lot of support there for them that's appropriate and quite often that's a real issue.

Although in the abstract these workers were sympathetic to the critical view that underscored the young women's questions, this did not resonate with their local experiences as service workers so were accorded little credence by them. In this excerpt, we see that these workers, most of whom subscribed to critical perspectives, found it difficult to accept that the general criticisms of human service workers could apply to them. Indeed, they differentiate themselves from the stereotype of the professionals by pointing to the changes that they have made in their own practice (for example, 'I'm sure that you would agree today that the workers who have come here with you are positive workers'). While acknowledging the prejudicial treatment to which the young women had been subjected, they refuse to occupy the oppositional category of dominator ('we feel that obviously it would make you very ANGRY if I stood up here and started saying those things'). The young women, whose position of powerlessness depended on a contrast with the powerful, were dissatisfied with this response. As one participant lamented 'They [the workers] wouldn't admit ANYTHING was wrong.' Neither the questions of the young women nor the response of the workers allowed complex relations of power, beyond that of 'powerful' or 'powerless', to come to the fore.

While many of the workers shared the young women's critique of social service workers, they nonetheless considered their own situations to be considerably more complex than a simple dualism between themselves as 'oppressors' and the young women as 'oppressed'. In the context of what they saw as their own complex relation to power, some workers experienced the young women's inference about the prejudicial actions of workers as an attack on them. This extract is from field notes taken during a phone call with a human services worker who had attended the forum:

> [The worker stated that] the young women wanted us to say that we were lousy, they wanted us to say that we stereotyped . . . [the worker] also talked about the powerless-ness of workers. She [the worker] stated that in her work with the young women she felt like saying 'I'm just as powerless as you to fix the situation', she further commented that 'They see me as having power, particularly when I say no.' [The worker] seemed distressed about the negativity expressed toward workers . . . [she said] 'you create an environment that's safe for them, but we're not safe ourselves.'

The dualistic view of power that was adopted by the young women was experienced as unfair by workers, particularly those who sought to enact a social justice agenda in their work practices. These claims, whilst perhaps true of human service activities generally, did not, in their view, take account of the differences they attempted to achieve in their work practices.

The workers' attendance at the public forum would seem to indicate an interest in young women's issues. Most of the workers were employed in small non-government organizations and most identified as feminists. Yet despite their professional and personal investment in critical practices, or perhaps because of it, they would not tolerate a general critique of their power that failed to engage with the complexities around their experiences of power and their attempts to do things differently.

Power and powerlessness

Whatever uses the oppositional approaches to power may have for increasing sensitivity to certain kinds of power differentials in the practice context, it is not transformative (Yeatman, 1997). Ironically, rather than help to dismantle and trans-form power relations, these representations construct and reinforce oppositions. Within the project group, the collapsing of all power relations into two opposed positions constrained the development of shared participation in the achievement of activist processes and outcomes. On the one hand, the power of my co-worker and me was exaggerated, with the consequence that we could be held responsible for achievement of the highly utopian goals of the project. These ideals, such as that of total equity, were not subject to question. On the other hand, the representation of participants as outside 'positive political capacity' (Yeatman, 1993, p. 220) glossed over the actuality of their power in relation to one another and their potential to exercise power for change.

The following excerpt illustrates how the oppositions between powerful and powerless suppressed recognition of alternative operations of power in the practice context. Just prior to this excerpt, a participant, Annette, had raised the dissonance between the egalitarian ethos underpinning the project and the differences that prevailed between workers and participants, and she illustrated her claim by pointing to the workers' role in the organization of the child-care arrangements.

Worker 2: I HAVE TROUBLE WHEN YOU SAY, when people or someone organizing *(Worker 1: yeh)* what is it that doesn't make you feel equal in the fact that someone's organizing it?

Annette: because somebody's choosing the child-care worker that's lookin' after my children, somebody's choosing the facility

Worker 1: hhhh (exasperated sound)

Annette: that my children are gonna be catered for at that's the problem that I have it's like, there's no, I WOULD LIKE TO KNOW WHO THE CHILD-CARE WORKERS ARE, because at the you know, the two people, I don't have a problem with any of 'em, don't get me wrong, but I DON'T KNOW WHO THESE PEOPLE ARE, I've never been introduced to these people, BAR Lena [the key child care-worker] saying, this is such and such, helping me, you know what I mean

Worker 2: that's an expectation, I mean, could you go an' introduce yourself an' ask them?

Brooke: but they're paid to be there, it's their job, shouldn't they

Worker 2: but even when I pay for my child care NOBODY introduces anybody to

Annette: but the child care was chosen and

Worker 2: no but I've got to initiate it all, I've gotta go up and say, 'WHAT'S your name? My name is so and so, I'm ahh, I'm gonna leave my child here, I have to everytime

Annette: but THAT'S IN A CENTRE, I'M TALKIN about PEOPLE THAT ARE COMING HERE that

Worker 2: na, ANYWHERE.

From a critical perspective the arguments presented by Annette and Brooke are difficult to fault. It was true that my co-worker and I organized the child-care arrangements and that we had failed to introduce the participants to the child-care workers; nor had the child-care workers initiated introductions to participants. The assumption was that the workers had failed in their responsibility to equalize power. In the context of a polarized understanding of power that was fostered in the project, the workers were held responsible for the continuing power inequities ('I've never been introduced to these people' and 'but they're paid to be there, that's their job') even though the issue of participant involvement in the child-care arrangements was not previously raised by the young women or the project workers. There is an irony that in the identification of power relations, these oppositional approaches reinforce inequities in that the 'powerless' are rendered incapable of challenging their circumstances except via securing agreement of the powerful to protect and to empower them.

Through the assumption that the achievement of the values of activist practice, such as equity and service user participation, are the responsibility of the powerful, oppositional approaches minimize the shared capacity and shared responsibility for achieving participatory processes. From within the positions of the powerful worker and the powerless client, it was difficult to contest the oppositions on which the critical social work discourses depended. Instead, my co-worker uses her identification as a mother (but even when I pay for my child care NOBODY introduces anybody) to unpack the implicit claim that the workers are the only site at which power is possible. In this way, the worker highlights the capacity and the responsibility of the young women to exercise power to address and change the things that concerned them ('could you go an' introduce yourself an' ask them').

The oppositional approach to power was also contested by some of the participants within the practice context. The general critique of human service workers' power that emerged amongst the participants over the course of the project had limited utility in explaining the local power relations in the practice context. Indeed, one of the empowering aspects of the project for many of the participants was the recognition that the power of human service workers, such as ourselves, was not necessarily insurmountable, and that they were not powerless in relation to us. As one young woman pointed out in reflecting on the project, almost two years after it began:

> We could say we had all this knowledge that you didn't have, 'you don't know what it's like to be in domestic violence, you don't know what it's like to be a young mother, we know this and you don't', it balances it out because you have the technical knowledge and we don't.

Similarly, over the course of the project it was difficult for some participants to develop and sustain a sense of us as opposite to them because of the recognition of the commonalities we shared. For instance, sometimes the young women and I would talk about experiences of harassment in night clubs, while the participants would often refer to my co-worker's identity as a mother as a site of commonality with her. Although there were ongoing inequities in the project context, the power relations were not static and through regular and continuing reflection on the power relations significant changes had occurred. The conflation of power as domination provided no avenue for acknowledging these local changes or for negotiating change in power relations other than through contesting those associated with power. Indeed, over the course of the project an oppositional approach risked becoming 'a pseudo-politics, namely a politics without contestation or dialogue, wherein the ethical features of political discourse become empty and righteous slogans' ignoring the multiple and shifting power relations amongst us (Yeatman, 1993, pp. 236–7).

Although the participants were willing to use oppositional tactics to human service workers and other powerful groups, in general, there was considerable ambiguity about the use of these strategies in the project meetings. Some participants were intimidated by the conflictual approaches used by some others, even when directed at my co-worker and me. In contrast to the caricature of working class women as comfortable with 'conflict ridden, tactical, ends oriented' political practices (Dixon, 1993, p. 26), some of the participants found these approaches to be reminiscent of the violence they had experienced. As one participant, Leah, described it: 'it's just like domestic violence, except this time it's women doing it to me'. This statement was all the more remarkable, given that at no stage was Leah the direct focus of condemnation; rather, for her, the oppositional tactics contributed to an environment of fear. Throughout the practice process there was an important balance to be struck in developing activist practices that were sensitive to the victimization the young women had experienced without confining them to the status of victim. A polarization of power relations to the recognition only of extreme positions of the powerful and the powerless was not helpful for grasping the operations of power beyond them.

The 'powerless' as authors and subjects of disciplinary power

In this analysis, I have considered how critical assumptions about power impeded understanding of power relations amongst workers and participants in the practice context and in the public activism undertaken by the project group. An oppositional approach to power was limited for helping the young women to unravel their own complex experiences of domination and in understanding their relations to power, both as authors and as subjects of it. For example, in the lives of the young women, men were responsible for the physical and sexual abuse they had experienced, yet, women were also agents of some forms of domination. In particular, in their discussions about their bodies the young women emphasized that they and other women (such as their peers, their mothers and even themselves) were primarily responsible for the surveillance of themselves in relation to particular (unattainable) standards of beauty and perfection. The young women's reflections on the subtle operations of power are consistent with Bartky's observations about patriarchical power. Referring to Foucault's work, Bartky (1988) argues that 'The disciplinary power that inscribes femininity on the female body is everywhere and it is nowhere; the disciplinarian is everyone and yet no-one in particular' (p. 74). Thus, rather than a clear delineation between oppressor and oppressed, according to Bartky one can be both disciplinarian and subject of patriarchal power.

In critically reflecting on their experiences, the young women recognized that they were not only the subjects of patriarchal power but also the conduits of it. Although the young women were critical of the extent to which their parents, particularly their mothers, had reinforced patriarchal standards of feminine appearance upon them, they also recognized the pervasiveness of these standards in their own parenting. An excerpt illustrating this point is taken from a discussion which occurred in the fifth month of the project, by which stage the participants had been involved in extensive consciousness raising processes.

Melissa: We pass it on to our kids, if we've got GIRLS, I mean. I like always make
             sure that Lizzy, I mean she doesn't get out of the house until she's lookin'
             perfect, she's got her hair nice and she's just lookin' like a doll ya know,
             and then it gets passed on to her. Even at this age, she knows when she
             looks PRETTY and ya know when she's got her PRETTY dress on
Worker 1:   so we pass this on to our children
Melissa: we DO, unconsciously, we definitely do it
Jo: you like, Leah, you might not want Maggie to go through what you went
             through [being very concerned about weight], but even though you might
             not realize it
Leah: like hung up on food, ya know, like little things like that and I mean I know,
             I know that I watch what the kids eat. The girls, I can't say that I watch
             what Nathan eats, probably, if anything, I encourage him to eat yeah,
             'cause he's male *(Worker 1: yeh)* but I don't feel that with the girls 'cause,
             yeh, I don't want them to have a weight problem, 'cause of the problems I
             had with it.

Again, although the young women acknowledge the damaging effects of maintaining certain standards of thinness and beauty, they recognize that they reinforce
these expectations in their parenting ('we DO, unconsciously, we definitely do it').
For whatever damage these standards have had in their own lives these expectations
may, paradoxically, have enabling effects for their children. For example, Leah
suggests that by controlling the eating habits of her female children she may help
them to avoid 'a weight problem' and thus the difficulties she experienced with
such issues in her own life.

The recognition that the young women consider that these standards have both
disabling and enabling effects for their children suggests a significant limitation to
activist processes, particularly consciousness raising processes, aimed at the critical
evaluation and refusal of oppressive practices. Bartky (1988) observes that:

> Whatever its ultimate effect, discipline can provide the individual on whom it is
> imposed with a sense of mastery as well as a secure sense of identity . . . Women, then,
> like other skilled individuals, have a stake in the perpetuation of their skills, whatever it
> may have cost to acquire them and quite apart from the question whether, as a gender,
> they would have been better off had they never had to acquire them in the first place.
> Hence, feminism, especially a genuinely radical feminism that questions the patriarchal
> construction of the female body, threatens women with a certain deskilling, something
> people normally resist; beyond this, it calls into question that aspect of personal identity
> that is tied to the development of a sense of competence. (p. 77)

An oppositional approach to activism that posits one identity group (such as, in
this instance, one sex class) over another, erases the subtle and pervasive ways
in which oppressive practices are produced and reproduced through the 'powerless' as well as the 'powerful'. For whereas critical social science theories have
acknowledged that the oppressed may be complicit in their own marginalization,
poststructural theory further suggests that the very processes through which
oppression occurs may also induce forms of power and pleasure. Poststructural
theory demands, then, an approach to activism that recognizes the complex and

contradictory processes through which oppression occurs. The radical potential of activist practice strategies to overcome domination is tempered by the recognition that one may willingly perpetuate and actually *benefit* from (albeit in a limited sense) those practices through which one is also oppressed.

In this section, I have critically examined the utility of the oppositional approaches as a basis for understanding and responding to domination. Although critical social workers claim to expose the power relations of practice, in this analysis I have demonstrated that the critical social science assumptions on which these practice theories are premised can also obscure alternate operations of power. Alongside a structural analysis of power, the practice group required also an understanding of the local nuances of power, in other words a micro-physics of power, if we were to grapple with the complexity of power in our activist practices and in our own lives.

Moving to action in the public sphere

As part of a broad vision of social change, activists urge the transformation of private concerns into public issues (see, for example, Maguire, 1987; Finn, 1994). This means that at some point oppressed populations must publicly contest the injustices they face. In this section, I explore the extent to which critical practice strategies, through which the participants moved to public action, unsettled existing social relations, and to what extent these practice strategies effected the extension of domination and surveillance.

The young women anticipated an antagonistic reception to their contest of the representations and policies that disadvantaged them. Yet, although the project group was subject to some opposition, typically, we experienced considerable ambiguity and even support in the responses from representatives of the state and the media. We were able to attract interest from representatives of the state, such as bureaucrats involved in social policy development and magistrates who presided over domestic violence matters, and the media; for instance, aspects of the project were given lengthy attention in two national radio programmes. Partly in response to this profile, the project group received financial support from the state to continue the development of a peer support and advocacy network for and by young women (see Healy and Walsh, 1997). To point to the ambiguous operations of powerful institutions such as the state and the media is not to be naive about the disciplinary power these institutions wield in the lives of service users. Certainly, vigilance about the operations of the government and the media are imperative but the state is not a monolith and we were able to identify sympathetic people within these institutions who could help us achieve our change objectives.

Critical social workers are united in their quest to develop practices free from domination. Such a quest is further challenged by the recognition of critical post theorists that activist strategies themselves can be used to extend the power of the activist and the operations of discipline and surveillance. Thus rather than confining our reflections to institutions or particular types of people (for example, people inside or outside 'the system'), it was important to turn our critical attention also to the local effects of critical practice strategies. The insights of critical post theories are useful for grappling with the limitations encountered by the project group in using collective identifications as a basis for public action. As the young women moved to public dialogue and debate they found that their participation in the public domain, in the media and with policy makers, was conditional upon their speaking from their position as young mothers and as victims of violence. Members of the project group encountered significant pressure, particularly from the media, and on occasion from human service professionals, to reveal intimate details of their personal lives. This level of personal openness in public forums was never requested of professionals (including myself and my co-worker) nor of the media personnel who were in contact with the young women.

Initially, rather than resist this concentration on their personal experiences (particularly those of victimization), the young women actively engaged with it. Indeed, when my co-worker and I raised concerns about public self-revelation, the young women fervently defended the importance of their speaking about their personal experiences. The participants argued that telling their stories was liberating for them and that it could assist others to break the cycle of violence. Yet the expression of collective identifications in the public sphere set up an unequal dialogue in that the young women revealed a great deal but had little power to demand anything in return.

However, in the latter stages of the project the young women who had initially engaged willingly in public discussions about their personal experiences became more ambivalent about doing so. In the second year of the project, the participants began to resist requests from professionals to speak at public meetings and there was some questioning amongst the young women about the constraining and even the potentially embarrassing effects their personal disclosures had had upon them. In response, the women's network had begun to formulate a media policy cautioning against too much self-revelation and encouraging, instead, the discussion of the network's work rather than individual experiences.

Foucault (1980a, 1981a) has written extensively on the role of confession in modern systems of surveillance and control. His work is useful for understanding the disempowering potential of activist strategies which encourage the claiming of a collective identification and speaking out from the basis of it. Foucault (1981a) has argued that:

> the agency of domination does not reside in the one who speaks (for it is he who is constrained), but in the one who listens and says nothing; not in the one who knows and answers, but in the one who questions and who is not supposed to know. And this discourse of truth finally takes effect, not in the one who receives it, but in the one from whom it is wrested. (p. 62)

Indeed, whilst the women's speaking out contributed to greater community awareness of young mothers' vulnerability to violence, their entry to public debate has been largely dependent on their willingness to publicly confess their experiences of violence. Although these actions may have challenged professional and community attitudes, it also provided the audiences with significant personal information about the young women's lives. Moreover, the young women were positioned as knowledgeable only in relation to their victim status and to the experiences of other victims. Indeed, whilst in the short term such acts of speaking out may be empowering in the sense that those who were previously silenced have the opportunity to contest representations about them, the longer term effects for empowerment and change cannot be assumed. For, according to Foucault, power accrues not to those who speak (in this instance, the young women) but to those who listen and say nothing (in this instance the community members and professionals). Through reliance on public acts of self-revelation, activist practices can further processes through which the oppressed are romanticized and made over into objects of interest rather than as interlocutors in processes of transformation (see Frost, 1977, p. 72).

While in activist practices the use of identifications may be necessary, critical poststructural theory alerts us to the dangers of approaches deriving from this foundation. Collective identifications provide a conduit for the discipline and surveillance of marginal populations by confining them to ways of being, thinking and acting (see Butler, 1990; Foucault, 1992; Cixous, 1994a, 1994b). For example, the collective identity of the young women as victims and survivors of violence gave them a public voice but also constrained them to speak from that voice, whilst marginalizing other identifications that were relevant to them. Even if, as activists, we cannot forgo identity because of its political utility, we can be more cautious in invoking identifications and more self-reflexive about their effects upon those with whom we work for social transformation.

Conclusion

In this chapter, I have used poststructural perspectives to critically review the effects of activist practice strategies upon and amongst the participants as we moved to public action. Notwithstanding the empowering effects of these strategies, they were also implicated in the operations of surveillance and disciplining through and upon the participants. The insights of post theories draw activists to recognize that there is no space innocent of the operations of power to which we can turn and no pure practices of emancipation. Instead of assisting the search for a core to critical social work, poststructural theories can lead activists to increased sensitivity to the contextual variations in practice sites and the multiple operations of power within them. In the next chapter, I will outline the implications of these insights for reconstructing emancipatory social work practices.

7   Reconstructing Critical Practices

Critical social work is in a period of transition. If there ever was a good time to be activist it seems it isn't now, as critical social work faces challenges from within, about the silencing and dominatory effects of its practices, and from without, as welfare states are significantly re organized. Apart from some attempts to revive a radical fundamentalism, many predict that, at the very least, the halcyon days of critical social work have now passed (Langan, 1998). In the context of this admittedly bleak outlook, critical 'post' theories provide troublesome but necessary challenges to critical forms of social work. Notwithstanding the profoundly destabilizing effects of these ideas, they also offer hope for the reconstruction and diversification of activist social work practices. Whilst not jettisoning critical social science ideas altogether, the disruptions of critical poststructuralism encourage more self-reflexivity and less grandiosity about the processes and goals of critical social work practices. In the 'hyper- and pessimistic activism' to which Foucault (1991b, p. 343) refers, change is possible, but it is recognized as limited and always dangerous.

In this chapter, I will outline how critical poststructural theory can be used as a resource in the emergence of diverse and vital activist social work practices relevant to the vastly transformed contexts of welfare practice that human service workers now face. Starting with a discussion of challenges to the theory/practice split, I will then outline the implications of critical poststructural theory for enhancing reflexivity about the context, power, identity and processes of change in activist social work. I will conclude with an overview of the limits of these theories for activism as part of an argument for why, even in the context of the important recent inroads made by 'post' theories, progressive workers cannot yet do without insights of critical social science as well.

Deconstructing the theory/practice split

On the basis of critical social science assumptions, activists proclaim the truth about what social work is and what it should be. However, in recent years a growing chorus of discontent has emerged contesting the capacity of critical practice theories to apprehend the complex, contradictory and compromised worlds of social change, social work and policy practices (see Wise, 1990; Bennett, 1998; Healy, 1998). For despite an emphasis on 'praxis' in activist practice theories, these understandings remain impervious to criticisms, even those that arise through practice, that undermine core critical social science assumptions.

Poststructuralists show the schism between theory and practice to be more than a superficial problem requiring a fundamental rethinking of the position of both in critical social work. In their respect for local diversities, critical post-structural theorists challenge the use of theory to explain and to guide local activity. Poststructuralism shows the total explanations of the social whole on which critical practice theories have relied to be misguided, in so far as they seek to impose order on that which is fragmented, and arrogant, in that they operate to suppress alternate understandings and practices (Grosz, 1989; B. Davies, 1994). For example, in Chapters 5 and 6 I used practice illustrations to show complexities in the operations of power, identity and change. It could be suggested that the local dimensions focused upon in the analysis could be explained via small group theories or other interpersonal analyses. Yet, my point is precisely to challenge a central assumption of critical social work theories that local analyses can be deduced from an understanding of the social totality. Instead, I suggest that local analysis can extend and complicate the structural foundations of critical practice approaches.

In contrast to the priority given to grand social explanations in critical social work practice, poststructural thinkers, such as Foucault and the French feminist author Le Doeuff, propose approaches to knowledge that are respectful of the limits of theory to know the truth and to guide practice. Foucault (1991e) argues for a more partial role for theory and critique thus:

> Critique doesn't have to be the premise of a deduction which concludes: this then is what needs to be done. It should be an instrument for those who fight, those who resist and refuse what is. Its use should be in the processes of conflict and confrontation, essays in refusal. It doesn't have to lay down the law for the law. It isn't a stage I programming. It is a challenge directed to what is. (p. 84)

Of course, social work theorists are in a different position to philosophers such as Foucault in the sense that their field of inquiry, 'social work', refers to a range of activities, not only ideas. Yet, even so, Foucault's advocacy of a less deterministic role for philosophy is relevant to destabilizing the schism between theory and practice that endures in critical social work much more than it should. In respect for the diversity of local contexts of practice, poststructuralists, such as Foucault, recognize that theory can provide at best partial understandings and critique directed to 'what is'. In contrast to the truth status attached to critical social work assumptions, Foucault insists that activists must be free to accept or reject theoretical critique in accordance with its usefulness for achieving critical processes and change in local contexts of practice.

Critical poststructural theory contributes to the repositioning of theory in practice. In this new position, theory is a tool, something that can be used to critique practice but also something practitioners and service users can speak with and against. The reinvention of critical social work, from this viewpoint, does not involve jettisoning critical practice ideas, for there is important political work that these ideas make possible. Instead, critical poststructural theory destabilizes the truth status of the critical social science claims. For it is this position of unquestionable truth that creates a monologue in which theory is privileged over practice and structural over local analyses.

Critical poststructural theory shows the truths proclaimed in critical social work to be partial truths and the voices of the theorist/researcher to be situated rather than universal voices. This recognition can contribute to different ways of theorizing, to greater openness to those aspects of social work practice that defy explanation in traditional scientific terms or through reference to the social 'whole'. These more open ended approaches to theorizing are required if social work theory is to engage with those aspects of social work knowledge which are 'intensely subjective, interpersonal, idiographic, value laced and interpretive and often takes a narrative form' (Gorman, 1993, p. 252).

To advocate incompleteness in theory building is not to suggest an uncritical 'anything goes' approach to activism. Rather, the contribution that critical post-structural theories can make at this point in the history of critical social work is to renew appreciation of local 'everyday' contexts of practice as sites for disrupting established critical theories about practice and constructing new ones.

Social work in context

Poststructuralists emphasize the 'pragmatic, ad hoc, contextual and the local' and in so doing challenge the priority accorded to the social totality in contemporary approaches to activism (Fraser and Nicholson, 1990, p. 21). The radical social constructionist position adopted by poststructuralists challenges any attempts to define a core or a truth of critical practice. Instead, social work practices are recognized as fluid entities that are differently constituted across contexts of action. There is no one way of being a social worker and there can be no singular formula for activism. This recognition reopens critical social work to the questioning of its definitions of activism and to a search for answers grounded, at least in part, in the local contexts of practice. Thus, alongside the commonalities amongst critical workers there is also respect for differences in resources and contexts of change.

At one level, the recognition of the constitutive power of the historical and local contexts is constraining as it undermines claims about the emancipatory potential of critical social work. While critical social workers emphasize the role social workers have played in the subordination of oppressed populations, both historically and contemporarily, they tend to locate their own practices outside this history, as innately different to the practices which precede them. Yet, in so far as critical social workers uncritically pursue goals of liberating others in accordance with the truth claims of modern critical social theories, they too participate in the project of modernity, which must be regarded with scepticism by those on the margins. Critical poststructural theory challenges activists' attempts to position themselves as heroic agents who speak the truth to the powerful. Social workers, including activists, cannot evade the forces of histories through which we are constituted; instead, we must deal with the tensions of being inside systems of power whilst also seeking to subvert them.

By situating social work practices within their historical context, poststructural theories demand analysis of the relevance of activist practice goals to contemporary practice settings. Using a discourse analysis strategy, Rojek et al. (1988) argue that many of the ideals promoted in radical social work such as collectivism and commitment are 'drawn from the vocabulary of a very different kind of society' (p. 170). Even in the period since the initial emergence of a body of critical social work theories in the 1960s, the welfare state has undergone massive transformation. While many of the critical practice themes remain the same, such as the challenge of achieving just practices in the context of massive inequities, many of the former understandings are rendered defunct by the fundamental reorganization of welfare states. For instance, the significance of some of the earlier activist arguments against the welfare state is diminished with the destabilization of this entity. Indeed, some critical thinkers now find themselves in the sobering position of defending the remnants of the welfare states they have for so long contested. In addition, thinkers such as Esping-Andersen (1996) question whether the collectivist ideals that have long guided critical welfare practices are relevant to the 'more differentiated and individualistic demands of "post-industrial" society' (p. 26; see also Williams, 1994). At the beginning of the twenty-first century, a new set of questions looms large for critical social workers, particularly in relation to potential for practitioners to use or subvert the minimalist and increasingly corporatized welfare states in order that they might extend social citizenship to service users. At the very least, the radical reinvention and diversification of critical social work requires a willingness to acknowledge the limits of our current understandings to guide activism in the contemporary contexts of practice.

On another, more optimistic level, opportunities for the reinvention and diversification of activist practice theories emerge as critical 'post' theories destabilize the taken-for-granted assumptions of critical social work. This is important work: despite the heated debates that occur within critical social work, these representations have not been subjected to sustained scrutiny. The critical social work literature is riddled with dualisms which no longer make sense, if in fact they ever did, for supporting activist practices in the contemporary and diverse contexts of social work activity. These oppositions include:

Structural / local
Theory / practice
Dominance / egalitarianism
Community work / casework
Public sector / private or corporate sector
Rational / irrational
Care / control

The oppositional representations through which critical social work is constituted contribute to the minimization of the radical potential of everyday social work practices. For example, the conflation of activist practice with structural, meaning 'big', forms of change has led to the devaluation of much of the small-scale and localized activity in which human service workers are typically involved. The opposition between structural and local change provides an important contest to the individualistic emphasis that was dominant in social work theories prior to the emergence of a critical canon in the 1960s and that endures in the contemporary context. Yet, the emphasis on structural change leads not only to the minimization of the radical potential of local change practices but to the view that such practices are actually antithetical to radical transformation (see Mowbray, 1992, p. 66).

Similarly, these oppositional representations impede the emergence of critical practice theories that grapple with, rather than minimize, the challenges confronting workers in contexts characterized by competing demands from service users or their employing organization (Rojek et al., 1988; see also Bricker-Jenkins et al., 1991, p. 7). For instance, when critical approaches constitute ideals of service user empowerment and participation as requiring the minimization of worker power, they impede the development of critical practice strategies for statutory forms of social work where the explicit use of power is an irreducible aspect of practice (Clark, 1998; Healy, 1998). By destabilizing the taken-for-granted representations through which activism is constituted, critical poststructural theory can help to make visible the potential and actual practices of change in the diversity of practice contexts and obligations. For example, as the opposition between structural and local forms of change is dismantled, the local concerns and goals of service users can be valued as part of a continuum of social change rather than as the antithesis to it.

Critical social work theories are premised on the idea that there is a unified and identifiable set of activist practices. By contrast, the radical social constructionist position advocated through critical poststructural theories encourages social workers to take seriously the effects of context in shaping activism. This recognition is important for extending understanding of activist practices in the conventional, authoritarian and, increasingly, commercialized environments in which social work occurs. Working critically and subversively within these settings demands of social workers that they understand the other discourses, such as medical, legal and economic rationalist discourses, that are more visible and more powerful in shaping the practice context than either orthodox social work discourses or the critical social science ideals to which they subscribe. The reorientation of critical social work towards an engagement with the complexities and diversities of social work need not involve an abandonment of activist values, such as ideals of non-elitism. However, it requires a realization that definitions of activist practice cannot be determined outside specific, local contexts of practice.

In emphasizing the historical, local and organizational contexts through which social work practices are constituted, critical poststructural theories tear open critical orthodoxies about activism. Despite the loss of certainty about activism that this entails, it can also help in the reinvention and diversification of critical social work practices. In the next section, I will discuss the implications of critical poststructural theories for reconstructing understandings of power, identity and change in critical social work practices.

Power in practice

The poststructural work of Foucault challenges the primacy accorded to social structures and institutions such as the state in understanding local power relations. As Foucault (1980d) puts it: 'I don't want to say that the State isn't important; what

I want to say is that relations of power, and hence, the analysis that must be made of them, necessarily extend beyond the limits of the State' (p. 122). For Foucault, power and discourses are interrelated. There is no innocent space outside the operations of power. Because power is ever present, the challenge for critical social work is less one of minimizing power than of understanding how power can be used in ways that extend democracy and empowerment within the local contexts of practice and beyond them (Van-Krieken, 1992; Healy, 1998).

The poststructural reconceptualization of power to incorporate both its coercive and productive effects demands a fundamental reworking of the understandings of power on which critical practice approaches are based. In critical practice theories, domination and egalitarianism are paired dualistically as power is equated with domination and empowering practice is associated with its absence. A radical egalitarian position is promoted in a range of critical practice theories as a way of contesting the hierarchical and inequitable relation that is assumed to inevitably exist between workers and service users. Radical egalitarianism implies that power must be constantly given away to participants rather than held or possessed by workers.

The emphasis on the coercive effects of power in critical practice theories suppresses discussion of the productive functions of power. This has been a major weakness in the development of understanding and action in social work, even in relation to critical forms of practice. For, as I argued in Chapters 5 and 6, worker power is integral to the achievement of activist processes and goals. In relation to the young women's anti-violence project, worker power was used to: facilitate a critical reflection process through which participants developed new understandings and possibilities for action in relation to their vulnerability to violence; reinforce respect for participants' lived knowledge; manage the tensions between maximizing participation and achieving project outcomes; convey technical knowledge to participants. However, because of the equation of power with domination in critical practice theories, even the forms of power which activist approaches mandate and rely upon remain largely unarticulated.

In its celebration of differences, the work of poststructural theorists such as Cixous raises questions about the radical egalitarian claim that differences, such as the unequal distribution of skills, are inevitably correlated to an unequal distribution of power (see Phillips, 1991, p. 128). An egalitarian position that promotes sharing of skills and roles has merit for extending democracy and empowerment to excluded groups. Yet, by establishing standards for which any sign of difference becomes a threat to equity, radical egalitarianism is an ideal which is unreachable and which has undesirable effects for activist practice processes.

The premium placed on the overcoming of power differences in radical egalitarianism can lead workers to minimize the differences that remain and that are intrinsic to worker/researcher roles. Even when workers seek an equal relation with the service user, they are still bound by other professional, organizational and personal obligations, which shape the achievement of egalitarian ideals. In so far as the ideal of radical egalitarianism impedes workers from acknowledging these tensions in their practice, it contributes to exploitation and confusion for service users about the nature of their relationship with the service worker (Healy and

Young Mothers for Young Women, 1996). Reinharz (1993, p. 74) argues for relations of respect, shared information, openness and clarity of communication in place of the excessive and cynical demands for rapport found in some approaches to critical research and practice.

When the ideal of egalitarianism is coupled with notions of mutuality and trust it places unrealistic demands on both workers and service users. Such an ideal is problematic given the historical involvement of human services in the dispossession of oppressed populations. Service users are, quite rightly, wary of claims to an egalitarian ethos in the context of service workers' continuing access to technologies of power (such as tools of assessment) and official power which can be used to extend domination over them (Healy and Young Mothers for Young Women, 1996; Solas, 1996).

Without an appreciation of differences as part of equity, the radical egalitarian stance can contribute to patronizing and frustrating processes as those with advanced skills or abilities in a particular area are encouraged to camouflage them (Phillips, 1991, p. 129). Yet, as these differences become increasingly obvious to participants in the change process, it is easy for participants in a supposedly egalitarian context to feel duped and thus distrustful of the activist process (Healy and Peile, 1995). In addition, through concealing the skills and abilities of members, the activist process may be deprived of the important resources these differences can offer to the change process.

Finally, when the radical egalitarian stance is combined with a structural critique of power it contributes to a non-political practice of *ressentiment* rather than to transformation of relations of domination (Yeatman, 1997). The structural analysis fixes power to identities and so leads to a view of power as the possession of individuals who are privileged in structural terms; that is, middle class males, white and able bodied. This conflation of power and identity can lead political practice away from an emphasis on understanding how relations of domination are sustained and can be contested to a focus on attacking those who are associated with power and who are, therefore, evil (Tapper, 1993). As Gatens (1996) observes, 'The "good–bad" morality . . . locates the value – goodness or badness – in the object or class rather than in the relation between the object or class' (p. 129). One practical implication of the politics of *ressentiment* is that it defers responsibility for change to the powerful, who must be coerced into forgoing their power to the powerless. It also places the powerful in a precarious position, as the failure to achieve the highly utopian ideals of radical egalitarianism is attributed to the unwillingness of the 'powerful' to share power. Thus the ideal itself is sealed from contest.

Poststructural theory destabilizes the opposition between dominance and egalitarianism to reveal the coercive and the productive capacities of power. Yet, even in recognizing the positive effects of power, activists must hold to the critical social work insights about the links between social care and the practices of control. For example, in advanced Western countries, social work, like all human service occupations, has been implicated in the dispossession of people from their lands, from their families and from other basic human rights. It is vital that critical practice strategies contest the enormous disadvantages to which service users are subjected in contexts of practice and beyond them.

At the same, the poststructural recognition of the inevitable presence of power in all relationships, including human service relationships, can facilitate more humane and just practices *in the full knowledge* of the exercise of power that social work entails. Similarly, in contrast to the radical egalitarian equation of equity with sameness, poststructural theories support practices which celebrate diverse experiences, abilities and talents. From a poststructural perspective, equity is not opposed to difference but rather requires the 'recognition and inclusion of differences' (Scott, 1994, p. 297). In this view, differences, including differences in power, are not necessarily considered to be a threat to equity; rather, what matters most is how these differences are acknowledged and managed.

Power/knowledge in activist social work

Critical practice theories draw on critical social science assumptions, which locate power in overarching social structures and attach it to privileged subject positions, such as the advantaged position of the expert. By contrast, for Foucault, power and knowledge are inseparable. Foucault (1980b) insists that, 'it is not possible for power to be exercised without knowledge, it is impossible for knowledge not to engender power' (p. 52). In this section, I will consider the implications of the power/knowledge nexus for apprehending knowledge and power in social work generally and in its activist forms in particular.

Technical knowledge and power in social work

In a wide variety of critical social work theories and in the work of Foucault (1981a, 1991a) the helping professions, including social work, are implicated in the processes of domination. According to Foucault, the social sciences, on which the helping professions rely, have enabled the surveillance and disciplining of marginalized populations. Foucault (1980e, p. 82) and the radical poststructural feminists (see Grosz, 1990, p. 169) have argued that these scientific truth claims have served to marginalize non-rational and bodily forms of knowledge and ways of knowing. In addition, helping professions contribute to the domination of clients through processes of normalization. According to White and Epston (1990), helping professionals rely on certain scientific truth claims which 'are "normalizing" in the sense that they construct norms around which persons are incited to shape or constitute their lives' (p. 20). In the position of expert, social workers categorize and objectify service users and so extend discipline and surveillance over them (Howe, 1994).

Foucault's argument about the depowering effects of expert knowledge is doubtlessly an important one. However, its direct application to the diverse practices and knowledge bases of social workers is limited. In this analysis, I have critiqued the assumptions on which the Foucauldian critique of professional knowledge is based. First, I have argued that technical knowledge is not necessarily inconsistent with other ways of knowing; rather, what matters is whether this knowledge is used to extend the justice and humanity of social services or to confine it. In discussing the operations of worker power in the context of the young women's anti-violence project in Chapter 5, I showed that my co-worker and I often drew on and integrated the life experiences of the participants in exercising professional or technical knowledge. Similarly, the use of technical knowledge enabled the project group to produce an analysis rather than merely a description of young mothers' experiences of violence. This was important to the project group's aim of being taken seriously by professionals and bureaucrats, and in the longer run it helped to protect participants from the prying eyes of human service professionals, community and media about the individual experiences of the young women who participated in the project. Thus, while I acknowledge that professional knowledge can be used for dominatory purposes, professional knowledge can also take the form of a 'non-elitist expertise' which can be deployed for the purposes of 'serving and advancing the emancipatory demands for economic and social justice' of oppressed populations (Leonard, 1995, p. 15).

Second, the technical knowledge base is vulnerable to contest by other professionals and service users because of the perceived non-technical character of much social work activity. Indeed, in the activist practice context discussed in Chapters 5 and 6, the participants adopted an ambivalent attitude towards the 'technical' knowledge of my co-worker and me (see Chapter 5). In the context of the extensive consciousness raising that had occurred in the group, the participants articulated a strong critique of social services. This critique, which alluded to the perceived nature of social work practice as a non-technical or relational discipline, meant the knowledge of social workers was evaluated by participants in a different way from other forms of professional knowledge. Thus, even in the context of an extensive critique of social service workers, participants continued to value forms of professional knowledge they considered highly technical and necessary to the achievement of professional tasks, such as the provision of birthing services or education. The flaw in the critique of social workers as professional experts, found in both Foucauldian and critical social workers' accounts, is that in conflating social workers with other forms of modern human service practice it fails to account for the significant differences amongst the forms of power/knowledge to which these professions have access.

Critical perspectives and power/knowledge

While Foucault's notion of power/knowledge has been extensively used to explore traditional professional relations, its application to activist practices remains underdeveloped. Even as they critique the power of social workers, activists frequently represent themselves as contestants of the status quo (see Maguire, 1987; DeMaria, 1993; Fals-Borda, 1994). The critical discourses from which they speak are advanced as free of the investments of power that characterize social work and social research practices. Poststructural theory challenges this claim to a space of innocence by pointing to the relations of truth and power integral to the discourses of scientists and revolutionaries alike. Indeed, in some contexts of practice, policy making and social work education it is the critical discourses of activists that are hegemonic, 'official' and 'powerful' (Leonard, 1994, p. 16). Self-reflexivity is enhanced through the realization that all discourses, including critical practice theories, must be subject to critical interrogation of the forms of power discourses they effect. Foucault (1980d) asserts that: 'It is not a matter of emancipating truth from every system of power . . . but of detaching the power of truth from the forms of hegemony . . . within which it operates at the present time' (p. 133).

Poststructural theory calls into question not only the technical truths of the professional expert but also the critical truths of the activists (see Rojek et al., 1988; Leonard, 1996). From a poststructural perspective, claims to universal emancipatory insight and knowledge can reproduce the very processes of domination that activist practice is orientated towards overcoming (Leonard, 1995, p. 7). Cixous proposes that:

> the revolutionary himself [sic] can be a seducer. The discourse of seduction does not help people. Cixous questions both the politician and the revolutionary whose seductive discourse and lust for power are contrasted with the suffering of the people. (Conley, 1992, pp. 29–30)

Poststructural theory suggests that the discourses of liberation do not exist outside power. Indeed, these discourses can have oppressive effects. Ironically, these discourses can be used to accord power to their speakers, such as the revolutionary, whilst having little benefit for those whom the discourses claim to represent.

Critical truths can obscure participants' knowledge and resources for change just as traditional professional practice approaches have done. Although activists criticize the arrogance of professional practices, they too suppress differences in their own critical certainties about 'what kind of power is needed by the people, what constitutes their just interests' (Rahnema, 1990, p. 205). For example, in this analysis I have shown how the practice in which some critical social workers engage of labelling traditional ideas about motherhood as conservative glosses over the use of these ideas for the purposes of resistance. By drawing attention to the local effects of discursive practices, poststructuralism allows us to revalue the acts of resistance that are rendered invisible by the truth claims of the critical social sciences. Kingfisher (1996) observes that the reference to conservative ideas, 'may be construed as conservative in that it partakes of dominant views; but insofar as dominant views are appropriated for subversive purposes, this practice may be construed as resistance' (p. 541).

Critical social science perspectives silence through privileging rational ways of knowing. A fundamental assumption of the consciousness raising processes is that rational self-conscious thought will translate to transformed action. This emphasis on rationality minimizes the effects of things such as irrationality, traditions and social or institutional roles on activity. Fay (1987) acknowledges that:

> Certain of our inheritances are so deeply a part of who we are that it is psychologically naive to think that we can regard them with an objective eye, ready to discard them, when 'reason' shows them to be deficient. (p. 162)

The innumerable examples attesting to the dominatory and authoritarian actions of 'progressive' activists and educators (see hooks, 1994, p. 18) should of themselves be sufficient to urge greater caution in the claims about the emancipatory effects of critical awareness. Furthermore, there is potential also for critical ideals to contribute to individual blame in so far as they suppress the contradictions and complexities that continue even in the context of enhanced critical knowledge. For instance, in Chapter 6 I argued that the forging of collective and critical consciousness among the young women in the anti-violence project contributed to their sense of failure about those aspects of their lives that deviated from the ideals of strength, independence and defiance that had been fostered throughout the project.

To dismantle the critical truth claims of the activists is not to argue for the complete abandonment of critical social science analyses or the activist strategies that have been developed from them. Indeed, in the analysis (in Chapter 6), I have demonstrated that the critical perspectives did serve to disrupt some of the silences in the young women's lives. Rather, from a poststructural perspective it becomes necessary to adopt a sceptical stance towards the emancipatory claims of activists. Thus rather than *the* Truth, these perspectives become *a* truth, one set of a myriad of possibilities for working towards social transformation.

Lived experience and power/knowledge

Critical social work theory and poststructural perspectives emphasize the importance of developing dialogue in which people relate to one another as subjects rather than objects (see Alcoff, 1991, p. 23). Poststructural theory, however, contests the critical standpoint position suggesting that oppressed people experience enhanced access to truth by virtue of their marginalized social location (Harding, 1987, p. 26; Swigonski, 1993, p. 173). In the work of Foucault and the radical poststructural feminists there is recognition that all knowledge, including the lived experiences of oppression, is a function of discourse, so it is implicated in the operations of power.

By challenging the opposition between professional knowledge and lived experience in critical practice, poststructural theory can extend our understanding of the operations of power and knowledge in the local contexts of activist practice. Far from being innocent of the operations of professional power, lived experience can be used to extend professional power. For example, in Chapter 5 I showed that in the context of the young women's anti-violence project, my co-worker and I would sometimes use our knowledge of the participants' lived experience, gained over the course of the project, to challenge statements made by them. Often this was positive use of power in so far as we challenged negative or self-blaming statements through reference to examples of their own previously expressed understandings and action. Yet, the knowledge of the participant/service user can serve as a justification for suppressive forms of power, such as when activists claim their practices represent the true interests of oppressed people.

A second problem is that the dualistic representation of professional knowledge and lived experience can have non-dialogic effects (Gross, 1995, p. 211). While there are gains to be made in privileging lived experience, particularly when the voices of the marginalized have been long silenced, poststructuralism also points out that the mere inversion of a binarism between professional knowledge and lived experience keeps the opposition in place. The dualism suppresses insights that both workers and participants can bring to the processes of change. For example, to accord lived experience an unquestionable privilege can be to minimize alternative perspectives based on other knowledge sources (Alcoff, 1991, p. 17; Gross, 1995, p. 208). In addition, the reference to lived experience as though it is a unified category suppresses differences within it, so that the expression of experiences that do not conform to certain beliefs or images are marginalized. For example, in her well crafted discussion of critical practice with American Indians, Gross (1995) points out that unified representations of American Indian identity have, in some instances, suppressed the experiences of gay and lesbian indigenous Americans.

Poststructural theory challenges the search for knowledge that is innocent of the operations of power. This school of theory can be used to destabilize the opposition between professional knowledge and lived experience and to support practices which value the diverse contributions of both workers and service users (Fine and MacPherson, 1992, p. 201; Gross, 1995, p. 212; see also Pozatek, 1994, p. 402). Given the historical privilege accorded to the professional's voice, it is important that activists adopt a position of ongoing self-reflexivity in relation to their knowledge claims, including critical truths, as they seek to enter into dialogue with 'clients' or participants. Critical poststructural theory can support the development of critical and dynamic dialogues between service workers and service users based on an ongoing scrutiny of the knowledge that both bring to the practices of change.

Deconstructing the powerful worker and the powerless client

Activist social workers claim to reveal the 'true' nature of the identities of workers and service users and the relationship between them through extracting one aspect of identity (that of 'social workers' and 'service users') and basing all truth claims on it. Whilst this makes for a seamless and powerful critique of social work, it does little for apprehending the complexities and instabilities of identity and power in the everyday practices of social work. By contrast, poststructural theory shows us that critical discourses also constitute the entities they describe (Rojek, et al., 1988, p. 137). By tearing open the dualistic representation of workers and service users, poststructural theory allows more complex understandings of identities to emerge. One of the advantages of this approach is that it extends activist understanding about how workers and service users variously occupy the categories of 'powerful' and 'powerless' that critical social work theories have assigned to them.

Poststructuralism destabilizes the opposition between the 'powerful' worker and the 'powerless' service user by drawing attention to differences amongst subjects in their occupation of these categories. At one level, these identity categories are mediated by class, gender and race processes. It is important to recognize the influences of these processes without ontologizing them; that is, without making essentialist claims about them. For example, according to the critical literature, dialogical communication can only be achieved by the worker's willingness to step down from the hierarchical power relations that are considered to be a hallmark of professional power. Instead, workers must encourage service users to adopt a questioning stance towards them (see Leonard, 1995, pp. 10–12; see also Moreau, 1979, 1990). This approach to dialogue ignores that women, including women in high status professions such as medicine, have less access than male professionals to hierarchical forms of power, and that they are frequently subject to questions about their competence (see West, 1984, 1995). Ironically, in so far as the representations of power and authority are isolated from the differences amongst those who occupy the category of worker, both in terms of other identifications and work roles, they can reinforce discriminatory attitudes about some groups, such as women in the public sphere. Moreover, by ignoring the wide variety of sources of status within the general category of worker, the general critique of the professional power can leave the authority of others, such as men, privileged women or those in technical and high status occupations relatively untouched.

Yet, to point to differences in the occupation of identity categories, such as the 'powerful worker', is not to claim that these differences are uniform. Indeed, we need only to look at female leaders like the former British Prime Minister, Margaret Thatcher, to find a spectacular exception to typical differences amongst men and women in positions of official power (see Holmes, 1995; West, 1995). However, the recognition of general patterns of differences offers a profound challenge to the unified categories on which critical practice theories depend.

Poststructural theory further undermines the unified representations of the 'powerful worker' and the 'powerless service user' by drawing attention to the influence of local contexts and social practices on the ways in which individuals occupy these categories. In this analysis, I have challenged the equation between professional identity and power by showing that differences between my co-worker and me impacted on our access to and exercise of power. For example, my co-worker's status as a mother was a significant source of esteem and inclusion for her. Similarly, there were other points of commonality between the young women and me, such as my youth (I was only a few years older than some of the participants) and our shared experiences and interests that influenced my access to authority, both in enabling and constraining ways. Conversely, the value accorded to lived experience as a site of knowledge meant that my professional status was viewed ambivalently, commanding both respect and ridicule within the practice context.

The representation of the 'powerless service user' has also been subject to a growing chorus of discontent in recent years. This image is contested on the grounds that it downplays the capacities and the potential of individuals to resist domination and effect change (see McRobbie, 1991, p. 232; Crinnall, 1995, p. 45). Wearing (1996) argues that social structural explanations are limited for understanding local practices of resistance such as those she observed in her research:

> Australian women were resisting male domination at the micro social level, but the structuralist theoretical analysis construed such resistance as ineffectual, merely the result of false consciousness which located responsibility with the individual for lack of access to material resources. Yet such theoretical analysis was breeding a victim mentality which perpetuated subordination at an individual level. (pp. 32–3)

The deferment of analysis and action to overarching social structures devalues everyday practices of resistance. By destabilizing the unified categories of the powerful worker and the powerless service user, critical poststructural theories can reveal the potential for even relatively powerless people to participate in change. This involves a diversification of activist practice to include recognition of the capacities and potential of service users to act for their own empowerment.

Just as the representation of the 'powerless' participant has ignored the forms of power that service users exercise for change, it has also suppressed discussion of the exercise of dominatory power by relatively powerless people (Yeatman, 1997). The absence of discussion about the use of dominatory power amongst service users has significantly constrained the development of critical practices relevant to contexts involving the confrontation of such power. For example, feminist social work theory has been limited by the reticence of many feminist theorists to acknowledge violence by women (Featherstone and Fawcett, 1994; FitzRoy, 1997). Similarly, the proliferation of literature on working with the victims of violence is matched by a paucity of understanding about how to work progressively with the perpetrators of it, other than to minimize their responsibility for the exercise of the dominatory power. The failure to grapple with the use of dominatory power amongst service users has impeded the development of practice theories open to the complexities and contradictions about power and powerlessness that social workers must deal with in their everyday practices.

As critical post theories destabilize activist understandings of power and identity, operations of power that were previously unthinkable are revealed. The Foucauldian account of the complexity and contextual variance in the operations of power allows that even relatively powerless people, such as service users, may in some instances exercise power in relation to powerful others, such as service workers. Featherstone and Fawcett (1994) use this insight in their discussion of statutory family work, as they write:

> The recognition that mothers occupy a range of power positions which shift would enable an appreciation that they might be victims in one situation, for example in relation to their husbands, but in relation to the social worker or their children, they may be in a position of some power for a variety of reasons. They can therefore be both victim and victimiser and these positions themselves shift; for example, children grow up, agency policies change. (p. 75)

The recognition of the capacities of service users to exercise power both for their own empowerment and for domination is an issue that must be dealt with sensitively and cautiously. A critical appraisal of this power can only occur in the full recognition of the domination to which service users have been subjected by human services, both historically and contemporarily. By resisting the local relations of practice as more than an effect of structural forces, poststructuralism enables a fuller disclosure of the operations of power in practice than has been possible in the critical tradition alone.

Beyond the heroic activist

The work of feminist poststructural theorists highlights and contests the implicitly phallocentric assumptions on which modernist socio-political theories rest (see Lloyd, 1986, 1989; Gatens, 1992). The phallocentricism of these theories lies in their representation of those forms of power and agency available to the most privileged members of identity categories as though they were the norm. This limits understanding of the complex and often multiple positions of social actors who are 'other' to the most privileged individuals, even as they adopt 'powerful' roles. The critique of phallocentric representations is important for opening critical social work theories, including feminist theories, to differences within the identity category of human service worker.

One illustration of the phallocentric character of activist discourses is the representation of the activist workers as disembodied and heroic actors who stand outside the systems of power and speak the truth to them. This representation is dependent on a conception of agency as the rational, self-controlled activity of the individual (B. Davies, 1991, p. 42). For instance, activists are distinguished from orthodox workers by their willingness to rationally recognize systemic injustices and their preparedness to take a stand against the established order. DeMaria (1993) writes that:

> While the latter [the radicals] hold nothing sacred except their commitment, the former [the orthodox] still accept the unspoken, unreflected values of liberal capitalism including the twin cults of individualism and reformism. (p. 51)

By privileging the rational and heroic stance of individual workers, activist practice theories are premised on a conception of agency that is most relevant to those positioned powerfully across discourses (Benson, discussed in B. Davies, 1991, p. 44). The representation of the heroic activist is limited for understanding diverse and inconspicuous forms of activism. For in the majority of settings in which social workers act, agency is less a matter of standing out from the crowd in a heroic way than engaging in social change activities through the local networks and systems of which they are a part.

The heroic activist is a deeply gendered representation which is of limited relevance to the activism of those who are Other to the white, middle class and able-bodied male, and for those who are located in positions of limited authority within their organizational contexts. From a radical poststructural perspective it can be argued that these representations offer social workers, the majority of whom are women and many of whom experience Other identifications, two choices. Firstly, the worker can adopt the phallocentric terms of activist discourses; that is, to situate herself as powerful. For although modern feminist social work discourses recognize the shared gender oppression of service workers and service users, the class, professional and institutional status is considered to entirely overcome this commonality (see Rojek et al., 1988, ch. 3; see also E. Wilson, 1977; Dominelli and McLeod, 1989). Rojek et al. (1988) summarize this position thus, 'becoming a social worker changes you; to be "professional" you must often forget that you are a woman' (p. 113). From a radical poststructural feminist perspective, 'forgetting' one's gender is impossible, as this identification remains even in the presence of other identities, such as those of worker or service user (B. Davies, 1991, p. 43). It is questionable whether this representation of the powerful individual is relevant even to social workers and administrators who are privileged in structural terms, in so far as their access to power is also structured through processes and contexts in addition to identity. Gatens (1990) writes in questioning modern representations of power that: 'This house is proving to be inadequate shelter even for the purposes of sheltering its original architects' (p. 10).

The other option the dualistic representation provides is to identify oneself as entirely powerless. Thus, the worker can refuse to acknowledge power differences between themselves and their client. Indeed, this position is aligned with the identity politics that particularly characterized activist writings of feminist social workers active in the late 1970s. From this position, the worker and client were understood to share a basic gender identity and hence activist practice was developed around the 'commonalities' of being women (Hanmer and Statham, discussed in Rojek et al. 1988, p. 98). However, a poststructural approach does not aim for the occlusion of power differences, such as those between worker and service user. Rather, poststructuralism challenges activists to understand how power relations are discursively and multi-constructed within specific contexts, particularly specific practice contexts.

The work of radical poststructural feminists challenges the unified representations of the heroic activist. For them, the body is a signifier enabling certain kinds of identification and prohibiting others. Thus, even though bodily and other differences amongst workers remain unspoken in activist discourses and in the practice context, they are not simply shed as worker and client identities are outwardly adopted (see Gatens, 1991, 1992, 1996). The representations of social workers as 'powerful' and 'authoritative' fails to adequately recognize that workers who are women, indigenous people, disabled people, and so forth, occupy an ambivalent space within this phallocentric imagery.

If the activist canon is to be open to the multiple identifications and obligations of service workers, then it is necessary to develop conceptualizations of agency beyond that associated with the heroic individual. B. Davies (1991) offers a post-structural rethinking of the concept of agency that may be useful for recognizing differences amongst service workers and service users as they shape activist practices. B. Davies (1991) argues that:

> To conceive of agency once the male/female dualism is abandoned is to think of speaking subjects aware of different ways in which they are made subject, who take up the act of *author*ship, of speaking and writing in ways that are disruptive of current discourses, that inverts, invents and breaks old bonds, that creates new subject positions that do not take their meaning from the genitalia (and what they have come to signify) of the incumbent. (p. 50)

This approach to agency recognizes the embeddedness of action (and activism) within specific contexts of practice. The multiplication of definitions of agency allows that one may have access to some forms of agency and yet might be denied others. Thus, rather than see the activist as someone who stands outside the system and speaks the truth to it, activists are recognized as being embedded in the systems which both constrain and enable them to achieve progressive change.

The questioning of the heroic individual as the epitome of the activist social worker can open the activist canon to recognizing the diverse ways in which social workers in front line service roles (roles which are typically occupied by women) contribute to activism. For example, evidence from feminist discourse analytic research suggests that women typically demonstrate communication abilities such as a strong capacity for active listening and an orientation towards egalitarian communication processes (Fishman, 1983; Goodwin, 1988; West, 1995). Similarly, in her study of social workers in aged care, Opie (1995, p. 48) found that amongst the social workers she interviewed it was the experienced front line female practitioners who were best able to understand and respond to the complex and conflicting needs of service users and service organizations. While these practices are highly consistent with activist social work processes, the value these different contributions can make to activist practice is often questioned (see Mowbray, 1992). Yet, if activist practice theories are to recognize the diverse contributions social workers can make to activism it is important that we tear open the oppositions, such as that between hero and the conformist or structural and local changes, which have served to render these differences invisible.

Strategies for change

In contrast to the emphasis on the social totality that underpins activist analysis and action, poststructural theory assumes that social realities are 'unstable, complex and disorderly' (Flax, quoted in Ang, 1995, p. 67). This view contests the grand and utopian visions of change and replaces them with political practices that are anti-utopian and anti-dogmatic. As Leonard (1995) asserts, 'The embracing of diversity does not necessarily imply the end of mass emancipatory politics, but that it takes a more exploratory, pragmatic turn' (p. 14). In this section, I will discuss the implications of poststructural theory for rethinking change strategies advocated within activist social work theory, specifically processes of consciousness raising and collective action.

Rethinking consciousness raising

Poststructural theory challenges the premises of established critical practice strategies. From a poststructural perspective, the practice of consciousness raising is contested on the grounds that it:

- dictates what counts as 'conservative' and 'activist' in accordance with critical social science understandings and in so doing devalues local understandings and practices of resistance;
- promotes intolerance of differences in so far as the alternative perspectives, even those advanced by oppressed people, are readily dismissed as evidence of false consciousness;

- privileges rational ways of knowing and acting, thus downplaying the myriad of factors, including irrationality and local contexts, that impinge on human activity.

In its valuing of pragmatic and localized approaches to activism, poststructuralism encourages the retention of critical practice strategies such as consciousness raising, whilst opening these practices to critique. In this way, poststructural theory renews appreciation of local complexities and contradictions rather than view them as impediments to change. B. Davies (1994) asserts that:

> Understanding the political work that each discourse makes it possible to achieve, enables each person to access a range of speaking positions, to see the contradictions as inherent in the discourses rather than in themselves. While consistency and total coherence are pleasurable and satisfying, they involve a large degree of selective perception and ignorance: we need to live with contradictory discourses because we live in a profoundly contradictory world with multiple and contradictory positions and discourses which go to make up that world. (p. 35)

The inclusion of critical social science perspectives as a resource permits the important political work these ideas allow, whilst also acknowledging the limits of any singular perspective, critical or otherwise, to provide total guidance in the compromised and contradictory practices of change.

Poststructural theory compels activists to 'examine our assumptions about social justice, equality, and rationality in the light of our critique of the eurocentricism and androcentricism of modernist thinking' (Leonard, 1994, p. 15). From this perspective there can be no transcendent programme of change; rather, one must be prepared to articulate and interrogate the perspectives that are used within practices of change. The reflexivity toward critical perspectives demanded by poststructural theory should not be taken to imply an indifferent attitude towards questions of justice. However, it becomes necessary to consider the local implications of activist social work discourses, including the local knowledge and actualities of resistance and change obscured by these perspectives.

Rethinking collective identification and action

Poststructural theory calls into question the identity politics involving the formation of collective and oppositional identities. In this process the oppressed recognize their shared identifications and their shared interest in overcoming unjust social conditions. While many poststructural theorists concerned with emancipatory politics recognize the political potency of collective and oppositional identifications, they also raise questions about this approach to contestation. De Lauretis (quoted in Sawicki, 1991) observes that, 'identity formation is both strategically necessary and dangerous' (p. 108).

The formation of collective identifications is strategically necessary in the sense that it affords collective power. For if the poststructural emphasis on fragmentation is followed to its logical end, it means that one can never make claims beyond that of one's lived experience (Alcoff, 1991, p. 17). This runs the risk of fragmenting the shared political concerns of marginalized people. Yet, notwithstanding the strategic utility of collective identification and action for according power to marginalized people, these practices are also dangerous. The problem lies in the belief that identities, which are the foundation stone of collective politics, refer to fixed and stable essences. In order for this belief to be sustained it is necessary to suppress differences amongst those so identified. For example, over the past quarter of a century, women who are Other to the white, privileged, able-bodied heterosexual woman have contested the representations and interest which have dominated feminist theory and activism (see Hill-Collins, 1990; Asch and Fine, 1992). Ang (1995) asserts that for many women, 'other interests, other identifications are sometimes more important and politically pressing than, or even incompatible with, those relating to their being a woman' (p. 73).

Critical poststructural theorists have argued that identities are a product and conduit of power. This perspective suggests a cautious approach to the adoption of collective identifications in so far as through them modern practices of surveillance and discipline occur (Butler, 1995). Gatens (1996) contests the uncritical use of unified notions of sexual difference; she writes: 'to insist on sexual difference as the fundamental and eternally immutable difference would be to take for granted the intricate and pervasive ways in which patriarchal culture has made that difference its insignia' (p. 73).

Social theorists have used poststructural ideas to question the transformative potential of collective identification. Some point to the connection between an emphasis on identification and the development of a politics of *ressentiment* in which the focus is on attacking identities rather than on identifying and transforming social practices (see Tapper, 1993; Brown, 1995; Pringle, 1995; Gatens, 1996; Yeatman, 1997). Because power is equated with evil and powerlessness with innocence, this approach weakens the opportunity for mass political action. The politics of *ressentiment* has the contradictory effects of extending citizenship by enabling marginalized people to make a claim to representation in public policy and resource allocation, whilst confining individuals to speak from the position of outsider, victim or contestant of the established order of things.

The insights of critical poststructural theory can be used to prise open the assumptions on which the collective strategies of critical social work are based, without jettisoning these strategies altogether. Poststructural theory destabilizes shared and essential identifications as a foundation for action; for there is 'no collective movement that can speak for each of us, all the way through' (Rich, quoted in Pratt, 1993, p. 57). Mass action remains possible, though; because shared political interests can never be taken for granted, the ongoing negotiation of differences becomes a necessary feature of large-scale political action (Yeatman, 1993).

Critical cautions about post theories

Throughout this book, I have emphasized the potential contribution of recent 'post' theories to the disruption and diversification of activist social work. Yet, whatever uses critical post theories have for democratizing and diversifying critical social work practices, they should not be expected to provide a total alternative. In the absence of the insights that have emerged through critical social work theory, 'post' theories can contribute to some very uncritical practice directions, which I will outline here.

Maintaining a tension between the symbolic and the material

The first concern is that the poststructural emphasis on language and on the symbolic can elide the material realities of disadvantage. An important lesson of post-structuralism is that the local is more than an effect of the structural, and hence the broad overarching frameworks of critical social science are viewed as blunt instruments for understanding and action upon local experiences of power, identity and the practices of change. As Barrett (1992) asserts: 'Foucault challenged the familiar hierarchy of values of the materialist perspective, counterposing the dumb existence of reality with the ability of groups of signs [discourses] to act as "practices that systematically form the objects of which they speak"' (p. 202).

Even so, in the contemporary contexts of increasing material inequities, activists cannot turn their backs on the material experiences of poverty, sexism and racism (Hewitt, 1993; Taylor-Gooby, 1993; Leonard, 1995). Thus, critical social science theories in their emphasis on analysis categories of 'class', 'gender' and 'race' continue to provide important analytic and strategic resources for understanding and responding to disadvantage (Sands and Nuccio, 1992, p. 493). While post theories alert us to the limitations of claims of critical social science theories, at this point in the history of social work these perspectives continue to provide insights relevant to activist practices. To insist that activists must choose between post-structuralism and critical social science theories as a foundation for practice is to establish an unnecessary dualism between the two. Neither the critical post theories discussed in this book nor the critical social science ideas that have long provided a foundation for activism can provide insights or can provide total guides to activism. However, both can provide insights useful to understanding and responding to the interplay between the structural and the symbolic in the genesis of social disadvantage.

Acknowledging relations of domination

A second concern is that the poststructural reconceptualization of power as flexible, multifarious and contextually variable obscures those forms of power that are fixed and dominatory. For example, recently some feminist theorists have used the insights of critical poststructuralism to question the representations of victimhood in the feminist literature (see Crinnall, 1995; Pringle, 1995; Wearing, 1996). Using a Foucauldian analysis of power, it is argued that one actively participates in and gains power through the practices through which one is also oppressed (Bartky, 1988). Pringle's (1995) claim that 'Women actively produce the forms of femininity through which they are controlled: they are never merely victims' (p. 207), demands a radical rethinking of feminist analysis and action.

In this analysis, I have argued that poststructuralism compels activists to move beyond dualistic representations of the powerful and powerless and to recognize the complexities and contextual variability in the operations of power. However, I also recognize that there is considerable danger in relinquishing notions of victimhood and domination altogether. For example, although the young women who participated in the anti-violence project (discussed in Chapters 5 and 6) did exercise power in a range of contexts, there were forms of domination, such as acts of serious violence, that they were powerless to contest. Critical poststructural theories are useful for activism in so far as they expose the fiction and, indeed, the paralysing effects of an embrace of victimhood as the entire definition of an individual or a population. Yet, alongside the recognition of the limits of the identity of victim there must be room to identify relations of domination that are unilateral and firmly entrenched. In other words, it is just as dangerous to say that one is never a victim as it is to say that one is always a victim.

An uncertain certainty

A third concern revolves around the political costs of the renunciation of truth and certainty of politics based on 'ambiguity, complexity and partiality' (Pratt, quoted in Pringle, 1995, p. 199). Activists are reluctant to make this shift, Leonard (1995) asserts that:

> To give up this claim to *general truth* in favour of a theory of difference, of the diverse concrete social experiences of specific populations, is a painful renunciation which strikes at the impulse to generalization which often lies at the heart of 'progressive' approaches to social welfare. (p. 7)

The poststructural embrace of uncertainty can draw attention to the complexities and tensions at the local levels of activist practices. This openness to local differences and visions for change can be used to contest the orthodoxies that have settled in critical practice theories. For example, in this analysis I have argued that poststructuralism does not necessarily lead to a jettisoning of critical perspectives, but rather to a recognition of truth claims and activist strategies beyond critical social science perspectives.

At the same time, the embrace of difference can lead to uncertainty of direction and political strategy (see Dixon, 1993; Fals-Borda, 1994; Kenny, 1994). This is a high price to pay in so far as certainty is a powerful base to contest the truths of dominant groups. Howe (1994) warns: 'There is an irony that pluralism's dispersal of centres of truth and its tolerance of the different values and meanings found in various cultural and intellectual groups is overridden by those who claim to possess *the* truth' (p. 526). In the pragmatic approach to political action that post-structuralism embraces, there may be ways of allowing for certainties in so far as these are recognized as having relevance for the specific time and space of the change process. This approach can accord the power that certainties permit, without requiring that particular truths will provide a permanent guide for practice even within a specific context of change.

Ethical framework and the limits to an openness to difference

A final concern is the failure of critical poststructural theorists to identify the limits of the celebration of differences and plurivocality that they espouse. For even as Foucault and Cixous emphasize the notion of difference, it is apparent that not all difference is acceptable to them. Cixous, for instance, is committed to the celebration of cultural differences, and hence the 'different' view of the colonist or expansionist receive scathing condemnation in her writing (see Cixous, 1981b, 1994a; Conley, 1992). In recent years, a number of theorists have sought to address the problem of articulating the ethical frameworks that mediate the emphasis on locality and difference in poststructural/postmodern political practices (see Gatens, 1996, p. 105; see also Yeatman, 1993, 1994). A feature of these discussions has been an emphasis on openness to reflection on and contest of these foundations within local contexts of practice. According to Yeatman (1993, p. 231) a politics of difference requires both an openness about ethical commitments and a willingness to argue for these values in a 'logically coherent manner' (p. 231). This reflexivity about one's ethical commitments is intended to enhance greater openness to differences than is possible in the critical tradition alone, and hence to increase the potential for partnerships between activists and oppressed populations (Gatens, 1996, p. 105).

Yet, despite some recent attempts to locate ethical practices consistent with a politics of difference, the boundaries of such practice are likely to remain obscure. The emphasis on opening one's values to reflection and debate privileges rational ways of knowing, as it advantages those who are most able to articulate their position. Thus, despite an apparent openness to voices of difference, this approach can reinforce existing power relations including relations of privilege and domination. In addition, rational claims to openness gloss over the limitations to subjecting one's knowledge to critical scrutiny. This is a significant weakness in so far as the values that guide political practice arise not only through rationality but also develop through other ways of knowing, such as emotional and bodily knowledge (Fay, 1987, p. 162), which are perhaps less accessible to rational reflection. As Barrett (1992) contends: 'political objectives are in an important sense constituted on the basis of values and principles . . . they cannot be grounded in a scientific social analysis but spring from aspiration rather than proof' (p. 217). Thus, although poststructuralism provides the possibilities for the scrutiny of one's political values, it is important to acknowledge that limitations to reflexivity remain.

Conclusion

During the 1990s, critical social work began to articulate the value of critical 'post' theories for extending activist analyses of social work (see Howe, 1994; Parton, 1994a). Yet, the post theories of Foucault and the radical poststructural feminist are also profoundly disruptive to the orthodoxies that have settled in critical social work. Critical post theories destabilize the taken-for-granted critical social science truth claims about power, identity and change. As the foundations of critical social work are undermined, the search for a critical core to practice is abandoned in favour of the recognition of the diversity of social work *practices*.

The critical insights of post theories can reopen critical social work theory to questions about who is activist and what should count as activist practices. They make possible forms of activism that do not necessarily conform to the critical social science claims through which progressive practice has been constituted. They also enable new approaches to theorizing in which those who experience social work practices, as social workers and as service users, can speak back to the certainties that have been unassailable in critical practice approaches. Yet, this does not imply the rejection of critical social science altogether, for these perspectives have continuing relevance for understanding and responding to contemporary formations of social disadvantage. In the anti-dogmatic and anti-utopian re-orientation of change practice, critical social science perspectives have a place as one of a myriad set of possibilities for change. By interrogating and repositioning the critical social science foundations of social work, critical post theories contribute to activist practices relevant to the multiple and conflicting obligations through which much human service work is constituted and to the diverse contexts where contemporary social work practices occur.

8   Conclusions

The inroads being made by 'post' theories into critical social analyses are but one of a series of contests that are shaking the foundations of critical social work practices. Esping-Andersen (1990) asserts that, we are 'leaving behind us a social order that was pretty much understood and entering another, the contours of which can only be dimly recognised' (p. 223). The welfare systems which, in the second half of the twentieth century, were taken-for-granted features of most industrialized countries, are being dismantled and reorganized in line with corporate ideologies. The capacity of modern social theories to explain social realities and to direct social action are profoundly challenged by these contemporary transformations.

Disrupting activism

We are witnessing the end of certain aspects of the projects of modernity, such as the belief in rationality, faith in grand plans, and intentions to explain the social whole. Yet these contests do not necessarily signal the demise of critical social work. Indeed, now as ever, critical social workers seek understanding and practice approaches to assist them in working alongside service users for progressive change. What *is* at issue is the status of critical social science concepts as 'articles of faith'; that is, as unspoken and unquestioned truths for guiding activism. The failure of critical social workers to acknowledge the constraining effects of these core assumptions has proven to be a major weakness for the diversification of critical practice approaches. For example, to this point, critical perspectives have contributed little to the articulation of understanding and strategy relevant to authoritarian organizational contexts and to many occupations where the overt use of power is an unavoidable aspect of the social worker's role (see Healy, 1998; see also Clark, 1998). Indeed, critical social science ideals confine understanding of operations of power, identity and change processes even within those practice contexts that are most consistent with activist ideals; that is, small, non-bureaucratic practice contexts (see Healy and Mulholland, 1998).

At this point in the history of critical social work, post theories can make crucial interventions into the conventions of critical social work. Through destabilizing critical certainties, these interventions can reopen the activist canon to questions such as: What is the nature of power and identity in social work practices? When are social work practices activist and when are they conservative or orthodox? When are specific actions 'acts of resistance and when are they simply acts of accommodation?' (Cobb, quoted in Kingfisher, 1996, p. 531). Post theories challenge the assumption, central to activist social work, that the answers to these questions lie in critical social science theories, and lead instead to a recognition of the importance of context in defining processes of power, identity and change.

Reconstructing critical approaches

The impulses of critical post theories are not only destabilizing but also constructive for critical social work practices. Critical post theories invite activists to recognize the importance of historical and local contexts in shaping activism, rather than as something to be overcome. These contemporary theoretical insights make it possible to imagine, articulate and practice activisms that extend and even confound critical social work orthodoxies. In place of grand plans and utopian ideals, social work activism takes a pragmatic turn focused on local, contextual and modest proposals for change. In this new pragmatism, activism continues to be orientated towards extending social citizenship within local contexts of practice and service users' lives through, for example, enabling resistance to oppressive practices, and fostering more just, humane and accountable approaches within the human services. Yet, the local contexts of practice, expectations and obligations upon service providers and aspirations of service users take centre-stage in determining the course of activism.

Although activists cannot afford to jettison critical social science ideals altogether, critical post theories can enhance reflexivity about the constraining effects of them. As the limits of critical social science ideas are exposed, activists are encouraged to look to sources of understanding and action in addition to them. In contrast to the reticence expressed by many activists towards post theories, in this book I have argued that the critical poststructural work of Foucault and the radical post-structural feminists can help to reconstruct emancipatory practice approaches. I have shown how their work is useful for destabilizing unitary practice concepts and for recreating critical social work practices premised on the complexity, instability and, most importantly, the contextual variability in processes of power, identity and change. Yet, the investigation can be taken further. The field has yet to adequately explore the opportunities provided by major contemporary social thinkers whose critical engagements with postmodern and poststructural ideas in relation to power, subjectivity and social citizenship are of relevance to the on-going transformation of critical social work. I speak here, in particular, of the work of Bourdieu, Derrida, Deleuze, Lacan, Lyotard, Rorty and feminist authors such as Grosz, Gatens, Kristeva, Irigaray and Le Doeuff. Of course, the investigation of contemporary social theories should be undertaken in a spirit of dialogue and debate. For too long social workers have been positioned as the handmaidens of the grand narratives of the social sciences and humanities. This monologue has suppressed the diverse insights that can be brought from other sites to extend and complicate the theories on which social work has relied.

A further source of insight for understanding and action in critical social work are local organizations and practices of social work. Despite a claim to praxis, that is the linking of theory and practice, surprisingly little critical social work theory is derived from practice based research. One consequence is that the activism of social workers and policy makers is hidden. For example, in her recent study of activism and social policy processes Yeatman (1998) observed that: 'My evaluation work deepened my impression that here is a type of activist work that has been relatively unrecognised: namely, the highly skilled, strategic and visionary commitment to public policy and public service' (p. 2).

Foucault (1980d) calls for ascending orders of analysis; that is, for analyses that begin with the detail of social practices. This focus on the detail of social practices encourages empirical researches, which are locally and historically situated, that extend and develop the potential of critical practices based on understandings of what social work 'is' (see, for example, Fook, 1996). In this book, I referred to information from two contexts of social work practice to analyse and develop critical social work ideas. I am aware that the contexts of my investigations are local and specific and thus no assumption can be made that other local contexts would reveal similar processes.

Much more critical practice research is needed into the local contexts of social work practices. The value of such empirical research lies in its potential contribution to the practice theories that are sufficiently flexible to accommodate the diversities of critical social work practices and that engage critically and productively with the dilemmas faced in contemporary human welfare practices. At the very least, these theories can encourage respect for the complexities inherent in the local contexts of social work practices. More ambitiously, the development of empirically based critical social work theories could assist workers and service users in the difficult and complex aspects of practice, such as the making of 'reasonable judgements in grey areas, where a wide range of professional and public opinion is encountered' (Clark, 1998, p. 397).

The emergence of broad based empirical research within the local organization of social work practices can enhance the sophistication and the relevance of critical practice theories, yet it is not a panacea. Not all aspects of practice can be articulated in terms of the discourses available to us. For example, change activity would seem, inevitably, to involve emotional and relational dimensions that are largely beyond the grasp of much current research methodology. There are dangers, also, that as social work enters an era of increasing accountability (Opie, 1995; Healy and Walsh, 1997), practice research can be employed for the surveillance of critical social work practices. This threat is greatest in organizations that are dominated by powerful and pervasive discourses such as biomedical or economic rationalist discourses. It may be that the lack of critical research into conventional practice settings has served a protective function in so far as activist social workers within these contexts have been shielded from particular forms of surveillance, whilst, of course, continuing to be subjected to others. The acts of making social work processes visible should be approached with some caution and with an ongoing reflexivity about the linkages between this project and the processes of governmentality to which social work practices in the postmodern era are increasingly subjected. As Foucault (1981a) warns, 'silence and secrecy are a shelter for power, anchoring its prohibitions; but they also loosen its holds and provide for relatively obscure areas of tolerance' (p. 101).

The dangers of activist practice research are real in many contemporary contexts of human service organization and need to be acknowledged alongside the potential benefits of critical practice research projects. The risks associated with practice research highlight the need for social workers themselves to be involved in this research, rather than for it be done externally by those who do not experience social work practice directly in a bodily and emotive way. The involvement of social workers may also assist them to understand and counteract (where possible) the potential for practice research to contribute to their increased surveillance. For example, practitioners could be involved in deciding what forms of information are 'safe' to circulate and what must, at least for the time being, remain relatively concealed.

Continuing challenges

In the current state of transformation in the theories and the organization of human welfare services there is much to be contested. Social workers concerned with developing critical service agendas must oppose the smug 'I told you it would never work' attitude that is fashionable amongst those unconcerned with progressive approaches to human welfare and which is being accorded increased legitimacy through the corporatization of welfare services. We are challenged also to move beyond the despair about the future of critical social work practices that seems to be engulfing many in the field. Although we must face squarely the limits of modern understandings to guide activism in the postmodern era, it is important that we also take pride in the rich tradition of critical social work practices.

We must resist an uncritical embrace of contemporary post theories. For although, as I have argued, these theories are useful to revaluing aspects of critical social work practices, such as the symbolic and the local dimensions, there are short-comings that should not be overlooked. Critical social work practices continue to be guided by political and ethical commitments, particularly to the extension of justice within practice contexts and beyond them. Given these concerns, we must exercise caution in relation to those aspects of post theorizing that evade the material dimensions of oppression and which lead to entirely relativist approaches to questions of social justice (Hewitt, 1993; Taylor-Gooby, 1993; Leonard, 1995). Yet, it is unhelpful and unnecessary to construct an opposition between the insights of critical social science and those of critical post theories. Indeed, in the pragmatism that flows from contemporary theoretical insights, activists are encouraged to 'think around'; that is, to investigate a wide range of perspectives to find what is useful for understanding and acting justly in relation to specific practice issues (Gibson-Graham, 1996). Thus we can acknowledge the important political work that critical social science makes possible whilst also benefiting from the understandings that critical post theories allow. At this point in the history of critical social work, the insights of both schools are needed to recognize the material and the symbolic dimensions of social practices.

Key understandings of critical post theories hold out a promise of increased reflexivity and openness to differences in social work practices (Parton and

Marshall, 1998). Yet, if this potential is to be realized there is much in the current post theorizing that we must overcome. The observation was made by hooks (1990) that:

> if radical postmodern thinking is to have any transformative impact, then a critical break with the notion of 'authority' as 'master over' must not simply be a rhetorical device. It must be reflected in the habits of being, including styles of writing as well as chosen subject matter. (p. 25)

The claim to respect differences, which is one of the attractions of critical post theories, is contradicted by the arcane language and abstract concerns within which these theories are couched (Leonard, 1995). It is important, therefore, that we orientate our energies to making these ideas accessible and to enhancing the possibilities for others to speak with and speak back to them.

Conclusion

As the orthodoxies that have settled in modern critical social work enterprises are exposed and unsettled, new sites of influence and new understandings about critical practices become possible. The impulses of contemporary post theories challenge the whole modern enterprise and, in turn, this can be used to contest attempts to unify critical social work practices around common causes and identifications. In the anti-dogmatic and pragmatic approaches to change that emerge, theories become a resource for, rather than the truth about, critical practices. Foucault (1988a) asserts that:

> My position is that it is not up to us to propose. As soon as one 'proposes' – one proposes a vocabulary, an ideology, which can only have effects of domination. What we have to present are instruments and tools that people may find useful. By forming groups specifically to make these analyses, to wage these struggles, by using these instruments or others: this is how, in the end, possibilities open up. (p. 197)

As critical post theories encourage an ongoing radical interrogation of the critical social work enterprise, we can learn from its successes and its failures. In the contemporary contexts of social work practices, these understandings can strengthen and diversify our capacities to extend social justice to those who would otherwise be denied it.

Appendix
Conversation Transcription Conventions

Many of the illustrations in Chapters 5 and 6 involve transcriptions of talk from practice sites. In order to give an indication of the tone and the pace of the conversations, in many of the transcripts I have included the conversational markers outlined here. These conversational transcription conventions have been adapted from the work of Atkinson and Heritage (1984).

A   Emphasis or loudness of tone: indicated by CAPITAL letters.

B   High pitch: indicated by ↑ ↑.

C   Quickness of speech: indicated by > >

D   Continuers: speech acts demonstrating acknowledgement in others' speech, such as 'hmm', 'yeh' are indicated on the transcript.

E   In the transcripts some priority is accorded to the replication of the actual sound of the speech. Thus, for example, 'out of' may be written as 'outta'.

F   Extension of a sound or a syllable: a colon ':' is used to indicate extensions in speech. Thus, for example, 'light' might be written as 'li:ght'. This is useful for showing emphasis in speech.

G   Audible aspirations: these were marked by 'hhh'

H   Uncertainty about content. Words within parentheses ( ) indicate some uncertainty in my interpretation of what was said. Empty parentheses indicate that I am unable to make any interpretation of the content of the talk.

J   Square brackets ([ ]) are used to indicate extra information that may be useful to the reader in interpreting the conversation. They enclose explanatory notes such as information that is common knowledge to the participants in the conversation but is unlikely to be unknown to the reader, such as Jean ([the midwife]). I also refer to ([talk over]) to indicate lapses in single group focus and the breaking up of the group talk into smaller and multiple conversations which were very difficult to transcribe.

References

Addams, J. (1961) *Twenty Years at Hull-house*. New York: Signet, Macmillan.

Agger, B. (1991) 'Critical theory, poststructuralism and postmodernism: their sociological relevance', *Annual Review of Sociology*, 17: 105–31.

Alcoff, L. (1991) 'The problem of speaking for others', *Cultural Critique*, 20: 5–32.

Alder, C. and Sandor, D. (1990) 'Youth researching youth', *Youth Studies*, 8 (3): 38–42.

Alinsky, S. (1969) *Reveille for Radicals*. New York: Vintage.

Andrews, D. (1992) 'Beyond the professionalisation of community work', *Social Alternatives*, 11 (3): 35–8.

Ang, I. (1995) 'I am a feminist but "Other" women and postnational feminism', in B. Caine and R. Pringle (eds), *Transitions: New Australian Feminisms*. St Leonard's, NSW: Allen and Unwin. pp. 57–73.

Aronson, J. (1995) 'Lesbians in social work education: processes and puzzles in claiming visibility', *Journal of Progressive Human Services*, 6 (1): 5–26.

Asch, A. and Fine, M. (1992) 'Beyond pedestals: revisiting the lives of women with disabilities', in M. Fine (ed.), *Disruptive Voices: The Possibilities of Feminist Research*. Ann Arbor: University of Michigan Press. pp. 139–71.

Atherton, C. (1993). 'Empiricists vs. social constructionists: time for a cease-fire', *Families in Society*, 74, 617–24.

Atkinson, J.M. and Heritage, J. (eds) (1984) *Structures of Social Action: Studies in Conversation Analysis*. Cambridge: Cambridge University Press.

Bailey, R. and Brake, M. (1975) 'Introduction: Social work in the welfare state', in R. Bailey and M. Brake (eds), *Radical Social Work*. New York: Pantheon Books. pp. 1–12.

Ban, P. (1992). 'Client participation: beyond the rhetoric', *Children Australia*, 21 (2): 23–30.

Barrett, M. (1992) 'Words and things: materialism and method in contemporary feminist analysis', in M. Barrett and A. Phillips (eds), *Destabilising Theory: Contemporary Feminist Debates*. Stanford, CA: Stanford University Press. pp. 201–19.

Bartky, S.L. (1988) 'Foucault, femininity and the modernization of patriarchal power', in I. Diamond and L. Quinby (eds), *Feminism and Foucault: Reflections on Resistance*. Boston: Northeastern University Press. pp. 61–86.

Bauman, Z. (1992) *Intimations of Postmodernity*. London: Routledge.

Bennett, T. (1998) *Culture: A Reformer's Science*. St Leonard's, NSW: Allen and Unwin.

Bernstein, R. (1983) *Beyond Objectivism and Relativism: Science, Hermeneutics and Praxis*. Oxford: Basil Blackwell.

Bogoch, B. (1994) 'Power, distance, solidarity: models of professional–client interaction in an Israeli legal aid setting', *Discourse and Society*, 5: 65–88.

Bordo, S. (1990) 'Feminism, postmodernism and gender-scepticism', in. L. Nicholson (ed.), *Feminism/postmodernism*. New York: Routledge. pp. 133–56.

Bordo, S. (1993) 'Feminism, Foucault and the politics of the body', in C. Ramazanoglu (ed.), *Up against Foucault: Explorations of Tensions between Foucault and Feminism*. New York: Routledge. pp. 179–202.

Bricker-Jenkins, M., Hooyman, N. and Gottlieb, N. (1991) *Feminist Social Work Practice in Clinical Settings*. Newbury Park, CA: Sage.

Brown, W. (1995) *States of Injury: Power and Freedom in Late Modernity*. Princeton, NJ: Princeton University Press.

Burke, B. and Harrison, P. (1998) 'Anti-oppressive practice', in R. Adams, L. Dominelli and

M. Payne (eds), *Social Work: Themes, Issues and Critical Debates*. London: Macmillan. pp. 229–39.

Butler, J. (1990) *Gender Trouble: Feminism and the Subversion of Identity*. New York: Routledge.

Butler, J. (1995) 'Contingent foundations: feminism and the question of "Postmodernism"', in S. Benhabib, J. Butler, D. Cornell and N. Fraser, *Feminist Contentions: A Philosophical Exchange*. New York: Routledge. pp. 35–57.

Calder, M. (1995) 'Child protection: balancing paternalism and partnership', *British Journal of Social Work*, 25: 749–66.

Cameron, J. (1992) 'Modern day tales of illegitimacy: gender, class and ex-nuptial fertility'. Unpublished Master's thesis, University of New South Wales, Sydney, Australia.

Campbell, L. (1997) 'Family involvement in decision-making in child protection and care: four types of case conferences', *Child and Family Social Work*, 2: 1–11.

Carniol, B. (1992) 'Structural social work: Maurice Moreau's challenge to social work practice', *Journal of Progressive Human Services*, 3(1): 1–20.

Carr, W. and Kemmis, S. (1986) *Becoming Critical: Education, Knowledge and Action Research*. London: The Falmer Press.

Carrington, K. (1993) *Offending Girls: Sex, Youth and Justice*. St Leonard's, NSW: Allen and Unwin.

Chesler, M. (1991) 'Participation action research with self-help groups: an alternative paradigm for inquiry and action', *American Journal of Community Psychology*, 19: 757–68.

Cixous, H. (1981a) 'The laugh of the Medusa', in E. Marks and I. de Courtivron (eds), *New French Feminisms: An Anthology*. Sussex: The Harvester Press. pp. 245–64.

Cixous, H. (1981b) 'Sorties', in E. Marks and I. de Courtivron (eds), *New French Feminism: An Anthology*. Sussex: The Harvester Press. pp. 90–8.

Cixous, H. (1994a) 'Three steps on the ladder of writing', in S. Sellers (ed.), *The Hélène Cixous Reader*. London: Routledge. pp. 199–205.

Cixous, H. (1994b) '(With) or the art of innocence' (trans. S. Flood), in S. Sellers (ed.), *The Hélène Cixous Reader*. London: Routledge. pp. 93–105.

Clark, C. (1998) 'Self-determination and paternalism in community care: practice and prospects', *British Journal of Social Work*, 28: 387–402.

Cloward, R. and Fox-Piven, F. (1975) 'Notes towards a radical social work', in R. Bailey and M. Brake (eds), *Radical Social Work*. New York: Pantheon Books. pp. vii–Lviii.

Conley, V.A. (1992) *Hélène Cixous*. New York: Harvester Wheatsheaf.

Corrigan, P. and Leonard, P. (1978) *Social Work Practice under Capitalism: A Marxist Approach*. London: Macmillan.

Crinnall, K. (1995) 'The Search for a feminism that could accommodate homeless young women', *Youth Studies Australia*, 14 (3): 42–7.

Dalrymple, J. and Burke, B. (1995) *Anti-oppressive Practice: Social Care and the Law*. Buckingham, England: Open University Press.

Davies, B. (1991) 'The concept of agency: a feminist poststructuralist analysis', *Social Analysis*, 30: 42–53.

Davies, B. (1994) *Poststructuralist Theory and Classroom Practice*. Geelong: Deakin University Press.

Davies, L. (1990) 'Limits of bureaucratic control: social workers in child welfare', in L. Davies and E. Schragge (eds), *Bureaucracy and Community*. Montreal: Black Rose Books. pp. 81–102.

Day, L. (1992) 'Women and oppression: race, class and gender', in M. Langan and L. Day (eds), *Women, Oppression and Social Work*. London: Routledge. pp. 12–31.

DeMaria, W. (1993) 'Exploring radical social work teaching in Australia', *Journal of Progressive Human Services*, 4 (2): 45–63.

Derrida, J. (1991) 'Of grammatology', in P. Kamuf (ed.), *A Derrida Reader: Between the Blinds*. New York: Harvester Wheatsheaf. pp. 34–58.

Dingwall, R., Eekalaar, J. and Murray, T. (1983) *The Protection of Children*. Oxford: Basil Blackwell.

Dixon, J. (1989) 'The limits and potential of community development for personal and social change', *Community Health Studies*, 13 (1): 82–92.

Dixon, J. (1993) 'Feminist community work's ambivalence with politics', *Australian Social Work*, 46 (1): 37–44.

Dominelli, L. (1989) 'An uncaring profession: an examination of racism in social work', *New Community*, 15: 391–403.

Dominelli, L. (1995) 'Women in the community: feminist principles and organising in community work', *Community Development Journal*, 30: 133–43.

Dominelli, L. and McLeod, E. (1989) *Feminist Social Work*. London: Macmillan.

Ellermann, A. (1998) 'Can discourse analysis enable reflective social work practice?', *Social Work Education*, 17 (1): 35–44.

Ellsworth, E. (1992) 'Why doesn't this feel empowering? Working through the repressive myths of critical pedagogy', in C. Luke and J. Gore (eds), *Feminisms and Critical Pedagogy*. New York: Routledge. pp. 90–119.

Esping-Andersen, G. (1990) *The Three Worlds of Welfare Capitalism*. Cambridge: Polity Press.

Esping-Andersen, G. (1996) 'After the golden age? Welfare state dilemmas in a global economy', in G. Esping-Andersen (ed.), *Welfare States in Transition: National Adaptations in Global Economies*. London: Sage. pp. 1–31.

Fabricant, M. (1988) 'Empowering the homeless', *Social Policy*, 18 (4): 49–55.

Fairclough, N. (1989) *Language and Power*. London: Longman.

Fairclough, N. (1992) *Discourse and Social Change*. Cambridge: Polity Press.

Fals-Borda, O. (1987) 'The application of participatory action-research in Latin America', *International Sociology*, 2: 329–47.

Fals-Borda, O. (1994) 'Postmodernity and social responsibility: a view from the third world', *Collaborative Inquiry*, 13: 2–4.

Fawcett, B. (1998) 'Disability and social work: applications from postmodernism, poststructuralaim and feminism', *British Journal of Social Work*, 28: 263–77.

Fay, B. (1975) *Social Theory and Political Practice*. London: George, Allen and Unwin.

Fay, B. (1987) *Critical Social Science: Liberation and its Limits*. Ithaca: Cornell University Press.

Featherstone, B. and Fawcett, B. (1994) 'Feminism and child abuse: opening up some possibilities?', *Critical Social Policy*, 14 (3): 61–80.

Featherstone, B. and Fawcett, B. (1995) 'Oh no! Not more isms!', *Social Work Education*, 14 (3): 25–43.

Fine, M. (1992) 'Passions, power and politics', in M. Fine (ed.), *Disruptive Voices: The Possibilities of Feminist Research*. Ann Arbor: The University of Michigan Press. pp. 205–31.

Fine, M. (1994) 'Working the hyphens: reinventing self and other in qualitative research', in N. Denzin and Y. Lincoln (eds), *Handbook of Qualitative Research*. Ann Arbor: The University of Michigan Press. pp. 175–203.

Fine, M. and Macpherson, P. (1992) 'Over dinner: feminism and adolescent female bodies', in M. Fine (ed.), *Disruptive Voices: The Possibilities of Feminist Research*. Ann Arbor: The University of Michigan Press. pp. 175–203.

Finn, J. (1994) 'The promise of participatory research', *Journal of Progressive Human Services*, 5 (2): 25–42.

Fishman, P. (1983) 'Interaction: the work women do', in B. Thorne, C. Kramarae and N. Henley (eds), *Language, Gender and Society*. Boston: Heinle and Heinle Publishers. pp. 89–101.

FitzRoy, L. (1997) 'The too hard basket is full: working with abusive mothers', *Proceedings of the 25th National Conference of the Australian Association of Social Workers*. Canberra, ACT, Australia.

Fook, J. (1993) *Radical Casework: A Theory of Practice*. St Leonard's, NSW: Allen and Unwin.

Fook, J. (ed.) (1996) *The Reflective Researcher: Social Workers' Theories of Practice Research*. St Leonard's, NSW: Allen and Unwin. Preface.

Forster, M. (1993) 'Hegel's dialectic method', in F.C. Beiser (ed.), *The Cambridge Companion to Hegel*. Cambridge: Cambridge University Press. pp. 130–70.

Foucault, M. (1977) 'History of systems of thought', in D. Bouchard (ed.), *Language, Counter-memory, Practice: Selected Essays and Interviews* (trans. D. Bouchard and S. Simon). Oxford: Basil Blackwell. pp. 199–204.

Foucault, M. (1978) Interview with Lucette Finas, in M. Morris and P. Patton (eds), *Michel Foucault: Power, Truth and Strategy*. Sydney: Feral Publications. pp. 67–75.

Foucault, M. (1980a) 'Body/power', in C. Gordon (ed.), *Power/knowledge: Selected Interviews and Other Writings 1972–1977*. New York: Pantheon Books. pp. 55–62.

Foucault, M. (1980b) 'Prison talk', in C. Gordon (ed.), *Power/knowledge: Selected Interviews and Other Writings 1972–1977*. New York: Pantheon Books. pp. 37–54.

Foucault, M. (1980c) 'Power and strategies', in C. Gordon (ed.), *Power/knowledge: Selected Interviews and Other Writings 1972–1977*. New York: Pantheon Books. pp. 134–45.

Foucault, M. (1980d) 'Truth and power', in C. Gordon (ed.), *Power/knowledge: Selected Interviews and Other Writings 1972–1977*. New York: Pantheon Books. pp. 109–33.

Foucault, M. (1980e) 'Two lectures', in C. Gordon (ed.), *Power/knowledge: Selected Interviews and Other Writings 1972–1977*. New York: Pantheon Books. pp. 78–108.

Foucault, M. (1981a) *The History of Sexuality*, Vol. 1 (trans. R. Hurley). London: Pelican Books.

Foucault, M. (1981b) 'The order of discourse', in R. Young (ed.), *Untying the Text: A Post-structuralist Reader*. London: Routledge and Kegan Paul. pp. 48–78.

Foucault, M. (1982) 'The subject and power', *Critical Inquiry*, 8: 777–95.

Foucault, M. (1988a) 'Confinement, psychiatry, prison' (a dialogue with M. Foucault, J.P. Faye, M.O. Faye and M. Zecca), in L. Kritzman (ed.), *Michel Foucault: Politics, Philosophy, Culture*. New York: Routledge. pp. 178–210.

Foucault, M. (1988b) 'Critical theory/intellectual history', in L. Kritzman (ed.), *Michel Foucault: Politics, Philosophy, Culture*. New York: Routledge. pp. 17–46.

Foucault, M. (1991a) *Discipline and Punish: The Birth of the Prison* (trans. A. Sheridan). London: Penguin.

Foucault, M. (1991b) 'On the genealogy of ethics: an overview of work in progress', in P. Rabinow (ed.), *The Foucault Reader: An Introduction to Foucault's Thought*. London: Penguin. pp. 340–72.

Foucault, M. (1991c) 'Polemics, politics and problemizations: an interview with Michel Foucault' (trans. L. Davis), in P. Rabinow (ed.), *The Foucault Reader: An Introduction to Foucault's Thought*. Penguin: London. pp. 381–90.

Foucault, M. (1991d) 'Politics and ethics: an interview' (trans. C. Porter), in P. Rabinow (ed.), *The Foucault Reader: An Introduction to Foucault's Thought*. London: Penguin. pp. 373–80.

Foucault, M. (1991e) 'Questions of method', in G. Burchell, C. Gordon and P. Miller (eds), *The Foucault Effect: Studies in Governmentality*. Chicago: University of Chicago Press. pp. 73–85.

Foucault, M. (1991f) 'What is enlightenment?' (trans. C. Porter), in P. Rabinow (ed.), *The Foucault Reader: An Introduction to Foucault's Thought*. London: Penguin. pp. 32–50.

Foucault, M. (1992) *The Use of Pleasure: The History of Sexuality*, Vol. 2. London: Penguin.

Fox Piven, F. and Cloward, R.A. (1993) *Regulating the Poor: The Functions of Public Welfare* (update edn). New York: Vintage Books.

Franklin, D. (1986) 'Mary Richmond and Jane Addams: from moral certainty to rational inquiry in social work practice', *Social Service Review*, 60 (4): 504–25.

Fraser, N. (1989) *Unruly Practices: Power, Discourse and Gender in Contemporary Social Theory*. Oxford: Polity Press.

Fraser, N. and Nicholson, L. (1990) 'Social criticism without philosophy: an encounter between feminism and postmodernism', in L. Nicholson (ed.), *Feminism/postmodernism*. New York: Routledge. pp. 19–38.

Freire, P. (1972) *Pedagogy of the Oppressed*. Harmondsworth: Penguin.

Freire, P. and Moch M. (1990) 'A critical understanding of social work', *Journal of Progressive Human Services*, 1 (1): 3–9.

Frost, S. (1977) 'Mothers in action', in M. Mayo (ed.), *Women in the Community*. London: Routledge and Kegan Paul. pp. 121–41.

Galper, J. (1980) *Social Work Practice: A Radical Perspective*. Englewood Cliffs, NJ: Prentice Hall.

Gatens, M. (1986) 'Feminism, philosophy and riddles without answers', in C. Pateman and E. Grosz (eds), *Feminist Challenges: Social and Political Theory*. Sydney, London, Boston: Allen and Unwin. pp. 13–29.

Gatens, M. (1990) *Women and Philosophy*. Anne Conlon Memorial Lecture. Published by the New South Wales Women's Advisory Council.

Gatens, M. (1991) *Feminism and Philosophy: Perspectives on Differences and Equality*. Cambridge: Polity Press.

Gatens, M. (1992) 'Power, bodies and difference', in M. Barrett and A. Phillips (eds), *Destabilizing Theory: Contemporary Feminist Debates*. Stanford, CA: Stanford University Press. pp. 120–37.

Gatens, M. (1996) *Imaginary Bodies: Ethics, Power and Corporeality*. London: Routledge.

Gatens, M. (1998) 'Institutions, embodiment and sexual difference', in M. Gatens and A. McKinnon, *Gender and Institutions: Work, Welfare and Citizenship*. Cambridge: Cambridge University Press. pp. 1–15.

Gaventa, J. (1993) 'The powerful, the powerless and the experts: knowledge struggles in the information age', in P. Park (ed.), *Voices of Change: Participatory Research in the United States and Canada*. Westport, CT: Bergin and Garvey. pp. 21–40.

Gibson-Graham, J.K. (1995) 'Beyond patriarchy and capitalism: reflections on political subjectivity', in B. Caine and R. Pringle (eds), *Transitions: New Australian Feminisms*. St Leonard's, NSW: Allen and Unwin. pp. 172–83.

Gibson-Graham, J.K. (1996) *The End of Capitalism (as We Knew It): A Feminist Critique of Political Economy*. Cambridge: Blackwell Publishers.

Goodwin, M. (1988) 'Co-operation and competition across girls' play activities', in A.D. Todd and S. Fisher (eds), *Gender and Discourse: The Power of Talk*. Norwood, NJ: Ablex. pp. 59–94.

Gordon, L. (1988) *Heroes of Their Own Lives: The Politics and History of Family Violence, Boston 1880–1960*. Viking: New York.

Gorman, J. (1993) 'Postmodernism and the conduct of inquiry in social work', *Affilia*, 8 (3): 247–64.

Groch, S.A. (1994) 'Oppositional consciousness: its manifestations and development. The case of people with disabilities', *Sociological Inquiry*, 64: 369–95.

Gross, E. (1995) 'Deconstructing politically correct practice literature: the American Indian case', *Social Work*, 40: 206–13.

Grosz, E. (1989) *Sexual Subversions: Three French Feminists*. St Leonard's, NSW: Allen and Unwin.

Grosz, E. (1990) 'Philosophy', in S. Gunew (ed.), *Feminist Knowledge, Critique and Construct*. London: Routledge. pp. 147–74.

Grosz, E. (1994) *Volatile Bodies: Towards a Corporeal Feminism*. St Leonard's, NSW: Allen and Unwin.

Gutierriez, L. (1995) 'Understanding the empowerment process: does consciousness-raising make a difference?', *Social Work Research*, 19: 229–37.

Habermas, J. (1978) *Knowledge and Human Interests*. London: Heinemann Education.

Habermas, J. (1983) 'Interpretive social science vs. hermeneuticism', in N. Haan, R. Bellah, P. Rabinow and W. Sullivan (eds), *Social Science as Moral Inquiry*. New York: Columbia University Press. pp. 251–69.

Hall, B. (1981) 'Participatory research, popular knowledge and power: a personal reflection', *Convergence*, 14 (3): 6–19.

Hanmer, J. (1977) 'Community action, women's aid and the women's liberation movement', in M. Mayo (ed.), *Women in the Community*. London: Routledge and Kegan Paul. pp. 91–108.

Harding, S. (1987) *The Science Question in Feminism*. Ithaca: Cornell University Press.

Hartsock, N. (1990) 'Foucault on power: a theory for women?', in L. Nicholson (ed.), *Feminism/postmodernism*. London: Routledge. pp. 157–75.

Healy, K. (1996) 'Participative action research and the process of feminist inquiry', in C. Alder and M. Baines (eds), . . . *And When She Was Bad? Working with Young Women in Juvenile Justice and Related Areas*. Hobart, Australia: National Clearinghouse for Youth Studies. pp. 89–96.

Healy, K. (1998) 'Participation and child protection: the importance of context', *British Journal of Social Work*, 28: 897–914.

Healy, K. (1999) 'Power and activist social work', in B. Pease and J. Fook (eds), *Transforming Social Work Practice: Postmodern Critical Perspectives*. St Leonard's: Allen and Unwin. pp. 115–34.

Healy, K. and Mulholland, J. (1998) 'Discourse analysis and activist social work: investigating practice processes', *Journal of Sociology and Social Welfare*, 25 (3): 3–27.

Healy, K. and Peile, C. (1995) 'From silence to activism: approaches to research and practice with young mothers', *Affilia*, 10: 280–9.

Healy, K. and Walsh, K. (1997) 'Making participatory processes visible: practice issues in the development of a peer support and advocacy network', *Australian Social Work*, 50 (3): 45–52.

Healy, K. and Young Mothers for Young Women (1996) 'Valuing young families: child protection and family support strategies with young mothers', *Children Australia*, 21 (2): 23–30.

Hegel, G.W.F. (1910) *The Phenomenology of Mind* (trans. J.B. Baille). London: Swan Sonnenschein.

Hegel, G.W.F. (1977) *Phenomenology of Spirit* (trans. A.V. Miller). Oxford: Clarendon Press.

Hewitt, M. (1993) 'Social movements and social need: problems with postmodern political theory', *Critical Social Policy*, 37: 52–74.

Hill-Collins, P. (1990) *Black Feminist Thought: Knowledge, Consciousness, and the Politics of Empowerment*. London: HarperCollins

Holmes, J. (1995) *Women, Men and Politeness*. London: Longman.

hooks, B. (1990) *Yearning: Race, Gender and Cultural Politics*. Boston, MA: South End Press.

hooks, B. (1994) *Teaching to Transgress: Education as the Practice of Freedom*. New York: Routledge.

Howe, D. (1994) 'Modernity, postmodernity and social work', *British Journal of Social Work*, 24: 513–32.

Hudson, A. (1989) 'Changing perspectives: feminism, gender and social work', in M. Langan and P. Lee (eds), *Radical Social Work Today*. Unwin Hyman: London. pp. 70–96.

Hutchinson-Reis, M. (1989). '"And for those of us who are black?" Black politics in social work', in M. Langan and P. Lee (eds), *Radical Social Work Today*. London: Unwin Hyman. pp. 165–77.

Ife, J. (1997) *Rethinking Social Work: Towards Critical Practice*. Melbourne: Longman.

Kellner, D. (1989) *Critical Theory, Modernity and Marxism*. Cambridge: Polity Press.

Kellner, D. (1993) 'Critical theory today: revisiting the classics', *Theory, Culture and Society*, 10: 43–60.

Kelly, A. (1995) 'A mud map for landcarers: the technique of participatory research', in S. Chamala and K. Keith (eds), *Participative Approaches for Landcare: Perspectives, Policies, Programs*. Brisbane: Australian Academic Press. pp. 93–106.

Kenny, S. (1994) *Developing Communities for the Future: Community Development in Australia*. South Melbourne: Thomas Nelson Australia.

Kenway, J. (1992) 'Feminist theories of the state: to be or not to be?', in M. Muetzelfeldt (ed.), *Society, State and Politics in Australia*. NSW: Leichhardt. pp. 108–44.

Killén, K. (1996) 'How far have we come in dealing with the emotional challenge of abuse and neglect?', *Child Abuse and Neglect*, 20: 791–5.

Kingfisher, C.P. (1996) 'Women on welfare: conversational sites of acquiescence and dissent', *Discourse and Society*, 7: 531–57.

Kravetz, D. (1976) 'Sexism in a woman's profession', *Social Work*, 21: 6, 421–7.

Kristeva, J. (1981) 'Women's time' (trans. A. Jardine and H. Blake), *Signs*, 7: 13–35.

Laird, J. (1995) 'Family centred practice in the postmodern era', *Family in Society*, 76 (3): 150–62.

Lane, M. (1990) 'Community work, social change and women', in J. Petruchenia and R. Thorpe (eds), *Social Change and Social Welfare Practice*. Sydney: Hale and Iremonger. pp. 166–80.

Langan, M. (1998) 'Radical social work', in R. Adams, L. Dominelli and M. Payne (eds), *Social Work: Themes, Issues and Critical Debates*. London: Macmillan pp. 207–17.

Langan, M. and Lee, P. (1989) 'Whatever happened to radical social work?', in M. Langan and P. Lee (eds), *Radical Social Work Today*. London: Unwin Hyman.

Larbalestier, J. (1998) 'Feminism, difference and social work: positions, practices and possibilities', in E. Fernandez, K. Heycox, L. Hughes and M. Wilkinson (eds), *Women Participating in Global Change*. Proceedings of the International Association of Schools of Social Work (IASSW), Women's Symposium (Hong Kong) Publications Committee.

Laursen, K. (1975) 'Professionalism', in H. Throssel (ed.), *Social Work: Radical Essays*. Brisbane: University of Queensland Press. pp. 47–71.

Lechte, J. (1994) *Fifty Key Contemporary Thinkers: From Structuralism to Postmodernity*. London: Routledge.

Leonard, P. (1975) 'Towards a paradigm for radical practice', in R. Bailey and M. Brake (eds), *Radical Social Work*. New York: Pantheon Books. pp. 46–61.

Leonard, P. (1984) *Personality and Ideology: Towards a Material Understanding of the Individual*. London: Macmillan.

Leonard, P. (1990) 'Contesting the welfare state in a neo-conservative era: dilemmas for the left', *Journal of Progressive Human Services*, 1 (1): 11–25.

Leonard, P. (1994) 'Knowledge/power and postmodernism: implications for the practice of a critical social work education', *Canadian Social Work Review*, 11 (1): 11–26.

Leonard, P. (1995) 'Postmodernism, socialism and social welfare', *Journal of Progressive Human Services*, 6 (2): 3–19.

Leonard, P. (1996) 'Three discourses on practice: a postmodern re-appraisal', *Journal of Sociology and Social Welfare*, 23 (2): 7–26.

Leonard, P. (1997) *Postmodern Welfare: Reconstructing an Emancipatory Project*. London: Sage.

Lloyd, G. (1986) 'Selfhood, war and masculinity', in C. Pateman and E. Gross (eds), *Feminist Challenges: Social and Political Theory*. Sydney, London, Boston: Allen and Unwin. pp. 63–76.

Lloyd, G. (1989) 'Women as other: sex, gender and subjectivity', *Australian Feminist Studies*, 10: 12–33.

Lowe, R. (1990) 'Reimagining family therapy: choosing the metaphors we live by', *Australian New Zealand Journal of Family Therapy*, 11 (1): 1–9.

Lugones, M. and Spelman, E. (1990) 'Have we got a theory for you! Feminist theory, cultural imperialism and the demand for "the woman's voice"', in A.Y. al-Hibri and M. Simons (eds), *Hypatia Reborn: Essays in Feminist Philosophy*. Bloomington: Indiana University Press. pp. 18–33.

Lukes, S. (1974) *Power: A Radical View*. London: Macmillan.

Lukes, S. (1977) 'Power and structure', in S. Lukes (ed.), *Essays in Social Theory*. London: Macmillan. pp. 3–29.

Lundblad, K.S. (1995) 'Jane Addams and social reform: a role model for the 1990s', *Social Work*, 40 (5): 661–9.

Lykes, M.B. (1988) 'Dialogue with Guatemalan Indian women: critical perspectives on constructing collaborative research', in R. Unger (ed.), *Representations: Social Constructions of Gender*. Amityville: Baywood Publishing Company. pp. 167–85.

Lynch, C. (1993) 'Politics versus psychology: ends, means and moral complexity', *AIDS and Public Policy Journal*, 8 (3): 109–14.

Lyotard, J.F. (1984) *The Postmodern Condition: A Report on Knowledge*. Manchester: Manchester University Press.

McDermott, F. (1996) 'Social work research: debating the boundaries', *Australian Social Work*, 49 (1): 5–10.

MacDonald, J. (1996) 'Dismantling the movement: feminism, postmodernism and politics', *Refractory Girl*, 50: 48–51.

McHoul, A. and Grace, W. (1991) *A Foucault Primer: Discourse, Power and the Subject*. Melbourne: Melbourne University Press.

McNay, M. (1992) 'Social work and power relations: towards a framework for an integrated practice', in M. Langan and L. Day (eds), *Women, Oppression and Social Work: Issues in Anti-Discriminatory Practice*. Routledge: London. pp. 48–66.

McNay, L. (1994) *Foucault: A Critical Introduction*. Cambridge: Polity.

McRobbie, A. (1991) *Feminism and Youth Culture: From Jackie to Just Seventeen*. Hampshire: Macmillan Education.

Maguire, P. (1987) *Doing Participatory Research: A Feminist Approach*. Amherst: University of Massachusetts Press.

Marchant, H. (1986) 'Gender systems thinking and radical social work', in H. Marchant and B. Wearing (eds), *Gender Reclaimed: Women in Social Work*. Sydney: Hale and Iremonger. pp. 14–32.

Marcuse, H. (1955) *Reason and Revolution: Hegel and the Rise of Social Theory* (2nd edn). London: Routledge and Kegan Paul.

Marx, K. (1972a) 'Alienation and social classes' (trans. R.C. Tucker), in R.C. Tucker (ed.), *The Marx–Engels Reader*. New York: W.W. Norton. pp. 104–6.

Marx, K. (1972b) 'Capital: Selections' (trans. S. Moore and E. Aveling), in R.C. Tucker (ed.), *The Marx–Engels Reader*. New York: W.W. Norton. pp. 191–318.

Marx, K. (1972c) 'The German ideology', Part 1 (trans. S. Ryazanskaya), in R.C. Tucker (ed.), *The Marx–Engels Reader*. New York: W.W. Norton. pp. 110–64.

Marx, K. (1972d) 'On the realm of necessity and the realm of freedom' (trans. S. Moore and E. Aveling), in R.C. Tucker (ed.), *The Marx–Engels Reader*. New York: W.W. Norton. pp. 319–20.

Marx, K. (1972e) 'Thesis on Feuerbach', in R.C. Tucker (ed.), *The Marx–Engels Reader*. New York: W.W. Norton. pp. 107–109.

Marx, K. and Engels, F. (1972). 'Manifesto of the Communist party', in R.C. Tucker (ed.), *The Marx–Engels Reader*. New York: W.W. Norton. pp. 331–62.

Mathrani, V. (1993) 'Participatory research: a potential for in-depth understanding', *Indian Journal of Social Work*, 54 (3): 345–53.

Middleman, R. and Goldberg, G. (1974) *Social Service Delivery: A Structural Approach to Social Work Practice*. New York: Columbia University Press.

Mies, M. (1983) 'Towards a methodology for feminist research', in G. Bowles and R. Duelli-Klein (eds), *Theories of Women's Studies*. Boston: Routledge and Kegan Paul. pp. 117–39.

Mittler, P. (1995) 'Rethinking partnerships between parents and professionals', *Children and Society*, 9 (3): 22–40.

Moore, R. (1992) 'Unemployment, the recession and pregnancy decisions', *Healthsharing Women*, 2 (5): 5–8.

Moreau, M. (1979) 'A structural approach to social work practice', *Canadian Journal of Social Work Education*, 5 (1): 78–94.

Moreau, M. (1990) 'Empowerment through advocacy and consciousness-raising: implications of a structural approach to social work', *Journal of Sociology and Social Work*, 17 (2): 53–67.

Morgen, S. and Bookman, A. (1988) 'Rethinking women and politics: an introductory essay', in A. Bookman and S. Morgen (eds), *Women and the Politics of Empowerment*. Philadelphia: Temple University Press. pp. 3–29.

Mowbray, M. (1992) 'The medicinal qualities of localism: a historical perspective', in R. Thorpe and J. Petruchenia (eds), *Community Work or Social Change?: An Australian Perspective*, (new edn). Sydney: Hale and Iremonger. pp. 50–66.

Mullaly, R. (1993) *Structural Social Work: Ideology, Theory and Practice*. Toronto: McClelland and Stewart.

Mullaly, R. and Keating, E. (1991) 'Similarities, differences and dialectics of radical social work', *Journal of Progressive Human Services*, 2 (2): 49–78.

Nes, J. and Iadicola, P. (1989) 'Towards a definition of feminist social work: a comparison of liberal, radical and socialist models', *Social Work*, 34: 12–21.

Opie, A. (1988) 'Qualitative methodology, process and textual analysis'. Paper presented at the Inaugural Social Research Conference, University of Queensland, Brisbane, Australia.

Opie, A. (1995) *Beyond Good Intentions: Support Work with Older People*. Wellington (New Zealand): Institute of Policy Studies, Victoria University of Wellington.

Pardeck, J., Murphy, J. and Choi, J. Min- (1994) 'Some implications of postmodernism for social work practice', *Social Work*, 39: 343–5.

Parker, N. (1961) 'Professional social work and community', *Australian Journal of Social Work*, 8 (2): 5–7.

Parton, N. (1994a) '"Problematics of government", (post)modernity and social work', *British Journal of Social Work*, 24: 9–32.

Parton, N. (1994b) 'The nature of social work under conditions of (post) modernity', *Social Work and Social Sciences Review*, 5 (2): 93–112.

Parton, N. and Marshall, W. (1998) 'Post-modernism and discourse approaches to social work', in R. Adams, L. Dominelli and M. Payne (eds), *Social Work: Themes, Issues and Critical Debates*. London: Macmillan. pp. 240–50.

Peile, C. (1988) 'Research paradigms in social work: from stalemate to creative synthesis', *Social Service Review*, 62: 1–19.

Peile, C. (1991) 'Towards a creative paradigm for social work: the creative synthesis of positivist, interpretivist, critical and ecological paradigms'. Unpublished doctoral dissertation, University of Queensland, Australia.

Peile, C. and McCouat, M. (1997) 'The rise of relativism: the future of theory and knowledge development in social work', *British Journal of Social Work*, 27: 343–60.

Petruchenia, J. (1990) 'Antiracist welfare practice with immigrants', in J. Petruchenia and R. Thorpe (eds), *Social Change and Social Welfare Practice*. Sydney: Hale and Iremonger. pp. 48–60.

Petruchenia, J. (1992) 'Multiculturalism in Australia: a new direction or consensus ideology?' in R. Thorpe and J. Petruchenia (eds), *Community Work or Social Change?: An Australian Perspective*, (new edn). Sydney: Hale and Iremonger. pp. 37–49.

Phillips, A. (1991) *Engendering Democracy*. Cambridge: Polity Press.

Pozatek, E. (1994) 'The problem of certainty: clinical social work in the postmodern era', *Social Work*, 39: 396–403.

Pratt, G. (1993) 'Reflections on poststructuralism and feminist empirics, theory and practice'. *Antipode*, 25: 51–63.

Pringle, R. (1995) 'Destabilising patriarchy', in B. Caine and R. Pringle, *Transitions: New Australian Feminism*. St Leonard's, NSW: Allen and Unwin. pp. 198–211.

Pritchard, C. and Taylor, R. (1978) *Social Work: Reform or Revolution*. London: Routledge and Kegan Paul.

Rahnema, M. (1990) 'Participatory action research: "The last temptation of saint" development', *Alternatives*, 15: 199–226.

Reason, P. (1994) 'Three approaches to participative inquiry', in N. Denzin and Y. Lincoln (eds), *Handbook of Qualitative Research*. Thousand Oaks, CA: Sage. pp. 324–39.

Rees, S. (1991) *Achieving Power: Practice and Policy in Social Welfare*. Sydney: Allen and Unwin.

Reinharz, S. (1993) 'Neglected voices and excessive demands in feminist research', *Qualitative Sociology*, 16: 69–76.

Resnick, S. and Wolff, R. (1987) *Knowledge and Class: A Marxian Critique of Political Economy*. Chicago: Chicago University Press.

Reynolds, B. (1963) *An Uncharted Journey: Fifty Years of Growth in Social Work*. New York: Citadel.

Rojek, C., Peacock, C. and Collins, S. (1988) *Social Work and Received Ideas*. London: Routledge.

Routledge, R. (1993) 'Grass tip consumer policy input', *Community Development Journal*, 28, 101–7.

Ryburn, M. (1991a) 'The myth of assessment', *Adoption and Fostering*, 15 (1): 20–7.

Ryburn, M. (1991b) 'The Children Act: power and empowerment', *Adoption and Fostering*, 15 (3): 10–15.

Sacks, H., Schegloff, E.A. and Jefferson, G. (1978) 'A simplest semantics for the organization of turn-taking in conversation', in J. Schenkein (ed.), *Studies in the Organization of Conversational Interaction*. New York: Academic Press. pp. 7–55.

Sands, R. (1988) 'A sociolinguistic analysis of a mental health interview', *Social Work*, 33: 149–54.

Sands, R. and Nuccio, K. (1992) 'Postmodern feminist theory and social work', *Social Work*, 37: 489–94.

Sarri, R. and Sarri, C. (1992) 'Organisation and community change through participatory action research', *Administration in Social Work*, 16 (3–4): 99–122.

Sawicki, J. (1991) *Disciplining Foucault: Feminism, Power and the Body*. New York: Routledge.

Schiele, J. (1994) 'Afrocentricity as an alternative world view for equality', *Journal of Progressive Human Services*, 5 (1): 5–25.

Schrijvers, J. (1991) 'Dialectics of a dialogical ideal: studying down, studying sideways and studying up', in L. Nencel and P. Pels (eds), *Constructing Knowledge: Authority and Critique in Social Science*. London: Sage. pp. 162–79.

Scott, J. (1992) 'Experience', in J. Butler and J. Scott (eds), *Feminists Theorise the Political*. New York: Routledge. pp. 22–40.

Scott, J.W. (1994) 'Deconstructing equality-versus-difference: or, the uses of poststructuralist theory for feminism', in S. Siedman (ed.), *The Postmodern Turn: New Perspectives on Social Theory*. Cambridge: Cambridge University Press. pp. 282–98.

Shah, N. (1989) 'It's up to you sisters: black women and radical social work', in M. Langan and P. Lee (eds), *Radical Social Work Today*. London: Unwin Hyman. pp. 178–91.

Shemmings, D. and Shemmings, Y. (1995) 'Defining participative practice in health and welfare', in R. Jack, (ed.), *Empowerment in Community Care*. Chapman and Hall: London, pp. 43–58.

Simon, B.L. (1990) 'Rethinking empowerment', *Journal of Progressive Human Services*, 1 (1): 27–38.

Smith, C. and White, S. (1997) 'Parton, Howe and postmodernity: a critical comment on mistaken identity', *British Journal of Social Work*, 27 (2): 275–95.

Solas, J. (1993) '(De)constructing social work education'. Unpublished doctoral dissertation. University of Queensland, Australia.

Solas, J. (1996) 'The limits of empowerment in human service work', *Australian Journal of Social Issues*, 31: 147–56.

Spicker, P. (1990) 'Social work and self-determination', *British Journal of Social Work*, 20: 221–36.

Stevenson, O. (1996) 'Emotional abuse and neglect: a time for reappraisal', *Child and Family Social Work*, 1: 13–18.

Stoecker, R. and Bonacich, E. (1992) 'Why participatory research?' Guest editors' introduction, *American Sociologist*, 23: 5–14.

Swigonski, M. (1993) 'Feminist standpoint theory and the question of social work research', *Affilia*, 8: 172–83.

Tandon, R. (1981) 'Participatory research in the empowerment of people', *Convergence*, 14 (3): 20–7.

Tannen, D. (1991) *You Just Don't Understand: Men and Women in Conversation*. London: Virago.

Tapper, M. (1993) 'Ressentiment and power: some reflections on feminist practices', in P. Patton (ed.), *Nietzsche, Feminism and Political Theory*. St Leonard's, NSW: Allen and Unwin.

Taylor, S. (1986) 'Teenage girls and the recession in Australia: some cultural and educational implications', *British Journal of Sociology of Education*, 7: 379–95.

Taylor-Gooby, P. (1993) 'Postmodernism and social policy: a great leap backwards', *Social Policy Research Centre, Discussion Paper, no. 45*. Sydney: University of New South Wales.

Taylor-Gooby, P. (1994) 'Postmodernism and social policy: a great leap backwards?', *Journal of Social Policy*, 23 (3): 385–404.

Thoburn, J., Lewis, A. and Shemmings, D. (1995) *Paternalism or Partnership? Family Involvement in the Child Protection Process*. London: HMSO.

Thorpe, R. (1992) 'Community work and ideology: an Australian perspective', in R. Thorpe and J. Petruchenia (eds), *Community Work or Social Change: An Australian Perspective* (new edn). Sydney: Hale and Iremonger. pp. 20–36.

Throssell, H. (1975) 'Social work overview', in H. Throssell (ed.), *Social Work: Radical Essays*. Queensland: University of Queensland Press. pp. 3–25.

Tucker, R.C. (1972) 'Introduction: The writings of Marx and Engels', in R.C. Tucker (ed.), *The Marx–Engels Reader*. New York: W.W. Norton. pp. xv–xxxiv.

Van Den Bergh, N. and Cooper, L. (1986) *Feminist Visions of Social Work*. Silver Springs, USA: National Association of Social Workers.

Van Krieken, R. (1992) *Children and the State: Social Control and the Formation of Australian Child Welfare*. Sydney: Allen and Unwin.

Walby, S. (1992) 'Post-post-modernism? Theorising social complexity', in M. Barrett and A. Phillips (eds), *Destabilising Theory: Contemporary Feminist Debates*. Cambridge: Polity Press. pp. 31–52.

Ward, D. and Mullender, A. (1991) 'Empowerment and oppression: an indissoluble pairing for contemporary social work', *Critical Social Policy*, 11 (2):21–30.

Wartenberg, T.E. (1993) 'Hegel's idealism: the logic of conceptuality', in F.C. Beiser (ed.), *The Cambridge Companion to Hegel*. Cambridge: Cambridge University Press. pp. 102–29.

Wearing, B. (1986) 'Feminist theory and social work', in H. Marchant and B. Wearing (eds), *Gender Reclaimed: Women in Social Work*. Sydney: Hale and Iremonger. pp. 33–53.

Wearing, B. (1996) *Gender: The Pain and Pleasure of Difference*. Melbourne: Longman.

Weatherley, R. (1987) 'Teenage pregnancy, professional agendas and problem definitions', *Journal of Sociology and Social Welfare*, 14 (2): 5–35.

Weedon, C. (1987) *Feminist Practice and Poststructuralist Theory*. Oxford: Basil Blackwell.

West, C. (1984) *Routine Complications: Troubles with Talk between Doctors and Patients*. Bloomington: Indiana Press.

West, C. (1995) 'Women's competence in conversation', *Discourse and Society*, 3: 107–31.

White, M. (1992) 'Deconstruction and therapy', in D. Epston and M. White (eds), *Experience, Contradictions, Narratives and Imagination*. Adelaide: Dulich Centre Publications. pp. 109–51.

White, M. and Epston, D. (1990) *Narrative Means to Therapeutic Ends*. New York: W.W. Norton.

White, S. (1997) 'Not always suffered, but sometimes enjoyed: power contra-Porter', *Sociology*, 31 (2): 347–51.

Williams, F. (1994) 'Social relations, welfare and the post-Fordist debate', in R. Burrow and B. Loader (eds), *Towards a Post-Fordist Welfare State?* London: Routledge. pp. 49–73.

Wilson, E. (1977) 'Women in the community', in M. Mayo (ed.), *Women in the Community*. London: Routledge and Kegan Paul. pp. 1–11.

Wilson, J. (1989) 'Decision making by adolescents about pregnancy', *Youth Studies and Abstracts*, 8 (2): 19–24.

Wilson, K., Wicker, L. and Price, J. (1994) 'Social rules for interpersonally effective behaviour in coflict situations. Paper presented to the Fifth International Conference on Language and Social Psychology, University of Queensland, Australia.

Wise, S. (1990) 'Becoming a feminist social worker', in L. Stanley (ed.), *Feminist Praxis: Research, Theory and Epistemology in Feminist Sociology.* London: Routledge. pp. 236–49.

Wood, G.G. and Middleman, R.R. (1991) 'Advocacy and social action: key elements in the structural approach to direct practice in social work', *Social Work in Groups*, 14 (3–4): 53–63.

Yeatman, A. (1993) 'Voice and the representation of difference', in A. Yeatman and S. Gunew (eds), *Feminism and the Politics of Differences*. St Leonard's, NSW: Allen and Unwin.

Yeatman, A. (1994) *Postmodern Revisionings of the Political*. New York: Routledge.

Yeatman, A. (1995) 'Interlocking oppressions', in B. Caine and R. Pringle (eds), *Transitions: New Australian Feminisms*. St. Leonard's, NSW: Allen and Unwin. pp. 42–56.

Yeatman, A. (1997) 'Feminism and power', in M.L. Shanley and U. Narayan (eds), *Reconstructing Political Theory: Feminist Perspectives*. Oxford: Polity Press.

Yeatman, A. (1998) 'Introduction', in A. Yeatman (ed.), *Activism and the Policy Process*. St Leonard's, NSW: Allen and Unwin. pp. 1–15.

Young, I.M. (1990) *Justice and the Politics of Difference*. New Jersey: Princeton University Press.

Index

  sense of, 109–10
  suppression of, 40
discourse
  definition of, 39
  in activist social work, 61–2
  role of, 45–6, 131
  rules of, 40–1
discourse analysis, 58, 67–8, 91, 93, 123,
    137
Dixon, J., 26, 63–4
domination
  power seen as, 111–16, 126
  processes of, 17–19
  social work as a vehicle for, 21, 45, 59,
    71–2
  within oppressed groups, 104, 134
  see also oppression
Dominelli, L., 29
  and McLeod, E., 23, 27
dualisms, 42, 49–50, 53, 64–6, 73, 113,
    124, 126, 131–2, 135–6, 140–1

écriture féminine, 50–1
egalitarian ethos, 79, 83, 87, 114, 127
egalitarian practice, 24, 27–9, 33, 91; *see
    also* radical egalitarianism
Ellermann, A., 58
emancipatory doctrines and practices, 3–9
    passim, 14, 21, 26, 32, 38, 41, 51, 55,
    58–9, 66, 111, 130–1, 145
embeddedness, 95–6, 136–7
empowerment, 28, 52, 120, 125–6
Engels, F., 16
Enlightenment philosophy, 14, 18
  criticisms of, 6
Epston, D. *see* White, M.
equitable practice relations, 29–30, 33,
    72–3; *see also* inequality
Esping-Andersen, G., 124, 144
essence of social work, 49, 51, 53, 55
essential meanings and beliefs, 39
essentialism, 27, 132
ethical frameworks, 142
evolutionary social change, 130
exteriority, principle of, 41

Fawcett, B., 37
Fay, B., 15, 18, 21, 130
Featherstone, B. and Fawcett, B., 37, 134
feminist analysis, 13, 18, 25–6, 34, 40,
    42, 46–55, 64–6, 90, 117, 128, 134,
    136
Fine, M., 65
Fook, J., 23–4, 69

Foucault, M., 5–9, 38–66 *passim*, 71, 73,
    79, 87, 90, 93–4, 95–6, 101, 119–34
    passim, 140–8 *passim*
Fox Piven, F. *see* Cloward, R.
Frankfurt school, 17–18
Fraser, N., 13–14
Freire, P., 18, 35, 83

Galper, J., 35
Gatens, M., 7, 42, 47–50, 65, 90, 127, 136,
    139, 145
gender, social construction of, 101
Gibson-Graham, J.K., 35
globalization, 57
Goldberg, G. *see* Middleman, R.
Gordon, L., 76
grand narratives of modernity, 6, 51, 54–5,
    63, 67, 70, 145
Groch, S.A., 32
Gross, E., 132
Grosz, E., 7, 47–9, 145

Habermas, J., 17–18
Harrison, P. *see* Burke, B.
Hartsock, N., 30, 57–8
Hegel, G.W.F., 14–16, 29, 41, 48
helping professions, the *see* human service
    workers
'heroic activists', 135–7
hooks, b., 147–8
Howe, D., 141
Hudson, A., 34
human service workers, 8, 44–5, 59–60,
    74–5, 87–90, 93, 112–13, 115, 128
Hutchinson-Reis, M., 25

identification with issues and populations,
    29
identity
  collective, 32, 46, 53, 108, 110, 119–20,
    138–9
  cultural, 61
  fragmentation of, 57
  hierarchically-structured, 64
  humanist notion of, 45
  multi-faceted nature of, 54
  professional, 72–3, 89
  social, 27
  see also oppositional consciousness;
    subjectivity
identity formation, 138
identity politics, 53, 136, 138
ideology, definition of, 20–1
individualistic emphasis in social work,
    22, 124

pragmatism of activist social work, 145, 147
praxis, 145
prefigurative strategy, 28
prejudices, 112–13
Pringle, R., 96, 140
Pritchard, C. and Taylor, R., 24
professionalism, 23, 72–5, 88–9, 93, 135–6
proletariat, the, 15–17, 33
public dialogue and debate, 107, 118–19

racism, 25–6
radical analysis and practice, 4–5, 7, 12, 25, 37, 124–5
radical egalitarianism, 77, 126–8
radical poststructural feminism, 46–51, 54–5, 128, 136
Rahnema, M., 104–5
rational self-consciousness, 20–1
rationalism and rationality, 52, 66, 130, 142
Reinharz, S., 127
relativism, 63, 147
research, need for, 146–7
Resnick, S. and Wolff, R., 17
ressentiment, politics of, 53, 127, 139
restructural theory, 132
revolutionary social change, 24
Rojek, C., 8, 123–4, 135–6
Routledge, R., 26

Sawicki, J., 43
self, sense of, 46, 53, 110; *see also* rational self-consciousness
self-reflexivity, 31–2, 63, 65, 96, 121, 129–30, 132
self-revelation, 119–20
sexism, 93
Shah, N., 25
single parents, 97–8
Smith, C. and White, S., 7
social categorization, 27, 140
social change, evolutionary and revolutionary, 24, 130
social constructionism, 101, 123, 125
social control, 21, 44–5, 59, 71–7 *passim*, 94, 127
social justice, 138, 147–8
social structure
    explanations of, 19–20
    prioritization of, 25–6
social transformation, 24, 32–5, 77, 96
social work, definition of, 146
social workers, role of, 33
speech, male and female, 91–3, 137

standpoint epistemology, 29, 33
stereotypes, 112–13
structural (as opposed to local) change, 124–5
structural social work, 27
subjectivity, 38, 45–6
surveillance of social workers, 146–7

Tapper, M., 53
Taylor, R. *see* Pritchard, C.
Taylor-Gooby, P., 57
technical knowledge, 79–81, 87–8, 128–9
Thatcher, M., 133
theory and practice, schism between 121–3
totality, social, 15–16, 19, 26, 41, 47, 51, 122–3
traditional values, 97, 99–100, 103, 130
transformative agenda, 24–5; *see also* social transformation
truth, regimes of, 40–1
truth claims, 40–2, 54–5, 62–3, 95, 101, 105, 141–2
    scientific, 128

utopian ideals, 66, 127, 137

values *see* bourgeois values; political values; traditional values
Van-Krieken, R., 76
vested interests of professionals, 72
victimhood, sense of, 141
violence
    by women, 134
    domestic, 40, 116; *see also* young women's anti-violence project

Wearing, B., 20, 47, 133
welfare state, 1–3, 124
West, C., 91–2
White, M. and Epston, D., 128
White, S. *see* Smith, C.
Wilson, E., 22–3
Wilson, J., 97
Wise, S., 45, 73
Wolff, R. *see* Resnick, S.
'woman', notion of, 47
women professionals, 93, 133
working class *see* proletariat

Yeatman, A., 6–7, 47, 53, 95, 142, 146
'Young Mothers for Young Women' network, 105–6
young women's anti-violence project, 68, 78–92, 95–113 *passim*, 120, 126, 129, 131, 141